Praise for

THE DARKENING A̶G̶E̶

A *New York Times* Notable Book
A *New York Times Book Review* Editors' Choice
Named a Book of the Year by the *Telegraph*,
the *Spectator*, the *Observer*, and *BBC History Magazine*
Winner of the Royal Society of Literature
Jerwood Award for Nonfiction

"A searingly passionate book . . . Nixey writes up a storm. Each sentence is rich, textured, evocative, felt . . . Nixey delivers this ballista-bolt of a book with her eyes wide open and in an attempt to bring light as well as heat to the sad story of intellectual monoculture and religious intolerance."
— *New York Times Book Review*

"Nixey paints with a wide brush . . . A fine history that is surely controversial in its view of how victims become victimizers and how professions of love turn to terror."
— *Kirkus Reviews*

"Nixey clearly but untendentiously summarizes phenomena that led up to the elimination of classical polytheism."
— *Booklist*

"[An] impassioned account . . . Nixey acutely and thunderously reminds us that many used the Christian project as an excuse to destroy rather than to love."
— *BBC History Magazine*, "Books of the Year"

"A book for the twenty-first century . . . Nixey has a great story to tell, and she tells it exceptionally well. As one would expect from a distinguished journalist, every page is full of well-turned phrases that leap from the page. She has an expert eye for arresting details, and brings characters and scenarios to life without disguising anything of the strangeness of the world she describes. Most of all, she navigates through these tricky waters with courage and skill . . . A finely crafted, invigorating polemic against the resilient popular myth that presents the Christianisation of Rome as the triumph of a kinder, gentler politics . . . [*The Darkening Age*] succeeds brilliantly."
—Tim Whitmarsh, *Guardian*

"[A] vivid and important new book . . . Nixey is a funny, lively, readable guide through this dark world of religious oppression . . . The book is also an essential reminder . . . that intolerance, ignorance and hostility to cultural diversity are sadly nothing new."

—*New Statesman*

"Exceptionally well written . . . [A] clever, compelling book."
—Thomas W. Hodgkinson, *Spectator*

"Sardonic, well informed and quite properly lacking in sympathy for its hapless target . . . *The Darkening Age* rattles along at a tremendous pace, and Nixey brilliantly evokes all that was lost with the waning of the classical world."
—Peter Thonemann, *Sunday Times* (UK)

"Nixey has done an impressive job of illuminating an important aspect of late-antique Christianity."
—Levi Roach, *Literary Review*

"A delightful book about destruction and despair. Nixey combines the authority of a serious academic with the expressive style of a good journalist. She's not afraid to throw in the odd joke amid sombre tales of desecration. With considerable courage, she challenges the wisdom of history and manages to prevail. Comfortable assumptions about Christian progress come tumbling down."

—Gerard de Groot, *Times* (UK)

"Captivating and compelling, *The Darkening Age* challenges our whole understanding of Christianity's earliest years and the medieval society that followed. A remarkable fusion of riveting narrative and acute scholarly judgment, this book marks the debut of a formidable classicist and historian."

—Dan Jones, best-selling author of
The Plantagenets and *The Templars*

"Catherine Nixey has written a bold, dazzling and provocative book that challenges ideas about early Christianity and both how and why it spread so far and fast in its early days. Nixey is a witty and iconoclastic guide to a world that will be unfamiliar, surprising and troubling to many."

—Peter Frankopan, best-selling author of
The Silk Roads

"Engaging and erudite, Catherine Nixey's book offers both a compelling argument and a wonderful eye for vivid detail. It shines a searching spotlight onto some of the murkiest aspects of the early medieval mindset. A triumph."

—Edith Hall, author of
Introducing the Ancient Greeks

"A devastating book, written in vivid yet playful prose. Catherine Nixey reveals a level of intolerance and anti-intellectualism which echoes today's headlines but is centuries old."

—Anita Anand, author of *Sophia* and
coauthor (with William Dalrymple) of *Koh-i-Noor*

"Nixey's elegant and ferocious text paints a dark but riveting picture of life at the time of the 'triumph' of Christianity, reminding us not just of the realities of our own past, but also of the sad echoes of that past in our present."

—Michael Scott, author of
Ancient Worlds

The
DARKENING AGE

———

The Christian Destruction
of the Classical World

Catherine Nixey

MARINER BOOKS
HOUGHTON MIFFLIN HARCOURT
BOSTON   NEW YORK

To T.,
for deciphering my handwriting

First Mariner Books edition 2019

Copyright © 2017 by Catherine Nixey

First published 2017 by Macmillan,
an imprint of Pan Macmillan
www.panmacmillan.com

hmhco.com

Library of Congress Cataloging-in-Publication Data
Names: Nixey, Catherine, author. Title: The darkening age : the Christian destruction
of the classical world / Catherine Nixey. Description: First U.S. edition. | Boston :
Houghton Mifflin Harcourt, 2018. | Includes bibliographical references and index.
Identifiers: LCCN 2017056985 (print) | LCCN 2017045347 (ebook) | ISBN 9780544800939
(ebook) | ISBN 9780544800885 (hardcover) | ISBN 9781328589286 (pbk.) Subjects:
LCSH: Church history—Primitive and early church, ca. 30-600. | Rome—Civilization—
Christian influences. | Greece—Civilization—Christian influences. Classification:
LCC BR162.3 (print) | LCC BR162.3 .N59 2018 (ebook) | DDC 270.2—dc23
LC record available at https://lccn.loc.gov/2017056985

Printed in the United States of America
24 25 26 27 28 LBC 11 10 9 8 7

Map by ML Design

Contents

List of Illustrations

Bust of Lucretius, 96?–55 BC, the Roman philosophical poet
© Granger

Emperor Constantine and the Council of Nicea, with the burning of
Arian books illustrated below, Italian manuscript, 9th century AD
Getty Images / ullstein bild

Fresco of the raising of Lazarus, catacombs of Via Latina, Rome, 4th
century AD
Catacomb of Via Latina, Rome / Bridgeman Images

Triumph of Faith—Christian Martyrs in the Time of Nero, 65 AD by
Eugène Romain Thirion
Private collection / Photo © Bonhams, London / Bridgeman Images

Colossal head of Emperor Constantine I ("the Great"), AD 270–337
Pinacoteca Capitolina, Palazzo Conservatori, Rome / Bridgeman Images

Emperor Theodosius I at the Council of Constantinople, Latin
manuscript, Turkey, 9th century
© De Agostini Picture Library / A. Dagli Orti / Bridgeman Images

Temple of Diana at Ephesus, engraving, English School, 19th century
Private collection / © Look and Learn / Bridgeman Images

FOLLOWING PAGE 222

Green basanite bust of Germanicus Caesar, Roman, Egypt
© The Trustees of the British Museum. All rights reserved.

Saint Apollonia Destroys a Pagan Idol by Giovanni d'Alemagna, c. 1442–45
© Daderot

Cult statue of the deified Augustus, in the Ephesus museum in
Selçuk, Turkey
Alamy / Odyssey-Images

Theophilus standing on the Serapeion, Goleniscev papyrus, 5th
century AD
Alamy / ART Collection

Byzantine chapel in Roman amphitheatre, Duresi, Albania
Julian Chichester / Bridgeman Images

Hypatia by Charles William Mitchell, 1885, Laing Art Gallery, Newcastle-upon-Tyne, UK
© Tyne & Wear Archives & Museums / Bridgeman Images

Archimedes palimpsest, *c.* 10th–13th century
Private collection / Photo © Christie's Images / Bridgeman Images

Theological debate between Catholic and Nestorian Christians at Acre, 1290
Pictures from History / Bridgeman Images

Fresco of satyr and maenad at Pompeii, 1st century BC
Private collection / Bridgeman Images

Fresco of Priapus, from the Casa dei Vettii *c.* 50–79, Pompeii
Bridgeman Images

Hell, Portuguese School, 16th century
Museu Nacional de Arte Antiga, Lisbon / Bridgeman Images

St. John Chrysostom, Panagia Ties Asinou church, Nikitart, Cyprus
De Agostini Picture Library / A. Dagli Orti / Bridgeman Images

Roman women playing sports, in one of the so-called Bikini Mosaics at Villa Romana del Casale, 4th century
Pictures from History / Bridgeman Images

St. Simeon Stylites sitting on his column, 5th–6th century
Werner Forman Archive / Bridgeman Images

St. Shenoute, secco painting, *c.* 7th century, north lobe of sanctuary, Red Monastery Church, near Sohag, Egypt
Photo by E. Bolman, © American Research Center in Egypt (ARCE)

Mosaic of Emperor Justinian I, Byzantine School, *c.* 547
San Vitale, Ravenna, Italy / Bridgeman Images

Roman Empire at the end of the first century AD

PROLOGUE: A BEGINNING

———

Palmyra, c. AD 385

There is no crime for those who have Christ.

—St. Shenoute

THE DESTROYERS CAME FROM out of the desert. Palmyra must have been expecting them: for years, marauding bands of bearded, black-robed zealots, armed with little more than stones, iron bars and an iron sense of righteousness, had been terrorizing the east of the Roman Empire.

Their attacks were primitive, thuggish and very effective. These men moved in packs—later in swarms of as many as five hundred—and when they descended utter destruction followed. Their targets were the temples and the attacks could be astonishingly swift. Great stone columns that had stood for centuries collapsed in an afternoon; statues that had stood for half a millennium had their faces mutilated in a moment; temples that had seen the rise of the Roman Empire fell in a single day.

This was violent work, but it was by no means solemn. The zealots roared with laughter as they smashed the "evil," "idolatrous" statues; the faithful jeered as they tore down temples, stripped roofs and defaced tombs. Chants appeared, immortalizing these glorious moments. "Those shameful things," sang pilgrims, proudly; the "demons and idols . . . our good Saviour trampled down all together."[1] Zealotry rarely makes for good poetry.

In this atmosphere, Palmyra's temple of Athena* was an

---

* In Palmyra the goddess became associated with the local goddess Allat, to become "Athena-Allat."

obvious target. The handsome building was an unapologetic celebration of all the believers loathed: a monumental rebuke to monotheism. Go through its great doors and it would have taken your eyes a moment, after the brightness of a Syrian sun, to adjust to the cool gloom within. As they did, you might have noticed that the air was heavy with the smoky tang of incense, or perhaps that what little light there was came from a scatter of lamps left by the faithful. Look up and, in their flickering glow, you would have seen the great figure of Athena herself.

The handsome, haughty profile of this statue might be far from Athena's native Athens, but it was instantly recognizable, with its straight Grecian nose, its translucent marble skin and the plump, slightly sulky mouth. The statue's size — it was far taller than any man — might also have impressed. Though perhaps even more admirable than the physical scale was the scale of the imperial infrastructure and ambition that had brought this object here. The statue echoed others that stood on the Athenian Acropolis, well over a thousand miles away; this particular version had been made in a workshop hundreds of miles from Palmyra, then transported here at considerable difficulty and expense to create a little island of Greco-Roman culture by the sands of the Syrian desert.

Did they notice this, the destroyers, as they entered? Were they, even fleetingly, impressed by the sophistication of an empire that could quarry, sculpt then transport marble over such vast distances? Did they, even for a moment, admire the skill that could make a kissably soft-looking mouth out of hard marble? Did they, even for a second, wonder at its beauty?

It seems not. Because when the men entered the temple they took a weapon and smashed the back of Athena's head with a single blow so hard that it decapitated the goddess. The head fell to the floor, slicing off that nose, crushing the once-smooth cheeks. Athena's eyes, untouched, looked out over a now-disfigured face.

Mere decapitation wasn't enough. More blows fell, scalping

Athena, striking the helmet from the goddess's head, smashing it into pieces. Further blows followed. The statue fell from its pedestal, then the arms and shoulders were chopped off. The body was left on its front in the dirt; the nearby altar was sliced off just above its base.

Only then does it seem that these men—these Christians—felt satisfied that their work was done. They melted out once again into the desert. Behind them the temple fell silent. The votive lamps, no longer tended, went out. On the floor, the head of Athena slowly started to be covered by the sands of the Syrian desert.

The "triumph" of Christianity had begun.

INTRODUCTION: AN ENDING

Athens, AD 532

We see the same stars, the sky is shared by all, the same world surrounds us. What does it matter what wisdom a person uses to seek for the truth?

— the "pagan" author Symmachus

That all superstition of pagans and heathens should be annihilated is what God wants, God commands, God proclaims!

— St. Augustine

THEY MUST HAVE BEEN a melancholy party. In AD 532, a band of seven men set out from Athens, taking with them little but works of philosophy. All were members of what had once been the most famous of Greece's philosophical schools, the Academy. The Academy's philosophers proudly traced their history back in an unbroken line—"a golden chain"[1] as they called it—to Plato himself, almost a thousand years before. Now, that chain was about to be broken in the most dramatic way possible: these men were abandoning not just their school but the Roman Empire itself. Athens, the city that had seen the birth of Western philosophy, was now no longer a place for philosophers.

Their leader, Damascius, must have been some comfort to them as they set out on this trip into the unknown. By the standards of the time, he was old, elderly even—almost seventy when their journey began—but he was formidable. Damascius was a brilliant, densely subtle thinker who peppered his writings with mathematical similes—and he did not suffer fools gladly. An acerbic "who's who" he wrote on his fellow philosophers is full of crushing comments on anyone whose intelligence or courage he considered wanting. In life, he could be as immoderate as in his writings: he had once almost drowned in a river when, too impatient for a boatman to take him across, he had decided to swim instead and nearly been swept away.

Many of Damascius's greatest risks were run in the service

of his beloved philosophy. He had already sheltered a wanted philosopher in his own home, embarked on perilous thousand-mile journeys into the unknown, and braved the risk of torture and arrest himself. No man, he felt, should do any less. "Men tend to bestow the name of virtue on a life of inactivity," he once wrote, with scorn. "But I do not agree . . . the learned, who sit in their corner and philosophise at length in a grand manner about justice and moderation, utterly disgrace themselves if they are compelled to take some action."[2]

This was no time for a philosopher to be philosophical. "The tyrant,"[3] as the philosophers put it, was in charge and had many alarming habits. In Damascius's own time, houses were entered and searched for books and objects deemed unacceptable. If any were found they would be removed and burned in triumphant bonfires in town squares. Discussion of religious matters in public had been branded a "damnable audacity" and forbidden by law.[4] Anyone who made sacrifices to the old gods could, the law said, be executed. Across the empire, ancient and beautiful temples had been attacked, their roofs stripped, their treasures melted down, their statues smashed. To ensure that their rules were kept, the government started to employ spies, officials and informers to report back on what went on in the streets and marketplaces of cities and behind closed doors in private homes. As one influential Christian speaker put it, his congregation should hunt down sinners and drive them into the way of salvation as relentlessly as a hunter pursues his prey into nets.[5]

The consequences of deviation from the rules could be severe and philosophy had become a dangerous pursuit. Damascius's own brother had been arrested and tortured to make him reveal the names of other philosophers, but had, as Damascius recorded with pride, "received in silence and with fortitude the many blows of the rod that landed on his back."[6] Others in Damascius's circle of philosophers had been tortured, hung up by the wrists until they gave away the names of their fellow scholars. A fellow philosopher had, some years before, been flayed alive. Another had been beaten before a judge until the blood flowed down his back.

The savage "tyrant" was Christianity. From almost the very first years that a Christian emperor had ruled in Rome in AD 312, liberties had begun to be eroded. And then, in AD 529, a final blow had fallen. It was decreed that all those who labored "under the insanity of paganism"—in other words Damascius and his fellow philosophers—would no longer be allowed to teach. There was worse. It was also announced that anyone who had not yet been baptized was to come forward and make themselves known at the "holy churches" immediately, or face exile. And if anyone allowed themselves to be baptized, then slipped back into their old pagan ways, they would be executed.

For Damascius and his fellow philosophers, this was the end. They could not worship their old gods. They could not earn any money. Above all, they could not now teach philosophy. For a while, they remained in Athens and tried to eke out a living. In AD 532, they finally realized they could not. They had heard that in the East there was a king who was himself a great philosopher. They decided that they would go there, despite the risks of such a journey. The Academy, the greatest and most famous school in the ancient world—perhaps ever—a school that could trace its history back almost a millennium, closed.

It is impossible to imagine how painful the journey through Athens would have been. As they went, they would have walked through the same streets and squares where their heroes—Socrates, Plato, Aristotle—had once walked and worked and argued. They would have seen in them a thousand reminders that those celebrated times were gone. The temples of Athens were closed and crumbling and many of the brilliant statues that had once stood in them had been defaced or removed. Even the Acropolis had not escaped: its great statue of Athena had been torn down.

Much of Damascius's writing has been lost, but occasional phrases remain; certainly enough to discern his feelings. His entire way of life, he wrote, was being "swept away by the torrent."[7] The writings of another Greek author from some years earlier show similar despair. We are, he wrote, "men reduced to ashes . . . for today everything is turned upside down." In another bleak epigram this same anguished poet asked: "Is it not true that we are dead and only seem to live, we Greeks . . . Or are we alive and is life dead?"[8]

When modern histories describe this period, this time when all the old religions died away and Christianity finally became pre-eminent, they tend to call it the "triumph of Christianity." It is worth remembering, however, the original Roman meaning of the word "triumph." A true Roman triumph wasn't merely about the victory of the winner.[9] It was about the total and utter subjugation of the loser. In a true Roman triumph the losing side was paraded through the capital while the winning side looked on at an enemy whose soldiers had been slain, whose possessions had been despoiled and whose leaders had been humiliated.

A triumph was not merely a "victory." It was an annihilation.

Little of what is covered by this book is well known outside academic circles. Certainly it was not well known by me when I grew up in Wales, the daughter of a former nun and a former monk. My childhood was, as you might expect, a fairly religious one. We went to church every Sunday, said grace before meals, and I said my prayers (or at any rate the list of requests which I considered to be the same thing) every night. When Catholic relatives arrived we play-acted not films but First Holy Communion and, at times, even actual communion. A terrible sin (and not a wonderful game, either), this was at least an opportunity to glean extra blackcurrant juice from adults.

So there was a lot of God, or at any rate of Catholicism, in my childhood. But despite having spent a combined twenty-six years inside monastic walls, my parents' faith was never dogmatic. If I asked about the origins of the world, I was more likely to be told about the Big Bang than about Genesis. If I asked where humans came from, I would have been told about evolution rather than Adam. I don't remember, as a child, ever questioning that God existed—but equally as a teenager I remember being fairly confident that He did not. What faith I had had died, and my parents either didn't notice or didn't mind. I suspect that, somewhere between monastery and world, their faith had died too.

What never, ever died in our family, however, was my parents' faith in the educative power of the Church. As children, both had been taught by monks and nuns; and as a monk and a nun they had both taught. They believed as an article of faith that the Church that had enlightened their minds was what had enlightened, in distant history, the whole of Europe. It was the Church, they told me, that had kept alive the Latin and Greek of the classical world in the benighted Middle Ages, until it could be picked up again by the wider world in the Renaissance. On holidays, we would visit museums and libraries where the same point was made. As a young child, I looked at the glowing gold of the illuminated manuscripts and believed in a more metaphorical illumination in ages of intellectual darkness.

And, in a way, my parents were right to believe this, for it is true. Monasteries did preserve a lot of classical knowledge.

But it is far from the whole truth. In fact, this appealing narrative has almost entirely obscured an earlier, less glorious story. For before it preserved, the Church destroyed. In a spasm of destruction never seen before—and one that appalled many non-Christians watching it — during the fourth and fifth centuries, the Christian Church demolished, vandalized and melted down a simply staggering quantity of art. Classical statues were knocked from their plinths, defaced, defiled and torn limb from limb. Temples were razed to their foundations and mutilated. A temple widely considered to be the most magnificent in the entire empire was leveled. Many of the Parthenon sculptures were attacked, faces were mutilated, hands and limbs were hacked off, and gods were decapitated. Some of the finest statues on the whole building were almost certainly smashed off then ground into rubble that was then used to build churches. Books — which were often stored in temples — suffered terribly. The remains of the greatest library in the ancient world, a library that had once held perhaps 700,000 volumes, were destroyed in this way by Christians. It was over a millennium before any other library would even come close to its holdings. Works by censured philosophers were forbidden and bonfires blazed across the empire as outlawed books went up in flames.

Dramatic though all this was, far more destruction was achieved through sheer neglect. In their silent copying-houses the monks preserved much, but they lost far more. The atmosphere could be viciously hostile to non-Christian authors. In the silence in which monks worked, gestures were used to request certain books: outstretched palms and the mimed turning of pages signified that a monk wished a psalter to be passed over to him, and so on. Pagan books were requested by making a gagging gesture.[10]

Unsurprisingly, the works of these despised authors suffered. At a time in which parchment was scarce, many ancient writers were simply erased, scrubbed away so that their pages could be reused for more elevated themes. Palimpsests — manuscripts in which one manuscript has been scraped (*psao*) again (*palin*) — provide glimpses of the moments at which these ancient works vanished. A last copy of Cicero's *De re publica* was written over by Augustine on the Psalms. A biographical work by Seneca disappeared beneath yet another Old Testament. A codex of Sallust's histories was scrubbed away to make room for more St. Jerome. Other ancient texts were lost through ignorance. Despised and ignored, over the years, they simply crumbled into dust, food for bookworms but not for thought. The work of Democritus, one of the greatest Greek philosophers and the father of atomic theory, was entirely lost. Only one percent of Latin literature survived the centuries. Ninety-nine percent was lost. One can achieve a great deal by the blunt weapons of indifference and sheer stupidity.

The violent assaults of this period were not the preserve of cranks and eccentrics. Attacks against the monuments of the "mad," "damnable" and "insane" pagans were encouraged and led by men at the very heart of the Catholic Church.[11] The great St. Augustine himself declared to a congregation in Carthage "that all superstition of pagans and heathens should be annihilated is what God wants, God commands, God proclaims!"[12] St. Martin, still one of the most popular French saints, rampaged across the Gaulish countryside leveling temples and dismaying locals as he went. In Egypt, St. Theophilus razed one of the most beautiful buildings in the ancient world. In Italy, St. Benedict overturned a shrine to Apollo. In Syria, ruthless bands of monks terrorized the countryside, smashing down statues and tearing the roofs from temples.

The attacks didn't stop at culture. Everything from the food on one's plate (which should be plain and certainly not involve spices), through to what one got up to in bed (which should be likewise plain, and unspicy), began, for the first time, to come under the control of religion. Male homosexuality was outlawed; hair-plucking was despised, as too were makeup, music, suggestive dancing, rich food, purple bedsheets, silk clothes . . . The list went on.

Achieving this was not a simple matter. While the omniscient God had no trouble seeing not only into men's hearts but into their homes, Christian priests had a little more difficulty in doing the same. A solution was found: St. John Chrysostom encouraged his congregations to spy on each other. Enter each other's homes, he said. Pry into each other's affairs. Shun those who don't comply. Then report all sinners to him and he would punish them accordingly. And if you didn't report them then he would punish you too. "Just as hunters chase wild animals . . . not from one direction but from everywhere, and cast them into the net, so too together let's chase those who've become wild animals and cast them immediately into the net of salvation, we from this side, you from that."[13] Fervent Christians went into people's houses and searched for books, statues and paintings that were considered demonic. This kind of obsessive attention was not cruelty. On the contrary: to restrain, to attack, to compel, even to beat a sinner was — if you turned them back to the path of righteousness — to save them. As Augustine, the master of the pious paradox, put it: "Oh, merciful savagery."[14]

The results of all of this were shocking and, to non-Christians, terrifying. Townspeople rushed to watch as internationally famous temples were destroyed. Intellectuals looked on in despair as volumes of supposedly unchristian books — often in reality texts on the liberal arts — went up in flames. Art lovers watched in horror as some of the greatest sculptures in the ancient world were smashed by people too stupid to appreciate them — and certainly too stupid to recreate them. The Christians could often not even destroy effectively: many statues on many temples were saved simply by virtue of being too high for them, with their primitive ladders and hammers, to reach.

I had originally conceived of this book as a travelogue: it would be interesting, I thought, to follow Damascius as he zigzagged across the Mediterranean — a pagan St. Paul. Syria, Damascus, Baghdad, parts of Egypt and the southern border of Turkey, all places that he had traveled to, were by no means easy to reach but they were, just about, achievable. However, in the years between coming up with that idea, and writing this book, the reality of doing so became impossible.

Since then, and as I write, the Syrian civil war has left parts of Syria under the control of a new Islamic caliphate. In 2014, within certain areas of Syria, music was banned and books were burned. The British Foreign Office advised against all travel to the north of the Sinai Peninsula. In 2015, Islamic State militants started bulldozing the ancient Assyrian city of Nimrud, just south of Mosul in Iraq, because it was "idolatrous." Images went around the world showing Islamic militants toppling statues around three millennia old from their plinths, then taking hammers to them. "False idols" must be destroyed. In Palmyra, the remnants of the great statue of Athena that had been carefully repaired by archaeologists was attacked yet again. Once again, Athena was beheaded; once again, her arm was sheared off.

My imagined journey had become impossible. As a result, this book has become a sort of historical travelogue instead. It travels throughout the Roman Empire, pausing at certain places and certain times that are significant. As with any travelogue, each of the places I have focused on is a personal choice and, in a sense, an arguable one. I have chosen Palmyra as a beginning, as it was in the east of the empire, in the mid-380s, that sporadic violence against the old gods and their temples escalated into something far more serious. But equally I could have chosen an attack on an earlier temple, or a later one. That is why it is *a* beginning, not *the* beginning. I have chosen Athens in the years around AD 529 as an ending—but again, I could equally have chosen a city farther east whose inhabitants, when they failed to convert to Christianity, were massacred and their arms and legs cut off and strung up in the streets as a warning to others.

This is a book about the Christian destruction of the classical world. The Christian assault was not the only one—fire, flood, invasion and time itself all played their part—but this book focuses on Christianity's assault in particular. This is not to say that the Church didn't also preserve things: it did. But the story of Christianity's good works in this period has been told again and again; such books proliferate in libraries and bookshops. The history and the sufferings of those whom Christianity defeated have not been. This book concentrates on them.

The area covered is vast and so this is a piecemeal history that darts about through geography and time. It makes no apology for that. The period covered is too long for a linear crawl through the past and the resulting narrative would be, quite simply, too dull. This is also narrative history: I have tried to give a sense of what it felt like to stand before an ancient temple, what it smelled like to enter one; of how pleasing the afternoon light was as it fell through the steam in an ancient bathhouse. Again, I make no apology for that, either. This approach has its problems—who can really know what an ancient temple smelled like, without visiting one? But not to try to recreate the world is an untruthfulness of another kind: the ancients did not move through a world delineated merely by clean historical periods and battle dates. They lived in a world where the billowing smoke of sacrifices filled the streets on feast days; where people defecated behind statues in the center of Rome; where the light glistened on the wet, naked bodies of young "nymphs" in theaters. Both dates—and bodies—are essential to understanding people of this period.

Any attempt to write about ancient history is fraught with difficulty. Hilary Mantel once said that "history is not the past . . . It is what is left in the sieve when the centuries have run through it." Late antiquity offers slimmer pickings in the sieve than most. The little that does remain there is therefore often hotly contested, and some of it has been argued over by scholars for centuries. Something as simple-sounding as an edict can attract years of disagreement between those who consider it seminal and those who relegate it to the status of a mere letter. I have footnoted some of the most significant controversies but not every one: it would have been impossible —not to mention unreadable.

What remains—whether quarreled over or not—should be treated with caution. As with all ancient history, the writers I quote had limited viewpoints and their own agendas. When St. John Chrysostom gloated that the writings of the Greeks had been obliterated, he was more voicing a hope than stating a fact. When St. Martin's biographer wrote glowingly of how Martin had violently burned and demolished temples throughout Gaul, the aim was less to report than to inspire. Propaganda, we would call such writings now. Every point these authors make is arguable, every writer I quote is fallible. They were, in short, human—and we should read them with caution. But we should still read them, as their tales are still worth telling.

My narrative opens in Egypt, as monasticism is born, then moves to Rome as this new religion is beginning to make an appearance there. It then travels to northern Turkey, to Bithynia, where the very first record of the Christians by a non-Christian was written. It goes to Alexandria in Egypt, where some of the worst desecration of all took place; and it goes far into the deserts of Syria, where some of the strangest players in this story existed: monks who, for the love of God, lived out their entire lives standing on pillars, or in trees, or in cages. And it travels, in the end, to Athens, the city where Western philosophy may be said to have really begun and where, in AD 529, it ended.

The destruction chronicled in this book is immense—and yet it has been all but forgotten by the modern world. One of the most influential Church historians would describe the moment when Christianity took control as the moment at which all oppression ceased, a time when "men who once dared not look up greeted each other with smiling faces and shining eyes."[15] Later historians would join in a chorus of agreement. Why would the Romans not have been happy to convert? They were, runs this argument, sensible people and had never really believed their own religion anyway, with its undignified priapic Jupiters and lustful Venuses. No, runs this argument: the Romans had been Christians-in-waiting, ready and willing to give up their absurd and confusing polytheistic rituals as soon as a sensible (for which read "monotheistic") religion appeared on the scene. As Samuel Johnson would put it, pithy as ever: "The heathens were easily converted, because they had nothing to give up."[16]

He was wrong. Many converted happily to Christianity, it is true. But many did not. Many Romans and Greeks did not smile as they saw their religious liberties removed, their books burned, their temples destroyed and their ancient statues shattered by thugs with hammers. This book tells their story; it is a book that unashamedly mourns the largest destruction of art that human history had ever seen. It is a book about the tragedies behind the "triumph" of Christianity.

A note on vocabulary: I have tried to avoid using the word "pagan" throughout, except when conveying the thoughts or deeds of a Christian protagonist. It was a pejorative and insulting word and was not one that any non-Christian at the time would have willingly used of themselves. It was also a Christian innovation: before Christianity's ascendancy few people would have thought to describe themselves by their religion at all. After Christianity, the world became split, forevermore, along religious boundaries; and words appeared to demarcate these divisions. One of the most common was "pagan." Initially this word had been used to refer to a civilian rather than a soldier. After Christianity, the soldiers in question were not Roman legionaries but those who had enlisted in Christ's army. Later, Christian writers concocted false, unflattering etymologies for it: they said it was related to the word *pagus*, to the "peasants" and the field. It was not; but such slurs stuck and "paganism" acquired an unappealing whiff of the rustic and the backward —a taint it carries to this day.

I have also, where possible, generally avoided ascribing modern nationalities to ancient characters and have instead described them by the language they chiefly wrote in. Thus the orator Libanius, though he was born and lived in Syria, I describe not as "Syrian" but as Greek. This was a cosmopolitan world where anyone, anywhere from Alexandria to Athens, might consider themselves to be a "Hellene"—a Greek—and I have tried to reflect that.

I have, at times, for sheer ease of reading, used the word "religion" to refer to the broad spectrum of cults worshipped by Greco-Roman society prior to the introduction of Christianization. This word has its problems—not least the fact that it implies a more centralized and coherent structure than what, in practice, existed. It is, however, more elegant than many of the cumbersome alternatives.

One final note: many, many good people are impelled by their Christian faith to do many, many good things. I know because I am an almost daily beneficiary of such goodness myself. This book is not intended as an attack on these people and I hope they will not see it as such. But it is undeniable that there have been—that there still are—those who use monotheism and its weapons to terrible ends. Christianity is a greater and a stronger religion when it admits this—and challenges it.

———

CHAPTER ONE

The Invisible Army

Behold, I give unto you power to tread on serpents and scorpions, and over all the power of the enemy.

—Luke 10:19

SATAN KNEW HOW to tempt St. Antony. One day, in a far corner of the Roman Empire, in Egypt, this prosperous young man caught the attention of the Evil One when he did something that was at the time very unusual. Aged about twenty, Antony walked out of his house, sold his possessions, gave all his land away and went to live in a pigsty.[1]

The Roman world of AD 270 was not one that usually celebrated the simple life. Indeed, if he had looked out across this realm at this time then Satan might have allowed himself a satisfied glow that his work had been well done. The sins of lust, gluttony and avarice stalked the land. Where once the aristocrats of Rome had prided themselves on wearing simple home-woven tunics, now the wealthy strode about sweating under scarlet fabrics that gleamed with embroidered gold. Women were even worse, wearing jewel-encrusted sandals and expensive silk dresses so diaphanous that every curve of their bodies could be seen even when fully dressed. Where once upon a time Roman noblemen had boasted of enjoying fortifyingly cold swims in the swirling Tiber, this generation preferred to go to the baroquely decorated bathhouses, taking with them countless rattling silver bottles of ointment.

The behavior inside those steamy rooms was said to be wanton. Women stripped naked and allowed slaves, their fingers gleaming with oil, to rub every inch of their bodies. Men and women bathed together, each one "divesting themselves of their modesty," as one observer put it, "along with their tunic."[2] That writer, in his embarrassment, only managed to mutter in abstract nouns about the "lust" and "licentious indulgence" that might brew in those humid rooms. The frescoes in Pompeian bathhouses were rather more precise. In one changing room, above a shelf where bathers left their clothes, was a small painting of a man performing oral sex on a woman. Indeed, above each of the shelves in that room was a different image: a threesome above one, lesbian sex above another, and so on. A rather more memorable method, it has been speculated, of marking where you left your clothes than a locker number.

Had Satan looked at the empire's dining tables then he might have concluded with satisfaction that the behavior here was little better. Centuries before, the emperor Augustus had (somewhat ostentatiously) relished a simple diet of coarse bread and handmade cheese. Such parsimoniousness didn't last: soon, gourmands were supping one-hundred-year-old wines cooled with snow water out of jeweled goblets and sourcing their oysters from Abydos. All this, while many starved. Though not even those at the best tables could be sure of the best food and drink: in this showy, hierarchical world, hosts stratified the wine they served their guests, giving the worst wine to the least important diners, the mediocre wine to mediocre men and the best wine to the best men.

The young Antony, before he set out to that pigsty, had been the sort of man who could, in time, have earned the finer wines at dinner. He was a provincial, true, but he was also youthful, handsome, fit and healthy; he had been offered a reasonable education (even if, in the time-honored way of privileged young men, he had declined to make the most of it), and he was wealthy: he had recently inherited hundreds of acres of enviably good farmland. He was at just the age when a man ought to start making his mark on the world.

Instead, Antony abandoned it all. Not long after his parents' deaths, he had been in church when he heard a chapter from the Gospel of Matthew being read. "If thou wilt be perfect," it said, "go and sell that thou hast, and give to the poor, and thou shalt have treasure in heaven."[3] And he had promptly done so. Fifteen years later, Antony—soon he would become so famous that he could be known by this name alone—decided to go even farther, setting out to live in a deserted Roman fort on the edge of the Egyptian desert where he stayed for twenty years. Later, he would go farther still, making his home on a mountain by the Red Sea. He would stay there until he died in AD 356.

Antony was not one of the empire's gourmands. No Sicilian lampreys for him; instead he ate only bread, salt and water—and precious little of that, eating only once a day, after sunset. It can't have been a meal to look forward to: while he was in the fort, bread was brought to him only twice a year. Little about his life would have whetted the appetite of an aesthete. Antony slept on a simple rush mat, covering himself with a goats'-hair blanket. Often he didn't sleep at all, preferring to spend the whole night awake in prayer. While other young men daubed themselves with expensive perfumes and ointments, and plucked their hair so assiduously that (the moralists muttered) it was impossible to tell the jawlines of young men from those of women, Antony scorned his body. He assaulted it on a daily basis, refusing to use oils to anoint and clean it, and instead wore a hair shirt and never washed. He only cleaned the mud from his feet when he happened to cross a stream. It was said that no one saw his body naked until he died.

His was a life devoted to isolation, humility (or, to give it a less Christian gloss, humiliation) and self-abnegation. Yet just a few decades after his death, Antony became a celebrity. The story of his life, written down by a bishop named Athanasius, was a literary sensation, devoured by readers from Egypt to Italy, and remained a bestseller for centuries. Young men read this account of punishing self-denial and, inspired, headed out into the desert in imitation. So many men went, it was said, that the desert was made a city by monks. Centuries later, Antony would be revered as the founding father of monasticism, one of the most influential men in the history of Christianity. A few years after his death, people had already started to recognize his importance. When St. Augustine heard the story of Antony's austere life he was apparently so moved by its power that he rushed out of the house into the garden, tore his hair and beat his head with his hands. Such simple men, he said, were rising up and taking "heaven by force."[4]

Not everyone was so delighted. According to Antony's biographer, Athanasius, Satan looked on the hair shirt–wearing, sleepless saint and was revolted. This was intolerable virtue in one so young and so the Prince of Darkness had to act. He was in no doubt what form his attack should take: Antony was a man who scorned the pleasures of the flesh and so it was with the pleasures of the flesh that he would be tempted. Unclean thoughts were, Athanasius explains, Satan's standard weapon for tempting youths, and so he began sending seductive dreams to disturb the young innocent by night. Alas, the holy Antony was a match for this: he pushed them away with the power of constant prayer.

The Devil was forced to move to a second-tier temptation. One night the thwarted Satan turned himself into the form of a beautiful young woman omitting, adds Athanasius—a master of the intriguing aside—"no detail that might provoke lascivious thoughts." Antony struggled but stood firm by calling to mind "the fiery punishment of hell and the torment inflicted by worms."[5] Satan gnashed his teeth with fury; but he wasn't done yet. He decided to send his trump card: an apparition in the form of a young black boy who prostrated himself at Antony's feet. As he lay there the demon announced that he was the "friend of fornication" and bragged about how many chaste souls he had led astray. Antony responded by singing a psalm, an act that was, even then, so anaphrodisiac that the boy instantly vanished.[6]

Antony might have won these early battles but his war with evil was far from over. Over the following decades, as he moved about the emptiness of the desert, he faced repeated demonic onslaught. He was beaten so severely by demons that he was unable to speak. He saw the rules of nature flouted: thin air turned into silver that then disappeared like smoke; walls turned into air, and scorpions, lions and vipers streamed through and mauled him. He even saw Satan himself: he appeared to Antony just as he had appeared to Job. His eyes were like the morning star, his mouth poured forth incense, his hair was sprinkled with flames, his nostrils fumed with smoke, and his breath was like a glowing coal. Antony, his biographer recorded, found it "terrifying."[7]

Today, the story of how Christianity came to conquer Rome is told in reassuringly secular terms. It is a tale of weakened emperors and invading barbarian armies; of punitive taxation, gruesome plagues and a tired and weary populace. Where religion is mentioned in these narratives, it is often given a psychological role. This, runs the argument, was an age of anxiety. Disease, war, famine and death, not to mention the equally unavoidable horror of the tax collector, prowled the empire. During one fifty-year period in the third century, no fewer than twenty-six emperors and perhaps as many, if not more, usurpers claimed power. The barbarians, though not yet quite at the gate, were certainly massing nearby, launching raids on Britain, Gaul, Spain, Morocco and even Italy itself. Just when things seemed as though they couldn't get any worse, a terrible plague descended in which victims' intestines were "shaken with a continual vomiting," their eyes were "on fire with the injected blood"; the feet and parts of the limbs were "taken off by the contagion of diseased putrefaction," not to mention other, even less savory afflictions.[8]

Who, argue traditional narratives of Christianity, would not search for reassurance at such a time? Who would not be drawn to a religion that reassured its followers that, if not in this life then perhaps in the next, things would be a little more pleasant? Who would not long to be told that someone, some-where, had a plan—and that this was all part of it? As one twentieth-century historian put it: "In an age of anxiety any 'totalist' creed exerts a powerful attraction: one has only to think of the appeal of communism to many bewildered minds in our own day."[9]

But, continues this line of argument, the old religions of Rome did not offer such comfort. Far from it. The Greco-Ro-man underworld was a place where Tantalus was tortured by thirst and where Sisyphus spent his days rolling a stone uphill only to have it roll back down again. Hardly the sort of place one might wish to retire to. Nor did the Greco-Ro-man religious system offer much guidance to the living. These cults did not provide a moral handbook for everyday life. They issued no commandments or catechisms or creeds to guide the souls of the uncertain between birth and death. There were broad rules and demands for sacrifice. Admit-tedly, where the ambit of religion petered out then philos-ophy might step in to provide some solace—but given that the grin-and-bear-it philosophy of Stoicism was one of the most popular of the age, this was a cold comfort at best. "The world's a stage and life's a toy," as one Greek poet later wrote, bleakly:

> *Dress up and play your part;*
> *Put every serious thought away*
> *Or risk a broken heart.*[10]

Then, into this chilly, nihilistic world burst Christianity. Not only did the new religion offer comfort, companionship and purpose in this life, it also offered the promise of eternal bliss in the next. And as if all that wasn't tempting enough, it wasn't long before Christianity had even more to offer its converts. In AD 312 the emperor, Constantine, proclaimed himself a follower of Christ. Under his auspices, the Church was soon exempted from taxes and its hierarchy started to be richly rewarded. Bishops were paid five times as much as professors, six times as much as doctors — as much even as a local governor. Eternal delight in the next life, bureaucratic preferment in this. What more could one wish for?

So runs the traditional argument. And indeed there is a great deal of truth in it. No doubt the lure of money, wealth, status, as well as the thought of eternal life (quite apart from the sheer good sense and kindness of many of Jesus's teachings), must have had an effect on the numbers wishing to join this relatively young religion.

But that was not how Christianity was sold in the fourth century. The Church was not marketed as a way to improve a tax bill, or as a balm for anxiety. Christianity was not offered to the Roman Empire as an ecclesiastical comfort blanket against the ills of the world. This was not a lifestyle choice. This was not even about life and death. It was far more important than that.

This was a war. The struggle to convert the empire was nothing less than a battle between good and evil, between the forces of darkness and those of light. It was a battle between God and Satan himself.

The Battleground of Demons

My name is Legion: for we are many.

—Mark 5:9

THIS PERIOD WAS, for the later Church, an age of heroes. In those days the great giants of the Church still walked the earth; this was a time when St. Augustine might go to speak to St. Ambrose or write a letter to St. Jerome. Many of their names, even today, are well known. We have heard of the emperor Constantine, of St. Martin and of St. Antony — or at least of his monastery. We might even know the occasional humanizing detail about them: that Constantine founded Constantinople; that (less appealingly) he boiled his wife in a bath. We might well know that Augustine had an overbearing mother; or that as a young man he wished for God to make him chaste — but not yet.[1] This is a period that can seem familiar.

We should not be deceived. This was another country and they did things differently there. It was a time when a monk might talk personally with Christ, walk with John the Baptist and feel the tears of a prophet fall from heaven onto his skin. The world then still glimmered with miracles: the blind were still healed, the faithful still resurrected from the tomb, the holy still walked on water. It was a strange, ethereal place; a William Blakeish world where the doors of religious perception lay wide open; a world in which a holy man might transform into a flickering flame, travel on a shining cloud or single-handedly lay low a host of barbarians, armed solely with a flaming sword.

This was also a world of evil apparitions, not just holy ones: a place where Satan might walk past you in the road and a demon might sit down next to you at dinner; a world in which your immortal soul was in perpetual peril. The barbarian hordes that were beginning to nibble at the edges of the empire paled in comparison to the hideous army of demons that, according to Christian writers, was already swarming, slithering and loping across it. My name, the demon had announced in the Gospel of Mark, "is Legion: for we are many."[2] This, to many Christian writers of the time, was no mere metaphor. Demons and the threat they posed were real.

These demons may have been all but forgotten by modern historians, who tend to pass over demonologies with a silence that speaks eloquently of embarrassment, but such fiends obsessed, perhaps even possessed, some of the greatest minds of early Christianity. Demons stalk through the pages of Augustine's *City of God* — or to give it its full and often forgotten title, *The City of God Against the Pagans* — and they are a fearsome foe. They were, Augustine wrote, "teachers of depravity, delighting in obscenity."[3]

Faced with such a multifaceted threat, Christian writers mobilized. With the care of Victorian naturalists, the historians, theologians and monks of the late fourth century began to observe and record the habits of this breed. In writings of Linnaean specificity, one monk divided all demonic thoughts into eight main categories: gluttony, lust, avarice, sadness, anger, listlessness, vainglory and pride. If this list feels familiar it is because it would form the basis of the medieval world's concept of the deadly sins (listlessness, perhaps true to form, was subsumed into another sin to give the final total of seven).

These demonic descriptions were not, or not merely, done for their own interest — though some monks did admit a tendency to linger a little too long over the thoughts of the more pornographic apparitions. Instead, such precise accounts were seen as serving a valuable purpose in the Christian fight against evil. Knowledge, it was felt, was power. If you knew the demons' distinguishing features, habits and methods of attack then, just as a soldier might read Caesar's *Gallic Wars* before setting out to fight in northern Europe, so you would be better able to face down this frightening foe.

Complex demonologies appeared that explained everything from how these creatures were created (a Miltonian fall from grace), to their stench (revolting), their geography (Rome was a favorite haunt), the feel of their skin (deathly cold) and even their sexual habits (varied, imaginative and persistent). Everything was considered, including the ways in which the demons planned to overcome the logistical and linguistic difficulties involved in world domination. "We should not think that there is one spirit of fornication that seduces a person who, for example, commits fornication in Brittany," wrote one ancient observer, "and another for the person who does so in India." Instead, he explained, there were innumerable spirits, a whole "abominable army" that, under its leader, Satan, harasses the entire world, enticing it to sin.[4]

Part of the demons' power was their astonishing swiftness: they could appear almost anywhere, at any time. Like the angels that they had once been, these demons were winged and so able to travel astonishing distances at great speed to do their evil work—and generally alarm the populace. One man awoke to find a swarm of demons flying in his face like a flock of crows. "They are everywhere in a moment," wrote one ancient chronicler. "For them, the whole world is but a single place."[5] Demons, warned other writers, made terrible noises: they might shriek, howl, hiss or even (most insidious of all) speak. They could beat, punch, bite, burn and make marks on the skin "as if made by a cupping glass." Most foul of all was these creatures' aim: nothing less than "the subversion of mankind."[6]

The methods of demonic attack were numerous, and varied according to the person being attacked and the demon doing the attacking. Demons could and did appear as a flamboyant spectacle—though in general, they saved their most hellish displays for their holiest enemies. To Antony they appeared as wolves and scorpions. At other times, to less holy foes, they might appear as apparently innocuous, even pleasant, forms: as a fellow monk or as beautiful women, as naked boys or even as angels. One elderly monk found himself "beset" by naked women sitting next to him at dinner; while another found a demon sitting on his lap in the form of an Ethiopian girl he had once seen as a young man. Another monk was visited in his monastery by a particularly timeless apparition: a middle-ranking government official. The official then grabbed the monk, who started to wrestle him. As the struggle progressed, the monk realized that he was in the presence not of bureaucracy but (the distinction seems to have been a fine one) of pure evil. This, he realized, was a demon.

Some of the descriptions of demonic attack have an almost Proustian precision. One monk recorded the working of what he called the "noonday demon" that struck between the hours of 10 a.m. and 2 p.m. At this time the monk was supposed to be working, but this particular demon would thwart him and make "it seem that the sun barely moves, if at all, and that the day is fifty hours long. Then he constrains the monk to look constantly out the windows, to walk outside the cell, to gaze carefully at the sun to determine how far it stands from the ninth hour" — the hour of dinner. The demon might then force the monk to poke his head out of his cell to see if any other brethren are about. Then, in the warmth of the noonday sun, the monk finds that he "rubs his eyes and stretches his hands, and he takes his eyes off his book and stares at the wall. Then he returns to the book and reads a little. As he unfolds it, he becomes preoccupied with the condition of the texts . . . he criticizes the orthography and the decoration. Finally, he folds the book up and places it under his head, and he falls into a light sleep."[7]

For the majority of mankind, however, demons conducted their work through the more pedestrian yet insidious means of incitement and enticement, putting ideas into men's heads (and these accounts are all by men) that they were seemingly unable to resist. To counter these diabolic whispers one monk created a phrasebook of words with which one might respond to almost any such apparition. In much the same manner as old guidebooks would offer stock phrases for what to say at foreign railway stations, so this book offered handy phrases, all taken from the Bible, to use in the case of demonic assault. If one found oneself tormented by a thought that suggested a glass of wine would be good for you, one might piously reply: "He who takes pleasure in banquets of wine will leave dishonour in his strongholds"—and, hopefully, the temptation would flee.[8] The book is compendious, offering 498 passages to deploy as and when necessity demands. It is nice to wonder whether fourth-century monks, like contemporary travelers who can ask where the station is but cannot understand the answer, found themselves confounded when their interlocutor did not stick exactly to the prescribed script.

One consequence of the concept of demons was that wicked thoughts were the fault of the demon, not the man: an exculpatory quirk that meant even the most sinful thoughts could be —and were—freely admitted to. In writings of astonishing candor, the monkish id is laid bare as monks confess to being tormented by visions of naked women—not to mention other monks—"performing the obscene sin of fornication," visions that left their soul in torment and their thighs aflame. Monks write about being so overwhelmed by thoughts of sex that they are forced to "jump up at once and to use our cell for frequent and brisk walks." An erotic phantasmagoria danced —sometimes quite literally—before their eyes as the demon of fornication—a devious demon "that imitates the form of a beautiful naked woman, luxurious in her gait, her entire body obscenely dissipated"—turned on them.[9]

In one intriguing portmanteau temptation, an elderly monk suffered a vision in which he was lured not only by young bodies, but also by food and the forbidden fruit of "the other." As he sat in his cell a young "Saracen youth," as he describes him, wearing a bread basket, climbed through the window of his cell and started to sway, asking: "Elder, do I dance well?"[10] The blame was not always entirely lifted from the confessor. The same monk who wrote about his burning thighs also, in some distress, wrote about "the demon that threatens me with curses and said, 'I will make you an object of laughter and reproach among all the monks because you have investigated and made known all the kinds of all the unclean thoughts.'"[11] Even at this distance, the sense of a soul smarting at a confidence rebuffed is unmistakable.

But however alarming the demons of fornication may have been, the most fearsome demons of all were to be found, teeming like flies on a corpse, around the traditional gods of the empire. Jupiter, Aphrodite, Bacchus and Isis; all of them, in the eyes of these Christian writers, were demonic. In sermon after sermon, tract after tract, Christian preachers and writers reminded the faithful in violently disapproving language that the "error" of the pagan religions was demonically inspired. It was demons who first put the "delusion" of other religions into the minds of humans, these writers explained. It was demons who had foisted the gods upon "the seduced and ensnared minds of human beings."[12] Everything about the old religions was demonic. As Augustine thundered: "All the pagans were under the power of demons. Temples were built to demons, altars were set up to demons, priests ordained for the service of demons, sacrifices offered to demons, and ecstatic ravers were brought in as prophets for demons."[13]

The demons' motivation in all of this was simple: if they had human followers, then they would have sacrifices and these sacrifices were their food. To this end, Christian writers explained, demons had created the entire Greco-Roman religious system so that "they may procure for themselves a proper diet of fumes and blood offered to their statues and images."[14] It wasn't merely a question of nourishment, though: the demons also feasted on the very sight of people turning aside from the true Christian God.

Baroque explanations were brought to bear, explaining away all aspects of the old religious cults. One of the most devious demonic ruses was, it was said, to pretend that they could predict the future by prophecy, a talent so beguiling that it brought humans flocking to their altars. It was, Christians fulminated, nothing more than a trick. The demons achieved their so-called prophecies through that vestigial angelic power of swift flight: their wings enabled them to travel so fast that they could watch an event, then flit away and "prophesy" it to mankind. Thus the demons seem to be able to predict, say, the weather and thus "even promise the rain — which they already feel falling."[15]

Temples to the old gods served as centers of demonic activity. Here they settled in swarms, gorging on the sacrifices made by Romans to their gods. Creep into a temple late at night and you would hear petrifying things — corpses that seemed to speak, say — or you might even hear the demons themselves whispering together, plotting against mankind. Those who attempted to build Christian constructions on ruined temples did so at their own risk. In Turkey, a stonemason working on a new monastery found himself lifted into the air by outraged demons and tossed over a cliff. In front of his horrified companions he fell hundreds of meters, bouncing down the sides of the rocks, until he finally came to rest on a stone in the middle of the river far below. So great was the demons' fury at the advance of the Church.

In these early centuries, and in the face of this awful threat, Christian preachers began to exhibit a new, almost hysterical, desire for purity. It wasn't enough not to perform a sacrifice oneself: one had to avoid all contact with the blood, smoke, water and even the smell of other people's sacrifices. To be contaminated by the smoke or sacred water of the old cults was

utterly intolerable. Questions of religious contamination—
practical to the point of bathetic—were asked, and answered,
with great seriousness. At the close of the fourth century, a
faithful Christian wrote an anxious letter to Augustine. May a
Christian use baths which are used by pagans on a feast day, he
asked, either while the pagans are there or after they have left?
May a Christian sit in a sedan chair if a pagan has sat in that
same chair during the feast day celebrations of an "idol"? If a
thirsty Christian comes across a well in a deserted temple, may
they drink from it? If a Christian is starving and on the point of
death, and they see food in an idol's temple, may they eat it?[16]

This tension between the divine and the domestic would
persist. Over 1,500 years later, at the beginning of the twentieth
century, Stephen Dedalus, the protagonist of James Joyce's *Por-
trait of the Artist as a Young Man*, would find his mind winding
round such questions as whether baptism with mineral water
is valid; whether a tiny particle of the Eucharist contained all
the body and blood of Christ or only a part of it; and whether,
if the consecrated wine then went sour, Jesus was still in the
remaining vinegar or whether he preferred a fresher vintage.
Back in the fourth century, Augustine replied to his anxious
correspondent with a letter that concluded on a note of uncompromising rigidity. If a Christian is starving and on the
point of death, and the only food that they can see is food that
has been contaminated by pagan sacrifice, "it is better to reject
it with Christian fortitude." In other words, if it is a choice between contamination with pagan objects and death, the Christian must unhesitatingly choose death.[17]

The fathers of the early Church turned their full rhetorical
force on religious lapses. Time and time again they insisted
that Christians were not like other religions. Christians were
saved; others were not. Christians were correct; other religions were wrong. More than that: they were sick, insane,
evil, damned, inferior. A newly violent vocabulary of disgust
started to be applied to all other religions and anything to do

with them—which meant almost everything in Roman life. Religion ran through the Roman world like lines through marble. At that time, gladiatorial games were preceded by sacrifices; as were plays, athletic contests and even sessions of the Senate. But all, now, were demonic and to be avoided. One Christian soldier was obliged, in the course of military duty, to enter a temple to the old gods. As he went in, a drop of sacred water splashed onto his robe. Ostentatiously unable to bear it, he instantly slashed off that part of his cloak and flung it away. Christians, or so their preachers claimed, felt anxious when forced to inhale the smoke that drifted from altars in the Forum—the good Christian would rather spit on the altar of a pagan and blow out the incense than accidentally breathe in its fumes. The worship of the old gods began to be represented as a terrifying pollution and, like a miasma in Greek tragedy, one that might drag you to catastrophe.

The old laissez-faire Roman ways, in which the worship of one god might simply be added to the worship of all the others, were, preachers told their congregations, no longer acceptable. Worship a different god, they explained, and you were not merely being different. You were demonic. Demons, said the clerics, dwelt in the minds of those who practiced the old religions. Those who criticized Christianity, warned the Christian apologist Tertullian, were not speaking with a free mind. Instead, they were attacking the Christians because they were under the control of Satan and his foot soldiers. The "battleground" of these fearsome troops was nothing other than "your minds, which have been attuned to him by his secret insinuations."[18] Demons were able to "take possession of men's souls and block up their hearts" and so stop them believing in Christ.[19]

This talk of demons, at the distance of a millennium and more, can sound trivial, almost comical. It was not. Nor was it mere rhetoric. It concerned the salvation and damnation of mankind and nothing could be more important. When Con-

stantine had entered Rome in AD 312, it might at first have
seemed as though little would change. The emperor, for the
first time in the history of Rome, was a follower of Christ—
but he intended to allow citizens of the empire to continue
worshipping the gods that they had worshipped for centuries.
Or so he said. "No man whatever should be refused complete
toleration," announced his famous Edict of Milan of 313,* adding that "every man may have complete toleration in the practice of whatever worship he has chosen."

Fine words. And like many fine words, they proved empty.
Christian clerics could not—would not—allow such liber-
alism. The competing clamor of Roman religion did not, in
their eyes, provide different but equally valid opportunities for
worship: they were nothing more than different opportunities
for damnation. The Devil seized every newborn child and if
they were not baptized as Christian then the Devil would keep
them. How could a Christian, in good conscience, stand by and
watch as his brothers knowingly danced with demons?

It needn't have been this way. There is a significant amount
of evidence to suggest that while Christian preachers demanded complete purity, their congregations were much less
enthusiastic. An Augustine or a Chrysostom might believe that
worshipping the Christian God meant forsaking all others, but
many of their congregants were much less convinced. What
was even meant by "Christian" at this time? The habits of polytheism, in which each new god was merely added to the old,
died hard. Many "pagans" happily added the worship of new
Christian god and saints to their old polytheist gods and continued much as before. Gravestones happily reference Christ
and the old Roman gods of the underworld. Many "Christians"

---

* The status of what used to always be called the "Edict of Milan" is, and has been for the
past century, the subject of much academic debate. Many now argue that its importance
has been exaggerated and that it was, in fact, no more than a letter. The scholar H. A.
Drake argues convincingly that, letter or not, it was far from insignificant.

might turn up at church one day, and then the next, when a jubilant, drunken Roman festival started to whirl through town,
defect from the one true God and go and drink in celebration
of pagan ones, dancing late into the night. "Christians" might
pray to God for the truly substantial things in life and yet when
they desired something a little smaller—the return of their
cow, help with their bad knee—turn to slightly less awesome
spirits,[20] much to the despair of their preachers who argued
that God, while He might also have made heaven and earth,
could still find time for livestock. "Let us reduce it to the very
least things," Augustine told an (evidently wayward) congregation. "He sees to the salvation of your hen."[21]

Even the faith of the emperor Constantine himself seemed
troublingly ambiguous. A coin exists which shows Constantine
in profile alongside a god who looks very much like Apollo: as
well as his more famous Christian vision Constantine was also
said to have seen a vision of this decidedly pagan god.[22] Later
in life Constantine allowed a temple to be built to the imperial
family, as if they themselves were divine. With a confidence
that seems astonishing to modern Christians—but that would
have seemed much less so to ancient polytheists who were
used to their emperors being deified—he was titled Constantine "Equal-to-the-Apostles."

Such behavior might be overlooked in an emperor but it was
not what bishops wanted. In sermon after hectoring sermon
delivered by this new generation of rigidly unbending preachers, the people's choice was made clear. In deciding who to
worship, congregations were not choosing between one god
and another. They were choosing between good and evil; between God and Satan. To allow someone to follow a path other
than the true Christian one was not liberty; it was cruelty. Freedom to err was, Augustine would later vigorously argue, freedom to sin—and to sin was to risk the death of the soul. "The
possibility of sinning," as one pope later put it, "is not freedom,

but slavery."²³ To allow another person to remain outside the Christian faith was not to show praiseworthy tolerance. It was to damn them.

The preachers spoke and, eventually, the people — some of them, many of them — started to listen. The pace of Christianization started to increase.

In the nineteenth century, the Victorian poet Matthew Arnold would stand on Dover Beach and hear the "melancholy, long, withdrawing roar" as the sea of faith retreated, leaving man alone, confused, on a darkling plain. In the years of St. Augustine, Christians heard the counterpart of this noise. They called it the *strepitus mundi*, the "roar of the world."²⁴ This was not the roar of religion retreating but the sound of it advancing: the sound of Christianity pouring, as unstoppable as a tide, across towns, countries and continents. To Augustine, the sound of this change was as reassuring as to Arnold it had been melancholy. When Augustine came face to face with a group who had not yet converted to Christianity he told them that they should wake up, they should listen to the *strepitus mundi*.

But the definition of *strepitus* is not entirely straightforward. *Strepitus* is not a happy, reassuring sound in Latin. It is not even a neutral sound. It is not really a sound at all but a noise, and a stressful noise at that. It is the noise of wheels clattering over cobbles, the deafening roar of a river in full spate, the cacophony of an agitated crowd. *Strepitus* is at best an ambiguous word: something that if you are on the right side of it — standing above the flooded river, in the center of the jubilant crowd — can be exciting, even awe-inspiring. But rivers can drag you under; crowds, if they turn on you, can kill you. When Augustine told those people who had not yet converted that they should wake up and listen to the *strepitus mundi* it was, in part, an invitation to the Christian celebration. It was also, unmistakably, a threat.

To oppose another man's religion, to repress their worship

—these were not, clerics told their congregations, wicked or intolerant acts. They were some of the most virtuous things a man might do. The Bible itself demanded it. As the uncompromising words of Deuteronomy instructed: "And ye shall overthrow their altars, and break their pillars, and burn their groves with fire; and ye shall hew down the graven images of their gods, and destroy the names of them out of that place."[25]

The Christians of the Roman Empire listened. And as the fourth century wore on, they began to obey.

CHAPTER THREE

Wisdom Is Foolishness

Utter trash.

—the Greek intellectual Celsus evaluates
the Old Testament

IN EARLY AD 163, some of the most glamorous figures of sec-ond-century Rome gathered in a distinctly unglamorous-look-ing room. These people were not the merely rich, they were something that in those days was considered far more chic: they were the empire's intellectual elite. Eminent philosophers, scholars and thinkers could be glimpsed among the gathering crowd.

In front of this illustrious group, however, was one rather less distinguished guest: on a large board at the front of the room, tied fast by ropes around each limb, was one doubtless rather distressed-looking pig.

Then a young man stepped forward and assumed his place beside the pig. He was only in his early thirties, yet his manner was confident, arrogant even; he had the air of a performer who knew that he would soon have the audience in the palm of his hand. This was Galen. He would quickly become the most renowned doctor in Rome and within a few decades, the most famous physician in the Roman Empire. After his death his fame would spread throughout the entire Western Hemi-sphere. But all that was yet to come. On that day, in that room, Galen was little more than a man with a pig. And in a few mo-ments, through a bravura demonstration of surgical skill, he was going to steal its squeal.

Gatherings of this sort were not unusual in those days. At this time, the intellectual was also fashionable. Even the em-peror himself was a philosopher — and not a bad one: Mar-

cus Aurelius's *Meditations* are still widely read today. Surgery
had become a popular spectator sport and educated citizens
crowded round to watch an animal being vivisected with the
same enthusiasm with which they might once have listened to
the melodramatic declamations of a tragic poet. Those attending such performances needed inquiring minds, long attention
spans (for demonstrations could go on for days) and strong
stomachs. A favorite trick of Galen's was to tie an animal to his
board and lay bare its still-beating heart. Audience members
were then invited to squeeze the throbbing muscle—albeit
with care: the pulsing wet heart was apt to jump from between
inexperienced fingers. At times, for anthropomorphic drama,
Galen used an ape, though its agonized expressions could be
so vivid that they were off-putting. For this particular experiment he preferred pigs because, as he put it in one of his more
heartfelt asides, "there is no advantage in having an ape in such
experiments and the spectacle is hideous."[1]

And "hideous" was not what Galen wanted. Galen wanted
awe and admiration from his audience—and practiced relentlessly to get it. The whole Galenic performance—and make
no mistake, dissection for him was just that—had been cease-
lessly rehearsed. Everything, from the experiments he chose
to the way in which he flourished his glittering steel instruments, had been practiced with the same obsessiveness with
which a magician might burnish their sleight of hand. Galen
was a consummate showman. He was hardworking, brilliant
—and crashingly vain. "Even as an adolescent," he later wrote,
"I looked down on many of my teachers."[2] His skill as a healer
would later be rivaled only by his talent as an irritant.

But then, he was stupendously talented. It would take centuries for many of Galen's observations to be bettered. His
understanding of neuroanatomy would not be superseded
until the seventeenth century; his understanding of certain
functions of the brain would not be surpassed until the nineteenth.[3] It was Galen who proved that arteries contained blood

and not, as had been thought, air or milk. It was Galen who proved that the spinal cord was an extension of the brain and that the higher it was severed, the more movement was lost.

Note that word "proved." Galen knew vivisection was a good show, but it was not merely a show for him. It was utterly essential to understanding how bodies worked. As Galen wrote: "the anatomy of the dead teaches the position . . . of the parts. That of the living may reveal the functions." His writing is littered with the phrases of empiricism: "then you can show . . . ," he writes at one point; "you have seen all this publicly demonstrated," he adds at another; "you observed . . . ," he writes at a third.[4] He was a dedicated empiricist* and had nothing but the deepest scorn for anyone who was not. After describing the experiment to show what arteries contain, Galen writes contemptuously that he never saw milk in them and "nor will anyone who chooses to make the experiment."[5]

Back in Rome, the experiment went well. Galen tied some hair-like nerves in the pig's larynx, its squeal was silenced, and his reputation in the capital of the empire—and hence in history—was assured.

There was, however, one group of people who even the great Galen found himself unable to convince. This was a group who did not form their beliefs by basing them on experiments or on observations, but on faith alone—and who, worse still, were actually proud of this fact. These peculiar people were for Galen the epitome of intellectual dogmatism. When he wished to adequately convey the blockheadedness of another group of physicians, Galen used these people as an

---

* The term "empiricist," in the context of Galen, is a fraught one. Adherents in a medical school in Galen's time were actually known as the "empiricists." Galen, naturally, loathed them (Galen loathed everyone). Moreover, Galen was not a perfect empiricist in the modern sense of the term. His methodology leaves a lot to be desired: for instance, his experiments had no control group. However, Galen was considerably closer to the empirical ideal of observation and testing than many of his contemporaries—and certainly of his successors. Therefore I have used the term empiricist (with caution).

analogy to express the depths of his irritation. They were the Christians.

To show the extent of some doctors' dogmatism he used the phrase "one might more easily teach novelties to the follow-ers of Moses and Christ."[6] Elsewhere, he disparaged physicians who offered views on the body without demonstration to back up their assertions, saying that to listen to them was "as if one had come into the school of Moses and Christ [and heard] talk of undemonstrated laws."[7] Galen had little time for Moses himself, either. "It is his method in his books," wrote Galen, disapprovingly, "to write without offering proofs, saying 'God commanded, God spake.'"[8]

To a proto-empiricist like Galen, this was a cardinal error. Intellectual progress depended on the freedom to ask, ques-tion, doubt and, above all, to experiment. In Galen's world, only the ill-educated believed things without reason. To show something, one did not merely declare it to be so. One proved it, with demonstrations. To do otherwise was for Galen the method of an idiot. It was the method of a Christian.

At around the same time as Galen was torturing pigs in Rome, another Greek intellectual was performing a rather different sort of dissection: a merciless intellectual carving up of Chris-tianity.

This was a new experience for all concerned. For the first hundred-odd years of Christianity's existence, there are no mentions of Christianity in Roman writings. Then, around the turn of the second century, it started to appear, albeit in a piecemeal fashion, in the writings of non-Christians. In AD 111, there is a letter from Pliny, the Roman governor. Then a few years later come some tantalizingly brief references to it in Roman histories—a quick section in the historian Tacitus's *Annals* and another mention in a history by Suetonius. And that was it. None of these accounts were particularly detailed.

Certainly none were lengthy—a few paragraphs in total. But then why would they have been longer? Christianity may have seen itself as the only truth but to most people then it was little more than an eccentric and often irritating eastern cult. Why waste time rebutting it?

Then, about fifty years later, everything changed. Suddenly, in around AD 170, a Greek intellectual named Celsus launched a monumental and vitriolic attack against the religion. It is clear that, unlike the other authors who have so far written about it, Celsus knows a lot about it. He has read Christian scripture—and not just read it: studied it in great detail. He knows about everything—from the Creation to the Virgin Birth and the doctrine of the Resurrection.

It is equally clear that he loathes it all and in arch, sardonic and occasionally very earthy sentences, he vigorously rebuts it. The Virgin Birth? Nonsense, he writes; a Roman soldier had gotten Mary pregnant.[9] The Creation is "absurd"; the books of Moses are garbage; while the idea of the resurrection of the body is "revolting" and, on a practical level, ridiculous: "simply the hope of worms. For what sort of human soul would have any further desire for a body that has rotted?"[10]

What is also clear is that Celsus is more than just disdainful. He is worried. Pervading his writing is a clear anxiety that this religion—a religion that he considers stupid, pernicious and vulgar—might spread even further and, in so doing, damage Rome.

Over 1,500 years later, the eighteenth-century English historian Edward Gibbon would draw similar conclusions, laying part of the blame for the fall of the Roman Empire firmly at the door of the Christians. The Christians' belief in their forthcoming heavenly realm made them dangerously indifferent to the needs of their earthly one. Christians shirked military service, the clergy actively preached pusillanimity, and vast amounts of public money were spent not on protecting armies but squandered instead on the "useless multitudes" of the Church's monks and nuns.[11] They showed, Gibbon felt, an "indolent, or even criminal, disregard for the public welfare."[12]

The Catholic Church and its "useless multitudes" were, in return, magnificently unimpressed by Gibbon's arguments, and they promptly placed his *Decline and Fall of the Roman Empire* on the *Index Librorum Prohibitorum*, its list of banned books.* Even in liberal England, the atmosphere became fiercely hostile to the historian. Gibbon later said that he had been shocked by the response to his work. "Had I believed," he wrote, "that the majority of English readers were so fondly attached even to the name and shadow of Christianity . . . I might, perhaps, have softened the two invidious chapters, which would create many enemies, and conciliate few friends."[13]

Celsus did not soften his attack either. This first assault on Christianity was vicious, powerful and, like Gibbon, immensely readable. Yet unlike Gibbon, today almost no one has heard of Celsus and fewer still have read his work. Because Celsus's fears came true. Christianity continued to spread, and not just among the lower classes. Within 150 years of Celsus's attack, even the emperor of Rome professed himself a follower of the religion. What happened next was far more serious than anything Celsus could ever have imagined. Christianity not only gained adherents, it forbade people from worshipping the old Roman and Greek gods. Eventually, it simply forbade anyone to dissent from what Celsus considered its idiotic teachings. To pick just one example from many, in AD 386, a law was passed targeting those "who contend about religion" in public. Such people, this law warned, were the "disturbers of the peace of the Church" and they "shall pay the penalty of high treason with their lives and blood."[14]

---

* Those books that were approved of by the Catholic Church would be stamped or marked by the word "Imprimatur" — "let it be printed." As late as the 1950s, those who were educated in Catholic schools in this country would have seen books in their libraries so labeled.

Celsus paid his own price. In this hostile and repressive atmosphere his work simply disappeared. Not one single unadulterated volume of the work by Christianity's first great critic has survived. Almost all information about him has vanished too, including any of his names except his last; what prompted him to write his attack; or where and when he wrote it. The long and inglorious Christian practice of censorship was now beginning.

However, by a quirk of literary fate, most of his words have survived. Because eighty-odd years after Celsus fulminated against the new religion, a Christian apologist named Origen mounted a fierce and lengthy counter-attack. Origen was rather more earnest than his occasionally bawdy classical adversary. Indeed, it was said that Origen had even taken the words of Matthew 19:12 ("For there are some eunuchs . . . which have made themselves eunuchs for the kingdom of heaven's sake") a little too much to heart and, in a fit of heavenly self-abnegation, castrated himself.

Ironically, it was the very work that had been intended to demolish Celsus that saved him. No books of Celsus have survived the centuries untouched, true—but Origen's attack has and it quoted Celsus at length. Scholars have therefore been able to extract Celsus's arguments from Origen's words, which preserved them like flies in amber. Not all of the words—perhaps only seventy percent of the original work has been recovered. Its order has gone, its structure has been lost, and the whole thing, as Gibbon put it, is a "mutilated representation" of the original.[15] But nevertheless we have it.

It is easy to see why it upset the ancient Christians. Even by today's standards, Celsus's *On the True Doctrine* feels bracingly direct. It wasn't just Mary and Moses who were attacked. Everything was. Jesus was not, Celsus wrote, conceived through the Holy Spirit. This, he scoffs, was most unlikely because Mary wouldn't have been beautiful enough to tempt a deity.[16] Instead, he says, Jesus was conceived via the rather baser means

of that Roman soldier named Panthera.* When Mary's pregnancy and infidelity had been discovered, she was convicted of
adultery and "driven out by her husband."[17]

If that feels shocking, Celsus had barely begun. The divine
scriptures were, he said, rubbish; the story of the Garden of
Eden was "very silly" and Moses "had no idea" about the true
nature of the world.[18] The "prophecies" that had predicted Jesus's coming were also nonsense, since "the prophecies could
be applied to thousands of others far more plausibly than to
Jesus." Judgment Day also came in for scorn. How *precisely*,
asked Celsus, was this going to work? "It is foolish of them also
to suppose that, when God applies the fire (like a cook!), all the
rest of mankind will be thoroughly roasted and that they alone
will survive."[19] Cherished Christian beliefs were dismissed as
being the sort of tales that "a drunken old woman would have
been ashamed to sing . . . to lull a little child to sleep."[20]

Celsus professes himself baffled by the extent to which Jesus's teachings seem to contradict many of those laid down in
the Old Testament. Have the rules of an allegedly omniscient
god changed over time? If so, then "who is wrong? Moses or
Jesus? Or when the Father sent Jesus had he forgotten what
commands he gave to Moses?" Or maybe God knew he was
changing his mind, and Jesus was a legal messenger, sent to
give notice that God wished to "condemn his own laws and
change his mind."[21]

Celsus cannot understand, either, why there was such a
great gap between the creation of mankind and the sending

---

* This name is similar to the Greek word for virgin, *parthenos*, the insinuation—or perhaps pun—being that Jesus was not born from a virgin but from a man whose name
sounded like "virgin." This general story was one that would tempt humorists—and out-
rage Christians—for centuries. In the 1979 film *Life of Brian*, the father of the messiah-like
Brian turns out to be a Roman centurion called "Naughtius Maximus." The film was
banned in several countries. It was later marketed in Sweden as "So funny it was banned
in Norway."

of Jesus. If all who don't believe are damned, why wait so long to enable them to be saved? "Is it only now after such a long age that God has remembered to judge the life of men? Did he not care before?"[22] Moreover, why not send Jesus somewhere a bit more populous? If God "woke up out of his long slumber and wanted to deliver the human race from evils, why on earth did he send this spirit that you mention into one corner" of the world—and, Celsus implies, a backwater at that?[23] He also queries why an omniscient, omnipotent God would need to send someone at all. "What is the purpose of such a descent on the part of God?" he asks. "Was it in order to learn what was going on among men? . . . Does not he know everything?"[24]

Jesus's logistical abilities are, like God's, called into question. Celsus attacks the tendency for some of his most miraculous moments to be witnessed by the fewest number of people. "When he was punished he was seen by all; but by only one person after he rose again; whereas the opposite ought to have happened."[25] What witnesses the Bible did offer were, for Celsus, rarely reliable. Of the Resurrection he says: "Who saw this? A hysterical female, as you say"—and one other person who then went on to invent this "cock-and-bull story."[26] The Resurrection was therefore either "wishful thinking" or perhaps "a hallucination."[27]

The claim that Christ was divine seems to Celsus a logical impossibility: "How can a dead man be immortal?"[28] The idea that Jesus came to save sinners also comes in for short shrift. "Why on earth this preference for sinners?" he asks. "Why was he not sent to those without sin? What evil is it not to have sinned?"[29]

The arguments go on, hammering at Christianity's central beliefs. The Creation story itself takes a particular bashing. Celsus disdains the idea of an omnipotent being needing to piece out his work like a builder, to make so much on one day, so much more on a second, third, fourth and so on—and particularly the idea that, after all this work, "God, exactly like a bad workman, was worn out and needed a holiday to have a rest."[30]

To many intellectuals such as Celsus, the whole idea of a "Creation myth" was not only implausible but redundant. During this period in Rome, a popular and influential philosophical theory offered an alternative view. This theory — an Epicurean one — stated that everything in the world was made not by any divine being but by the collision and combination of atoms. According to this school of thought, these particles were invisible to the naked eye but they had their own structure and could not be cut (*temno*) into any smaller particles: they were *a-temnos* — "the uncuttable thing": the atom. Everything that you see or feel, these materialists argued, was made up of two things: atoms and space "in which these bodies are and through which they move this way and that."[31] Even living creatures were made from them: humans were, as one (hostile) author summarized, not made by God but were instead nothing more than "a haphazard union of elements."[32] The distinct species of animals were explained by a form of proto-Darwinism. As the Roman poet and atomist Lucretius wrote, nature put forth many species. Those that had useful characteristics — the fox and its cunning, say, or the dog and its intelligence — survived, thrived and reproduced. Those creatures that lacked these "lay at the mercy of others for prey and profit . . . until nature brought that race to destruction."[33]

The intellectual consequences of this powerful theory were summarized succinctly by the Christian apologist Minucius Felix. If everything in the universe has been "formed by a fortuitous concourse of atoms, what God is the architect?"[34] The obvious answer is: no god at all. No god magicked up mankind out of nothing, no divinity breathed life into us; and, when we die, our atoms are simply reabsorbed into this great sea of stuff. "No thing is ever by divine power produced from nothing," wrote Lucretius in his great poem *On the Nature of Things*, and "no single thing returns to nothing."[35] Atomic theory thus neatly did away with the need for and possibility of Creation, Resurrection, the Last Judgment, hell, heaven and the Creator God himself.

As indeed was its intention. Thinkers in the classical world frequently lamented the mortal fear of divine beings. Superstition, wrote the Greek biographer Plutarch, was a terrible affliction that "humbles and crushes a man."[36] People saw earthquakes and floods and storms and lightning and assumed, in the absence of any other explanation, that they are "done by divine power."[37] The consequence of this was that people tried to propitiate these temperamental gods. Writers such as Lucretius argued that atomism, correctly applied, could blast this fear into tiny pieces. If there was no Creator — if lightning, earthquakes and storms were not the actions of irate deities but simply of moving particles of matter — then there was nothing to fear, nothing to propitiate and nothing to worship.[38] Including no Christian God.

In the ensuing centuries, texts that contained such dangerous ideas paid a heavy price for their "heresy." As has been lucidly argued by Dirk Rohmann, an academic who has produced a comprehensive and powerful account of the effect of Christianity on books, some of the greatest figures in the early Church rounded on the atomists.[39] Augustine disliked atomism for precisely the same reason that atomists liked it: it weakened mankind's terror of divine punishment and hell. Texts by philosophical schools that championed atomic theory suffered.

The Greek philosopher Democritus had perhaps done more than anyone to popularize this theory — though not only this one. Democritus was an astonishing polymath who had written works on a breathless array of other topics. A far from complete list of his titles includes *On History, On Nature, The Science of Medicine, On the Tangents of the Circle and the Sphere, On Irrational Lines and Solids, On the Causes of Celestial Phenomena, On the Causes of Atmospheric Phenomena, On Reflected Images . . .*

The list goes on. Today Democritus's most famous theory is his atomism. What did the other theories state? We have no idea: every single one of his works was lost in the ensuing centuries. As the eminent physicist Carlo Rovelli recently wrote, after citing an even longer list of the philosopher's titles: "the loss of the works of Democritus in their entirety is the greatest intellectual tragedy to ensue from the collapse of the old classical civilisation."[40]

Democritus's atomic theory did, however, come down to us —but on a very slender thread: it was contained in one single volume of Lucretius's great poem, which was held in one single German library, which one single intrepid book hunter would eventually find and save from extinction. That single volume would have an astonishing afterlife: it became a literary sensation, returned atomism to European thought, created what Stephen Greenblatt has called "an explosion of interest in pagan antiquity" and influenced Newton, Galileo and later Einstein.[41]

In the Renaissance, Lucretius and his atomic theories were revolutionary. In Celsus's time they were utterly unremarkable. It wasn't just the fact that Christians were ignorant about philosophical theories that annoyed Celsus; it was that Christians actually reveled in their ignorance. Celsus accuses them of actively targeting idiocy in their recruitment. "Their injunctions are like this," he wrote. "Let no one educated, no one wise, no one sensible draw near. For these abilities are thought by us to be evils."

He went on: Christians "are able to convince only the foolish, dishonourable and stupid, and only slaves, women and little children."[42] They made overtures to children, cobblers, laundry-workers and yokels, then dripped honeyed intellectual poison into uneducated ears, claiming "that they alone . . . know the right way to live, and if the children would believe them, they would become happy."[43] Christianity's lack of intellectual rigor worried Celsus for the same reasons that it had bothered Galen. Christians, Celsus wrote, "do not want to give or to receive a reason for what they believe, and use such expressions as 'Do not ask questions; just believe,' and 'Thy faith will save thee.'"[44] To men as educated as Celsus and Galen this was unfathomable: in Greek philosophy, faith was the lowest form of cognition.

Celsus wasn't merely annoyed at the lack of education among these people. What was far worse was that they actually celebrated ignorance. They declare, he wrote, that "Wisdom in this life is evil, but foolishness is good"—an almost precise quotation from Corinthians. Celsus verges on hyperbole, but it is true that in this period Christians gained a reputation for being uneducated to the point of idiotic; even Origen, Celsus's great adversary, admitted that "the stupidity of some Christians is heavier than the sand of the sea."[45] This slur (and it almost certainly was a slur—Christians were no more likely, it is now thought, to be poorly educated than any other religious group) would make conversion socially awkward for Rome's upper classes for centuries to come. An educated man on the brink of becoming Christian would have to ask himself not only whether he was able to make the leap of faith but whether he was able to make the necessary social leap as well. Such a man would wonder to himself, as Augustine succinctly put it, "Shall I become what . . . my concierge, is and not a Plato, not a Pythagoras?"[46]

There is more than a whiff of actual as well as intellectual snobbery in Celsus's criticisms—and more than a dash of misogyny: Christianity is not something that educated men in Rome do: it is the habit of women and vulgar foreigners in foreign places. However, there was more to it than that. Lack of education, Celsus argued, made listeners vulnerable to dogma. If Christians had read a little more and believed a little less, they might be less likely to think themselves unique. The lightest knowledge of Latin literature, for example, would have brought the interested reader into contact with Ovid's *Meta-*

morphoses. This epic but tongue-in-cheek poem opened with a version of the Creation myth that was so similar to the biblical one that it could hardly fail to make an interested reader question the supposed unique truth of Genesis.

Even the most fervent Christian must notice the similarities between the two. Where the biblical Creation begins with an earth that is "without form," Ovid's poem begins with a "rough, unordered mass of things." In Genesis, the Creator God then "created the heaven and the earth" and ordered "the waters under the heaven be gathered together unto one place, and let the dry land appear." In Ovid's version, a god appears and "rent asunder land from sky, and sea from land" before instructing the seas to form and the "plains to stretch out."

The God of Genesis ordered that "the waters bring forth abundantly the moving creature that hath life, and fowl that may fly above the earth in the open firmament of heaven," while Ovid's deity ("whichever of the gods it was," he adds, somewhat vaguely) ensures that "the sea fell to the shining fishes for their home, earth received the beasts and the mobile air the birds." Both Creation stories culminate in the creation of man, who in Ovid is "moulded into the form of the all-controlling gods"; while in Genesis, "God created man in his own image."

In both, things then go wrong as mankind falls into wicked ways. The Ovidian god, at once grand and a trifle camp, looks down upon the world he has created, shakes his head in despair and groans. "I must," he declares, not without some melodrama, "destroy the race of men."[47] The God of Genesis looks down at the world and its wickedness and says: "I will destroy man whom I have created from the face of the earth."[48] In both accounts, the rainwaters fall, and the oceans rise across the lands. In both, only two humans, a man and a woman, survive.

The idea of "the Flood" was, to Celsus, "a debased" version of this classical flood, a "myth" for Christians to recount to small children.[49] To Christians it was the truth. Even in nineteenth-century England, the Church was still defending it as such. At this time, the story's authority was less in danger of erosion from scornful philosophers than from the new science of geology. The sheer age of the earth was beginning to make any belief in a Creation difficult—particularly in a Creation that had happened, as one Christian theologian infamously stated, on October 23, 4004 BC. Many pious Victorian academics fought back against this new and threatening science, including, somewhat bizarrely, some geologists. In his inaugural address, William Buckland, the first professor of geology at Oxford University, delivered a paper entitled "*Vindiciae Geologicae*, or, the Connexion of Geology with Religion Explained," in which he announced that a recent "deluge" is "most satisfactorily confirmed by every thing that has yet been brought to light by Geological investigations" and that "the Mosaic account is in perfect harmony with the discoveries of modern science."[50]

The Christian belief that their religion was unique—and uniquely correct—frequently grated on others. An educated critic of Christianity could point not only to other flood stories but to numerous characters who had made similar claims to those made by Jesus and his followers. The empire was not lacking, Celsus observed, in charismatic preachers who claimed divinity, espoused poverty or announced that they were going to die for the sake of mankind. There are "others who go about begging [and] say that they are sons of God who have come from above."[51] Nor, Celsus pointed out, was Jesus the only one to claim resurrection. Did the Christians believe that other tales of risings from the dead are "the legends which they appear to be, and yet that the ending of your tragedy is to be regarded as noble and convincing?"[52]

The Greek rhetorician Lucian, who described the Christians as those "poor wretches," wrote a satirical account of one such man, a charlatan (as Lucian saw him) named Peregrinus who lived in Greece. Desperate for fame, this pseudo-philosopher grew his hair long and traveled about the empire preaching platitudes. He lived off charity, gathered a reputation among the credulous, and eventually committed suicide by jumping into a fire "to benefit mankind by showing them the way in which one should despise death."[53]

Lucian, watching, learned not to despise death but he did learn to despise the "villainous reek" of an elderly man burning to death.[54] Before Peregrinus had died, he had hesitated, pausing on the edge of the flames, speechifying. As he hesitated, some of the assembled crowd begged him to save himself while others—the "more manly part," as Lucian approvingly describes them—bellowed, "Get on with it."[55] You can imagine, says Lucian, "how I laughed."[56]

After Peregrinus had been "carbonified" (as our unsympathetic narrator puts it) his stock only rose among his followers.[57] Before his end, Peregrinus had sent letters to all the great cities of the empire, bearing witness to his great life and encouraging and instructing his followers. He even "appointed a number of ambassadors for this purpose from among his comrades, styling them 'messengers'"—the Greek word is *angelos*, the same word translated in Christianity as "angel"—"from the dead."[58] Rumors that Peregrinus had indeed risen from the dead began to spread: one disciple declares that "he had beheld him in white raiment a little while ago, and had just now left him walking about . . . wearing a garland of wild olive."[59]

The Church was profoundly unamused by such irreverence. As one tenth-century Byzantine text explained, the nickname for Lucian was "the Blasphemer" because "in his dialogues he went so far as to ridicule religious discourse."[60] In the sixteenth century, the Inquisition also added Lucian to its list of banned books. Christianity found its own grimly humorless punch lines for such men. As the same Byzantine chronicle informed its readers, "the story goes that [Lucian] was killed by dogs, because of his rabid attacks on the truth, for in his *Life of Peregrinus* he inveighs against Christianity, and (accursed man!) blasphemes against Christ himself. For that reason he paid the penalty befitting his rabidity in this world, and in the life to come he will share the eternal fire with Satan."[61] An invigorating lesson for all satirists.

Celsus, however, implied that if people were better educated they would be more resistant to such hucksters as Peregrinus — or indeed to Jesus, whom Celsus considered little more than a "sorcerer."[62] The "miracles" that Jesus performed were, he felt, no better than the sort of thing that was constantly being peddled by tricksters to the gullible across the Roman Empire. In a world in which medical provision was rare, many laid claim to magical powers. Travel in the east and you would come across any number of men who "for a few obols make known their sacred lore in the middle of the market-place and drive daemons out of men and blow away diseases," and display "dining-tables and cakes and dishes which are non-existent."[63] Even Jesus himself, observes Celsus, admits the presence of such people when he talks about men who can perform similar wonders to his own. Modern scholarship supports Celsus's accusations: ancient papyri tell of sorcerers who had the power to achieve such biblical-sounding feats as stilling storms and miraculously providing food.[64]

Celsus touches on a sore point here. Early Christianity would have to spend a considerable amount of time and effort policing the boundaries between sanctity and sorcery. A large amount of ink was spilled on the subject of Simon Magus (the Magician). A quick summary of Simon's life makes it clear why he was so threatening: Simon performed various miracles, gathered a following of people who thought he was a god — including a former prostitute — and one of Simon's disciples "persuaded those who adhered to him that they should never die."[65] His followers even honored him with a statue inscribed with the words "To Simon, the Holy God" — in Latin, *Simoni Deo Sancto*. Interestingly, it is not Simon's supernatural abilities that are denied by Christian accounts — the texts admit he can perform amazing feats — merely his divine right to do so. The criticism seems to be not one of religious fakery but of religious fuel: Simon gains his power not from God but "by virtue of the art of the devils operating in him."[66]

Christians debunked pretenders. The ancient world debunked everyone else. Stories of witty atheists were treasured, told and retold. When one man asked a Greek philosopher to go with him to a shrine to pray, the friend replied that he must think the god was very deaf if he couldn't hear them from where they were.[67]

Some Romans had so little patience for Roman religious rites that they discarded them entirely. One moonlit night in the third century BC, a Roman consul called Publius Claudius Pulcher decided to launch a surprise attack against an enemy fleet. Before he moved, he took the usual auspices required before military action. In accordance with these rites, the sacred chickens were released from their cage. They refused to eat —a terrible omen and a clear sign to all that the gods did not favor this attempt and that it should be abandoned. It was not clear to Publius Claudius Pulcher. Throwing the chickens into the sea he scoffed: "Let them drink, since they don't wish to eat," and sailed into what would be a disastrous battle.[68]

There was a strong strain of skepticism in Greek and Roman thought. As Pliny the Elder put it: "I deem it a mark of human stupidity to seek to discover the shape and form of God. Whoever God is—provided there is a God—. . . he consists wholly of sense, sight and hearing, wholly of soul, wholly of mind, wholly of himself."[69] Pliny suggested that what divinity there was, was to be found in humanity itself: "God," he wrote, "is one mortal helping another."[70] Rome was not an empire of atheists—emperors were even deified after their death, and their "genius" (divine spirit) then worshipped. Nevertheless, even the emperors themselves didn't always take this too seriously. The emperor Vespasian is said to have announced the severity of his final illness by declaring: "Gah. I think I'm turning into a god."[71]

But Romans were not all cynics. "We too are a religious people," one nettled official tartly told some pious Christians.[72] It was a commonly held belief that Rome's great success depended on the goodwill of the gods. As a character in a Roman history observed: "All went well so long as we obeyed the gods, and ill when we spurned them."[73] This state of divine benevolence—the *pax deorum* or "peace of the gods"—was not manna that fell from heaven on the divinely deserving Romans. They weren't automatically gifted with the gods' favor and they were not automatically assured of this peace. Instead *pax* in that phrase was like the *pax* in *pax Romana:* less a state of eternal peace than the absence of war that had been negotiated through effort and could be lost by neglect. The real punch line of the Claudius Pulcher tale, retold by Cicero, is not the gag about chickens but what came next: after losing the battle, Claudius Pulcher was tried and died soon after.[74]

Religious they may have been; dogmatic and unbending they were not. Like the Roman Empire, the Roman pantheon could happily expand. Rome was not a paragon of religious pluralism. It had no scruples about banning or suppressing practices—whether Druidic or Bacchic or Manichaean—that seemed for any reason pernicious. But equally it could admit foreign gods—though as with so much else in Rome a bureaucratic process had first to be observed. To ignore this process and worship a foreign god that had not been accepted was a socially unacceptable act; it risked upsetting the contract with the incumbent gods and spreading disaster and pestilence. This was one of the problems with Christianity and its growth was, for some, nerve-racking: what effect would this new religion have on the *pax deorum?* "I cannot think there is anyone so audacious," wrote one, neatly summarizing this attitude, that they would "endeavour to destroy or weaken so ancient, useful and salutary a religion."[75] The old religions had served Rome well. Why abandon them now?

Despite his contempt for Christians, Celsus seems unsurprised that yet another religion had appeared in this world full of gods: religious diversity is precisely what one expects. Celsus shows an almost anthropological interest in the different sorts of worship that flourished across the Roman Empire. "The difference between each nation is very considerable," he writes. Some Egyptians "worship only Zeus and Dionysus. The Arabians worship only Ourania and Dionysus. The Egyptians all worship Osiris and Isis."[76] So what? is the implication. There is a strong strain of relativism in Celsus's work. At another point he states: "even if something seems to you to be evil, it is not yet clear whether it really is evil; for you do not know what is expedient either for you or for someone else or for the universe."[77] It was clear to Celsus that a person's religious affiliation was based less on any rational analysis of competing religious ideologies than on the geography of their birth. Every nation always, he points out, thinks its way of doing things is "by far the best."[78] He quotes Herodotus approvingly: "if anyone were to propose to call men and to tell them to choose which of all laws were the best, on consideration each would choose his own." But that didn't matter. As Herodotus himself said, "it is not likely that anyone but a lunatic would make a mock of these things."[79]

Christian observers would look on the tolerance of their non-Christian neighbors with astonishment. Augustine later marveled at the fact that the pagans were able to worship many different gods without discord while the Christians, who worshipped just the one, splintered into countless warring factions. Indeed, many pagans like Celsus seemed to actively praise plurality. To the Christians, this was anathema. Christ was the way, the truth and the light, and everything else was not merely wrong but plunged the believer into a demonic darkness. To allow someone to continue in an alternative form of worship or a heretical form of Christianity was not to allow religious freedom; it was to allow Satan to thrive.

Augustine, despite being impressed by the harmony of his

neighbors, was not willing to extend such tolerance himself. It was, he concluded, the duty of a good Christian to convert heretics—by force, if necessary. This was a theme to which he returned again and again.[80] Far better a little compulsion in this life than eternal damnation in the next. People could not always be trusted to know what was good for them. The good and caring Christian would therefore remove the means of sinning from the uncertain reach of the sinner. "For in most cases we serve others best by not giving, and would injure them by giving, what they desire," he explained. Do not put a sword in a child's hand. "For the more we love any one, the more are we bound to avoid entrusting to him things which are the occasion of very dangerous faults."[81]

A few decades after Celsus wrote *On the True Doctrine*, an even more monumental assault was made on the Christian faith by another Greek philosopher. It shocked the Christian community with its depth, breadth and brilliance. Yet today this philosopher's name, like Celsus's, has been all but forgotten. He was, we know, called Porphyry. We know that his attack was immense—at least fifteen books; that it was highly erudite and that it was, to the Christians, deeply upsetting. We know that it targeted Old Testament history, and poured scorn on the prophets and on the blind faith of Christians. We know some parts in more detail: that Porphyry felt that most people thought the story of Jonah and the Whale to be nonsense, as it "is utterly improbable and incredible, that a man swallowed with his clothes on should have existed in the inside of a fish."[82] It is also clear that Porphyry, like Celsus and Galen, accused Christianity of being an "unreasoning faith."[83] We know that Porphyry too found himself baffled as to why God had waited so long to save mankind: "If Christ declares Himself to be the Way of salvation, the Grace and the Truth . . . what has become of men who lived in the many centuries before Christ came?" he asked. "What, then, has become of such an innumerable multitude of souls, who were in no wise blameworthy" who

were born earlier? Why "did He who is called the Saviour with-
hold Himself for so many centuries of the world?"[84]

This much, then, is known—but not much more. And the
reason we don't know is that Porphyry's works were deemed
so powerful and frightening that they were completely eradicated. Constantine, the first Christian emperor—now famed
for his edict of "toleration"—started the attack. In a letter written in the early part of the fourth century, he heaped odium
on the long-dead philosopher, describing him as "that enemy
of piety," an author of "licentious treatises against religion."
Constantine announced that he was henceforth "branded with
infamy," overwhelmed "with deserved reproach," and that his
"impious writings" had been destroyed. In the same letter Constantine also consigned the works of the heretic Arius to the
flames and announced that anyone who was found hiding one
of Arius's books would be put to death. Constantine signed off
this aggressive epistle with the instruction "May God preserve
you!"[85] Presumably unless you were an admirer of Porphyry or
Arius. A century or so later, in AD 448, Porphyry's books were
burned again, this time on the orders of the Christian emperors Theodosius II and Valentinian III.[86]

This, the new generation of Christian preachers would argue, was loving, not repressive. To force someone to change
what they did, or what they believed, was to heal, not harm
them. In one of Augustine's many reassuring metaphors, he
explained that to restrain a sinner from being able to sin was
not a cruelty but a kindness. "If any one saw his enemy running headlong to destroy himself when he had become delir-
ious through a dangerous fever, would he not in that case be
much more truly rendering evil for evil if he permitted him to
run on thus, than if he took measures to have him seized and
bound?"[87] He went on: "Not every one who is indulgent is a
friend; nor is every one an enemy who smites. Better are the
wounds of a friend than the proffered kisses of an enemy."[88]

A new era was opening. To worship another god was no

longer to be merely different. It was to err. And those who erred were to be seized, struck and — if necessary — wounded. Above all, they were to be stopped.

"There is nothing wrong," Celsus had written, "if each nation observes its own laws of worship."[89] To many of the most powerful thinkers within the Christian Church, nothing could be more abhorrent.

CHAPTER FOUR

"On the Small Number of Martyrs"

Don't you see the beauty of this pleasant weather? There will be no pleasure to come your way if you kill your own self.

—a Roman official addresses a would-be martyr

IN CHRISTIAN MYTH, the persecution began with Nero. He, it was said, was "the first of the emperors to be the declared enemy of the worship of Almighty God."[1]

Few people, Christian or otherwise, had expected Nero to be a good thing. His breeding alone augured against it. His father, Domitius, had once, while driving his chariot through a village, run over and killed a young boy for fun. When another nobleman reprimanded him, Domitius turned and gouged out the man's eye. Nero's mother, Agrippina, was little more promising: a society beauty, in AD 54 she had murdered her third husband, the emperor Claudius, by poisoning him with his favorite food of mushrooms at a family dinner. Not even Nero's own father had high hopes for his offspring. When he was born, Domitius remarked sanguinely that "any child born to himself and Agrippina was bound to have a detestable nature and become a public danger."[2]

Nero did not disappoint. When he first came to power, his misdemeanors were mild. A little too much theater here, a little brawling there. But things soon deteriorated. Before long he was seducing freeborn boys and married women; had raped a Vestal Virgin; "married" a castrated young boy; and committed incest with his mother—it was said that whenever they rode together in the same litter they would seize the moment and "the stains on his clothes when he emerged proved it."[3] Like most of Nero's passions, this one didn't last and Nero soon had Agrippina murdered. Casting round for a new passion, he conceived a novel sexual entertainment. He ordered men and women to be tied to stakes then had himself released from a "den" and, dressed in wild animal skins, bounded forth and attacked the genitals of his trussed captives. Then, as his biographer Suetonius records with fastidiously phrased distaste (though not so fastidious that he doesn't record it at all), "after working up sufficient excitement by this means, he was despatched—shall we say?—by his freedman."[4]

This, then—or so the scurrilous historians said—was the character of the man who ruled the greatest city on earth. And what a city it was. Around a million people lived on its seven hills and they walked among world-famous monuments of awesome beauty and size. Even its infrastructure impressed: towering aqueducts disgorged millions of gallons of water a day, filling the city's drinking-water basins, its baths and even a massive fake lake on which mock naval battles could be staged. A million cubic meters of water flowed into the city every day —a thousand liters per head, double the amount available to those living in modern Rome. After Rome fell, no city in Europe would come close to matching its magnificence—and certainly not its plumbing—for well over a millennium.

This is the picture of Rome that we know. However, under the marble exterior lay a far less glossy reality. It is true that the city's sewers were, by the standard of the time, remarkable: as one Roman, with true Roman pragmatism, wrote, they were the city's "most noteworthy achievement of all." The tunnels were so massive that a man might ride a fully laden wagon along them.[5] But they were far from perfect. Despite the roomy vastness of the Cloaca Maxima, most people didn't have access to latrines and the streets of Rome provided de facto toilets for much of its population. Sometimes they used chamber pots; at other times they simply relieved themselves in streets, doorways and behind statues.

And while wealthy Romans lived in grand villas—the emperor Domitian later lived in a palace of 40,000 square meters

—most of the city's population existed in cramped and teetering apartment blocks. These buildings, many as high as seven stories, were jerry-built, poorly maintained by unscrupulous management agents and prone to falling down. "We inhabit a Rome for the most part supported by thin props," wrote the poet Juvenal, bitterly. Housing agents responded to their tenants' problems with minimal effort: after such an agent had "covered a gaping ancient crack, he tells us not to worry, as we sleep in a building on the point of collapse."[6]

Noise was an incessant problem. As well as thin walls there was no glass in the windows and most Romans—at least according to the grumbling of the city's satirists—suffered from chronic insomnia. Any peace was quickly interrupted by the clanging of braziers' hammers, or the clattering of carts as they rattled along the flagstones in the darkness. Daytime was little more serene: citizens were plagued by everything from the yells of salesmen to the floggings administered by shrill schoolmasters. No peace—and no peace of mind, either. For those who rented a home in those rickety apartment blocks, fire was a perpetual fear. Juvenal, evidently fed up with garret life, wrote: "if the alarm is raised at the bottom of the stairs, the person protected from the rain by only a little roof tile . . . will be the last to burn."[7]

One hot summer's day in AD 64, that fear came true. By nightfall on July 18 a fire had taken hold in some shops near the Circus Maximus. These buildings, fronted with wooden shutters and filled with inflammable goods, provided the conflagration with a wonderful start. Soon, houses along the whole length of the Circus were ablaze; before long, the fire had spread to the hills. As the blaze spread overnight, the sound of flames became mingled with the wailing of women and children as they tried to flee—often in vain. The flames, it was said, were so hot and so rapid that those who turned to look behind them found their faces burned by the heat. Rome had a (relatively) sophisticated fire service—but either the inferno was too fierce to control or something more sinister was going on. It was later said that as it raged, threatening men had appeared, forbidding anyone to extinguish the flames and even hurling firebrands into buildings which hadn't yet caught. Rome burned for almost a week. By the time the fire had finally gone out, three whole quarters of the city had been destroyed and thousands were homeless.

Rome was wretched; one man alone — so the historians said — was delighted. As his people fled, Nero was said to have spent the entire six days and seven nights of the disaster watching it from a high tower, enraptured by "the beauty of the flames."[8] He passed the time by getting into costume and singing a composition of his own ("The Sack of Ilium") about the burning of another famous city. He probably even played the cithara as he did so. Fiddling, as people later anachronistically described it, while Rome burned.

Nero looked at the charred ruins of Rome and, instead of seeing disaster, saw — or so it was said — the opportunity he had wanted. Building works began almost immediately; not to create homes for the thousands of newly homeless, but for himself. Nero's infamous Golden House rose, a palatial and tastelessly glitzy phoenix from the ashes. Where flames had once scorched the faces of the fleeing, now there was a bathhouse fed by sea water and sulfur water; where once the air had been so hot that buildings spontaneously burst into flame, there now lay a pond the size of a sea, surrounded by buildings made to look like miniature cities.

Even by Nero's standards this place was extravagant. The whole house glittered, so they said, like fire with overlaid gold, in which glowed jewels and mother-of-pearl. The roof of the dining room was fitted with ivory panels that could turn to release showers of petals upon the diners below, while pipes sprinkled a fine rain of perfume. Wild animals roamed through landscaped gardens. It was a rural idyll inside one of the largest

cities on earth. When the palace was completed Nero was finally content. "Good," he said. "Now I can at last begin to live
like a human being!"[9]

Listen carefully, however, and over the sound of splashing
water and the roars of those wild beasts, you might have heard
another noise: the murmurs of a deeply discontented populace. The citizens of Rome were angry, and they were suspicious. Nero, they whispered, had started the fire intentionally,
to clear space for the palace that gleamed where the flames had
glowed.

Nero himself—perhaps aware of the bitterness—blamed
a different group. A new cult had recently arrived in Rome.
The historian Tacitus later described it as a "pernicious superstition."[10] The followers of this superstition were said to be the
troublesome adherents of a man named "Christus" or possibly,
according to the historian Suetonius, "Chrestus."[11] They were,
Tacitus added, a group "popularly called Christians" and they
were "hated for their perversions." Tacitus added a little more:
"The name's source was one Christus," he wrote, "executed
by the governor Pontius Pilatus when Tiberius held power." A
significant sentence: this was the sole mention of this event in a
non-Christian source from this period. Tacitus was little more
enthusiastic about the Christians, adding the typically misan-
thropic, Tacitean conclusion that after Jesus's execution, "the
pernicious creed, suppressed at the time, was bursting forth
again, not only in Judaea, where this evil originated, but even
in Rome, into which from all directions everything appalling
and shameful flows and foregathers."[12]

By the time of the Great Fire in AD 64, it seems that there
were some Christians living in the capital. Certainly there were
enough that when Nero was looking for scapegoats for the inferno, not only did they seem a plausible target but he was able
to find a number of them (even if not quite the "huge multitude" that histories later said) to accuse. And to accuse, for

Nero, was to convict; and to convict was to punish. The actual crime was not arson, oddly, but "hatred of humankind."[13] The Christians were sentenced to death.

The mode of their execution showed, even by Nero's standards, a lunatic creativity. Some were dressed in animal skins and then torn to pieces by wild dogs. Others, convicted of making fire, died by it. As dusk fell in Nero's garden, Christians were nailed to crosses, then burned, serving as unusual nighttime illuminations. Nero threw open his gardens for the spectacle as a treat—or perhaps a warning—to others. As the killings were taking place, he wandered among his guests while dressed (for no clear reason other than perhaps that he liked chariot racing) as a charioteer. The display was so gruesome that even the Romans, not a people known to shirk the spectacle of painful death, were disconcerted. A feeling of pity started to grow among them since "the Christians' annihilation seemed to arise not from public utility but from one man's brutality."[14]

This, then, was where it began: the first imperial persecution of the Christians. According to Christian historians, it was very far from the last. Christian literature would go on to portray Roman emperors and their officials as demonically possessed servants of Satan who hungered insatiably for Christian blood.

It is a very potent picture. But it is not true.

Martyrs have always made good drama. When William Caxton introduced his printing press to London in the fifteenth century, one of the books he chose to print was the compilation of saints' lives—or more precisely their deaths—known as *The Golden Legend*. This collection, by Jacobus de Voragine, dating from around 1260, had already been a huge hit on the Continent. Caxton, a talented translator as well as a shrewd businessman, knew an opportunity when he saw one. He promptly translated (or, as his book's title page had it, "Englished") these verses into vividly salty prose. The description of the death of St. Alban provides a taste of the whole: St. Alban's torturer, this tale explains, "opened his navel and took out one end of his bowels, and fastened it to a stake which he pight in the ground, and made the holy man to go round about the stake, and drove him with whips, and beat him till that his bowels were wounden out of his body."[15] Caxton chose well: the book was a huge success, running to nine editions. A medieval bestseller.

The persecutions of Christians under the Romans had been a terrible time—but in the memory of the later Church it also became glorified as a wonderful one. According to the popular narrative, still widely believed to this day, all across the Roman Empire, Christians eagerly stepped forward to confess the risen Lord, whatever the cost. Stories hymned the thousands upon thousands of Christians who had died willingly, even joyfully, for their faith. "No sooner had the first batch been sentenced," wrote the historian Eusebius, "than others from every side would jump onto the platform in front of the judge and proclaim themselves Christians. They paid no heed to torture."[16]

Indeed, far from putting off potential converts, the Christians liked to say that the sight of their fellows being tortured to death merely tempted others to join up. This, Christian writers claimed, was a useful recruitment tool. The apologist Tertullian summed it up with his usual brio. "We become more numerous every time we are hewn down by you," he said. "The blood of the Christians is seed."[17] Another author saw the dead as playing a slightly different role in the garden of belief, explaining that "the blood of the martyrs water[ed] the churches."[18]

The martyrdoms also filled the inkwells of the later Church and martyr stories proliferated. These images exerted a powerful hold over European art for centuries. In the fourth century, poetic epics were written about the martyrs by the poet Prudentius, who lingered lovingly over details of torn flesh, consuming flames, and exposed and still throbbing organs. So influential were such tales that, as the academic Robin Lane Fox has pointed out, when a group of Christians were martyred by the Muslim authorities in Cordoba in the ninth century, the accounts of their trials set them before a "consul," as if this was all taking place in ancient Rome.[19] Walk around any great European art gallery today and the walls will be peopled by the most agonizing deaths depicted in lovingly—and often alarmingly—graphic detail.

Martyrs became art. And not always good art. While the earliest—and most reliable—martyr tales were often affecting in their simplicity and their honesty, many of the later and more fictional ones suffered from crass characterization, barely sublimated sexuality and lashings of gore. The Victorians, naturally, adored them. In the nineteenth century, hymns flowed from pious pens. "Bright the stones which bruise thee gleam," ran one verse on St. Stephen, who had been stoned to death, "Sprinkled with thy life blood's stream." Another hymned the saints who "met the tyrant's brandished steel / the lion's gory mane."[20]

Four centuries after Caxton, these lurid stories could still sell copies. In 1895 the Polish writer Henryk Sienkiewicz published a novel that became an international bestseller and contributed to his being awarded the Nobel Prize for literature. This seventy-three-chapter behemoth told the story of the Christian martyrs who were put to death by the emperor Nero. It concluded with the observation that "Nero passed on, as a whirlwind, as a storm, as a fire, as war or death passes, but the Basilica of Peter still stands on the Vatican Hill and rules over the city and the world."[21] Today, the book has been all but forgotten but its title, *Quo Vadis*, has not. Hollywood went on to make numerous film and television series by this name. The most famous was the 1951 swords-and-sandals epic in which a rotund Peter Ustinov as Nero smirkingly looks on while Christians, wearing white and looking pious, are pursued by lions in the arena, managing to sing hymns up to the very moment of mauling.[22]

But although martyr stories have often made for arresting and compelling drama, very few, if any, of these tales are based on historical fact. There were simply not that many years of imperially ordered persecution in the Roman Empire. Fewer than thirteen—in three whole centuries of Roman rule. These years may have loomed understandably large in Christian accounts but to allow them to dominate the narrative in the way that they have—and still do—is at best misleading and at worst a gross misrepresentation. During these first centuries of the new religion, local persecutions of Christians occurred. But we know of no government-led persecution for the first 250 years of Christianity with the exception of Nero's —and Nero, with even-handed lunacy, persecuted everyone. For two and a half centuries the Roman imperial government left Christianity alone.

The idea, therefore, of a line of satanically inspired emperors, panting for the blood of the faithful, is another Christian myth. As the modern historian Keith Hopkins wrote, "the traditional question: 'Why were the Christians persecuted?' with all its implications of unjust repression and eventual triumph, should be re-phrased: 'Why were the Christians persecuted so little and so late?'"[23]

Nevertheless, martyr tales have been hugely influential, not least on Christianity's image of itself. The academic Candida Moss has argued that in the years that followed the persecutions, Christianity came to see itself, with great pride, as a persecuted Church. Its greatest heroes were not those who did good deeds but those who died in the most painful way. If you were willing to die an excruciating end in the arena then, whatever your previous holiness or lack thereof, you went straight to heaven: martyrdom wiped out all sins on the point of death. As well as getting there faster, martyrs enjoyed preferential terms in paradise, getting to wear the much-desired martyr's crown. Tempting celestial terms were offered: it was said that the scripture promised "multiplication, even to a hundred times, of brothers, children, parents, land and homes."[24] Precisely how this celestial sum had been calculated is not clear but the general principle was: those who died early, publicly and painfully would be best rewarded.

In many of the martyr tales the driving force is less that the Romans want to kill—and more that the Christians want to die. Why wouldn't they? Paradoxically, martyrdom held considerable benefits for those willing to take it on. One was its egalitarian entry qualifications. As George Bernard Shaw acidly observed over a millennium later, martyrdom is the only way a man can become famous without ability. More than that, in a socially and sexually unequal era it was a way in which women and even slaves might shine. Unlike most positions of power in the highly socially stratified late Roman Empire, this was a glory that was open to all, regardless of rank, education, wealth or sex. The sociologist Rodney Stark has pointed out that—provided you believe in its promised rewards—martyrdom is a perfectly rational choice. A martyr could begin the day of their death as one of the lowliest people in the empire and end it as one of the most exalted in heaven. So tempting were these rewards that pious Christians born outside times of persecution were wont to express disappointment at being denied the opportunity of an agonizing death. When the later emperor Julian pointedly avoided executing Christians in his reign, one Christian writer, far from being grateful, sourly recorded that Julian had "begrudged the honour of martyrdom to our combatants."[25]

There were incitements for Christians not only to die but to die as painful a death as possible. As one soon-to-be martyred Christian irritably explained, the greater the pain, the greater the gain: "Those whose victory is slower and with greater difficulty, these receive the more glorious crown."[26] As martyr literature developed, the descriptions of the deaths became graphic to the point of prurient. In one gruesome account by Prudentius, a judge orders a Christian to be put on the rack, "till the joints of his bones in every limb are rent asunder with a crack. Then with cleaving strokes lay bare his ribs of their covering, so that his organs shall be exposed as they throb in the recesses of the wounds."[27]

The early martyrdom accounts are far stranger than is often remembered. Several verge on the salacious. Breasts, slim, naked or dripping with milk, are a theme. In later tales, female martyrs are frequently (and not entirely necessarily) required to strip naked, whereupon the crowd will be struck by their beauty. Toothsome beauties are often dispatched by lecherous governors to the brothel before death. In the apocryphal but once-popular *Acts of Paul and Thecla*, repeated paeans to virginity sit uncomfortably alongside passages that border on the titillating. Thecla is a great beauty who is determined (naturally) to remain a virgin. And of course, she is more than once required to strip off her clothes in front of a crowd. One night, she goes to visit Paul in prison and "her faith also was increased as she kissed his chains," a phrase to keep students of gender studies busy for decades.[28]

In martyr poems, mothers watch the martyrdom of their children with eager relish. In one story, a mother rejoices that she has borne a son who will die a martyr and, embracing his body, congratulates herself on her offspring. In another, the sight of a young boy being whipped is so atrocious that the eyes of all those present at the execution — even those of the Roman court stenographers — grow wet with tears. The boy's mother, by contrast, "showed none of this sorrowing, her brow alone was bright and clear with joy." The mother willingly carries her son in her arms to the executioner. As the boy's little head is severed from his neck she catches it and presses it joyfully "to her fond breast."[29]

Or did she? How many of these famous and emotive tales

actually happened? As the early Christian author Origen admitted, the numbers of martyrs were few enough to be easily
countable and Christians had died for their faith only "occasionally."[30] The stories might have proliferated but, as the Church
realized when it started to analyze them properly, many were
little more than stories. In the seventeenth century, one scholar
wrote a radical paper entitled *"De paucitate martyrum"* (On the
Small Number of Martyrs) that made just this point.[31] For all
the hyperbole, as Edward Gibbon crushingly put it, the aver-
age "annual consumption" of martyrs in Rome during the persecutions was no more than one hundred and fifty per year
during years of persecution.[32]

And there were few of those years. What state-sanctioned
attacks there were fall into three main phases: the Decian; the
Valerian, seven years later; and "the Great Persecution" fif-
ty-odd years after that in AD 303. And not all of these "persecutions" were intended to explicitly target Christians. The
Decian "persecution" began in AD 250 when Decius issued an
edict requiring everyone in the empire to sacrifice to him. True
Christians should refuse to sacrifice to anything. A request to
sacrifice to the emperor or gods became a common courtroom
test of someone's Christianity (or more precisely, their obedience) and these later formed the climax of many a martyr
tale. The intent of Decius's edict was to ensure loyalty from
his empire—but as Christians were not supposed to sacrifice
to such a "demon," some refused. But though Decius's edict
caught Christians, it almost certainly had not been aimed at
them. And it was brief: little more than a year after the first
persecution had been launched it had finished.

Valerian's persecution continued for approximately three
years and resulted in few deaths. Valerian himself was then
taken captive in Persia by the Persian king Shapur I.* It is true

---

* Where, as pious Christian historians would note with somewhat unchristian glee, he
spent his final years being used by King Shapur as a royal mounting block for his horse.

that the more substantial Great Persecution that followed was responsible for around half of all early Christian martyrdoms, but it petered out quickly in the West and officially ended after a decade. While it was going on, it was terrible. Scriptures were burned, Christians were tortured and executed and churches were destroyed. But it was limited. There were intermittent local persecutions too; but these were sporadic and had an inconsequential effect on the spread of the religion. The Romans did not seek to wipe Christianity out. If they had, they would almost certainly have succeeded.

Ever since the paper on the small number of martyrs, the death toll cited for the Roman "persecutions" has been dropping steadily. Detailed analysis of the calendar of saints' days revealed a picture that has been described as more romantic fiction than historical fact. Some saints appeared multiple times; other saints' names had clearly been at best misrecorded, mixed with the names of the consuls for that year. Several saints appear never to have existed at all. It is now thought that fewer than ten martyrdom tales from the early Church can be considered reliable. The martyr stories, inspiring and entertaining though they may be, show what the scholar G.E.M. De Ste. Croix called "an increasing contempt for historicity."[33]

To understand what really happened between the Christians and the Romans you must begin instead not with the martyr tales but with one of the most accurate historical accounts we have: you must begin with the very first mention of Christians by a non-Christian writer.

CHAPTER FIVE

───

These Deranged Men

Because they love the name martyr and because they desire human praise more than divine charity, they kill themselves.

—Pseudo Jerome

IN THE MIDDLE OF THE baking August of AD 111, as his ship rounded the foot of the Peloponnese in suffocating heat, Pliny the Younger looked little like the diabolical Roman governor of legend. The statue of Pliny in his hometown of Como shows him as a man with matinee-idol charms: a sternly square jaw set off by a sensuous mouth, a sensitive faraway gaze and lustrous curls. If Pliny was so dashing (which, given that he was then a middle-aged bureaucrat, seems improbable) then on that day he was very unlikely to have been looking his best. He was hot, he was flustered, and he was very late.[1]

The person for whom he was late was not a man one wanted to disappoint: the emperor Trajan himself had sent Pliny to Turkey to be its governor. Yet it was now late summer and Pliny was still nowhere near his destination. The intense heat had made land travel all but impossible; now unfavorable winds meant it was difficult to travel along the coast. Money could alleviate much in the Roman summer: it could buy you shady colonnades to walk in away from noonday sun; it could buy you fountains to play soothingly in the gardens beyond. It could even ensure your evening glass of wine was ice-cool. But it could not alter the weather nor make traveling enjoyable.

Whether over land or sea a voyage was in these times something to be dreaded and if possible avoided entirely. At sea, there were storms, shipwrecks and pirates. Travel on land was little better. Wealthy men like Pliny could move with armed bodyguards as protection; however, given that slaves might not only desert their owners in a fight but turn on them themselves, their presence was often less than reassuring. The atmosphere on the roads was tense. The highways of empire were decorated by the corpses of executed bandits, left impaled on stakes in the places where they had plied their trade.

To add to the other discomforts of his journey, Pliny had developed a fever and been forced to stay for a few days in the great city of Pergamum.* However, on September 17 he finally reached his destination, the province of Bithynia. He informed the emperor of this in a letter that, to modern eyes, looks more than slightly toadying: he had arrived, he wrote, "in time to celebrate your birthday in my province, and this should be a good omen."[2]

It seems unlikely that the citizens of Bithynia would have been as pleased to see Pliny as he was to get there. They appear to have been having a splendid time under their previous governor, embarking on expensive building projects that were then abandoned, diverting public funds into private hands and generally making merry. Pliny had been sent by Trajan with the express mission of whipping this errant eastern region into line—a task he would take on with zest and efficiency. Critical letters fly back to Rome, reporting some financial mismanagement here, some too-extravagant travel expenses there. A crumbling theater needs urgent attention; a canal is proposed to ease transport of raw materials to the sea; an aqueduct, begun at vast expense, has been left unfinished . . . The letters go

---

* This was not the first time Pliny had almost missed a date with history. On the morning of August 24, AD 79, he had been staying with his uncle's family in a villa on the Bay of Naples when they noticed a strange cloud emanating from the mountains across the bay. Pliny's uncle set out to investigate and asked his nephew whether he wished to go with him. The younger Pliny declined, giving the somewhat feeble excuse that he had homework to do: "I replied that I preferred to go on with my studies." So Pliny the Elder set out without him, declaring that "Fortune favors the brave." It did not favor him. Within less than twenty-four hours he was dead. Pliny the Younger's decision was undoubtedly a sensible one but it has hardly left him with a reputation for heroism.

on and on, a window onto Roman provincial life — and Roman imperial bureaucracy.

The emperor Trajan replies personally and promptly. He clearly knows and is fond of his emissary: "my dear Pliny," he calls him in one solicitous letter; "I wish you could have reached Bithynia without any illness yourself." In another he praises Pliny's energy and intelligence; another informs him, flatteringly, that Pliny has been "chosen as my representative" for a "special mission."[3] Trajan is remarkably closely involved in the minutiae of the province: when Pliny suggests getting a canal surveyed, Trajan replies that he will send out an engineer with experience in that line.[4] Trajan is friendly, helpful and fair — though there are glimpses of steel. When Pliny wishes to turn a blind eye to some elderly criminals who have wriggled out of their sentences, Trajan is intransigent. "Let us not forget," he writes, "that the chief reason for sending you to your province was the evident need for many reforms."[5] You can almost picture the middle-aged governor, eager celebrator of the imperial birthday, shifting uncomfortably in his seat as he reads that one.

These letters bear little trace of the figures who would later become such stalwarts of the martyr tales. In these stories, the Roman emperor is a villain who "feeds on innocent blood; hungering for the bodies of the godly"; he tears their flesh and "delights in torturing the faithful."[6] Satan himself, the "jealous and envious Evil One," is behind these attacks, which the Romans carry out "at the instigation of evil demons."[7] But far from showing demonic frothing, Trajan's letters show a man who is punctilious and practical, while Pliny gives the impression of a bookish, slightly fussy fellow whose greatest flaw seems to be his vanity. He is the sort of man who is more likely to pontificate on the correct wine to serve at dinner than to thunder about the importance of religion.

Then suddenly, among all the tales of provincial waterways and corrupt eastern officials, an unusual letter appears. It is now known by the unassuming name "Letter 10.96." It was almost certainly edited at some point later, yet the whole dispatch still has the feel of being somewhat carelessly drafted: it is full of omissions, assumptions and non sequiturs. There is no obvious reason why Pliny should have spent much more time over it than any of his other letters. To him, this was not of any great significance; it was merely the record of an inconsequential encounter with some of his subjects in his province, a footnote in a busy and ultimately successful imperial career.

Trajan's reply shows a similar lack of interest: he answers with his usual punctiliousness — but briefly. In their next letter, the two move on to the urgent need for new plumbing in a local city ("Among the chief features of Amastris, Sir . . . is a long street of great beauty. Throughout the length of this, however, there runs what is called a stream, but is in fact a filthy sewer, a disgusting eyesore which gives off a noxious stench").[8]

Letter 10.96 was not, however, inconsequential for the generations of Christians that followed. For Letter 10.96 is nothing less than the very first record of the Christians by a Roman writer.

It is clear from the moment the letter opens that Pliny is finding the Christians in his new province irksome. The "wretched cult" of Christianity has been spreading there and affecting the worship of the old gods. "Not only the towns, but villages and rural districts too . . . are infected," Pliny wrote. The temples of the old gods are becoming deserted.

Thus far at least, the letter bears some comparison to the martyr tales in which Roman governors are nettled by the neglect of the old gods. However almost immediately Pliny's approach diverges from stereotype. Life, as always, is more complicated than simple legend.

Pliny's problem with all of this is not religious. He is not upset because Jupiter has been neglected, or Hera has been slighted: he is upset because the citizens of his province are becoming disgruntled by the Christians' behavior. Anonymous pamphlets, containing the names of local Christians, have started to appear.

Whoever it is who has been writing these, Pliny is now obliged to react. Not because he is fervently religious—he is not—but because it is his job as governor to keep the province calm. The preservation of order is his primary duty. "It is proper for every good and worthy Governor," as one digest of Roman law put it, "to take care that the province over which he presides is peaceable and quiet." The digest goes on to add, confidently and somewhat blithely, that "this he will accomplish without difficulty if he exerts himself to expel bad men."[9] Discontented locals had to be taken seriously; if they were not listened to, a situation might develop where riots could break out—for which Pliny would be held responsible. Pontius Pilate might have been the first official to be reluctantly pressed into action against Christians by local agitators—but he was certainly not the last.

Even the locals who were forcing Pliny's hand might not have been complaining about Christians for religious reasons either: it has been speculated that what was really upsetting them was not theology but butchery. Local tradesmen were angry because this surge of Christian sentiment had led to a drop in the sales of sacrificial meat and their profits were suffering: anti-Christian sentiment caused less by Satan than by a slow trade in sausage meat.

This is a very different situation already to the martyr tales which, particularly later, portrayed Roman officials as at best piqued, and at worst obsessed, by Christians out of religious principle. A Christian historian would accuse a Roman governor of declaring that Christians "were all to be hunted out."[10] Some governors may well have said this; but vast numbers of Roman officials were far more ambivalent. There is clear evidence that, far from persecuting Christians, Roman officials actively supported some of the most prominent. None other than St. Paul—who preached so vigorously that he ensured the faith was being "proclaimed throughout the whole world" —was clearly on good terms with officials in his province: they are variously impressed by his teaching, apologize to Paul when he is mistreated and imprisoned, and even intervene to try to protect him from an angry mob.

This is not to say that Pliny had no time for the religions of his own nation; he did. In one letter he writes with lyrical enthusiasm about the shrine of a local river god that he has visited in Italy. There, he says, at the foot of a hill densely wooded with ancient cypresses, a spring gushes "into a pool as clear as glass. You can count the coins which have been thrown in and the pebbles shining at the bottom." The temple itself is, says Pliny, "venerable"—though as with so many Romans, there were limits to his veneration. The walls of this temple were covered with inscriptions, some of which, Pliny tells his friend, "will make you laugh—though I know you are really too charitable to laugh at any of them."[11] Pliny, once again, is the perfect Roman: too well educated to indulge in fervent belief of the gods; too well bred to spurn them.

So the famous first recorded encounter between Christians and Romans does not document a clash of religious ideals: it is about law and order. It was Pliny's duty as a governor, and as a Roman, to monitor and minimize discontent. Many future clashes would show a similar pattern. The main point of Letter 10.96 is not to fulminate about the Christian religion but to ask the correct method for dealing with it. "I have never been present at an examination of Christians," Pliny wrote. "I do not know the nature of the extent of the punishments usually meted out to them, nor the grounds for starting an investigation and how far it should be pressed." Pliny was by no means a modern champion of religious equality or human rights—at one point in his investigations he has two Christian women tortured with the same calm efficiency that he would have a canal surveyed—but nor is he the ranting, eager persecutor of Christian myth.

In fact, all over the empire, Romans are frustratingly unwilling to play their role as bloodthirsty martyr-makers. Many even refuse to execute Christians when they arrive in front of them. Arrius Antoninus was a Roman governor of Asia who in the late second century had executed a number of Christians in his province. He was perhaps unprepared for what came next. Instead of fleeing, local Christians suddenly turned up and, in one large mob, presented themselves before him. Antoninus did indeed dutifully kill a few (presumably there is only so much temptation a Roman can stand) but rather than dispatching the rest with pleasure, he turned to them with what, even with the passage of almost two millennia, sounds unmistakably like exasperation. "Oh you ghastly people," he said. "If you want to die you have cliffs you can jump off and nooses to hang yourself with."[12]

Other Christians were so eager to die that when they spontaneously turned up in front of officials they did so ready chained, much to the interest of bemused locals. As one Christian author excitedly said, "so far from dreading, we spontaneously call for tortures!"[13] Often with disappointing results. In AD 311, St. Antony, hearing that a persecution was in full swing in nearby Alexandria, hurried from his desert dwelling to the city. There, he went out dressed in white "to catch the judge's attention as he walked past, for Antony was burning with a desire for martyrdom." Alas for Antony, the judge either did not notice the saint or did not bother with him. Antony returned home, "saddened by the fact that despite his wish to suffer for the name of God, martyrdom was not granted him."[14] Once back in his cell, Antony consoled himself for his continuing existence by adding a hair shirt to his daily attire and never washing again.

Other Christians who were deprived of execution turned instead to suicide. In fourth-century North Africa, locals watched in horror as faithful and "deranged men . . . because they love the name martyr and because they desire human praise more than divine charity, they kill themselves."[15] The methods of suicide varied but drowning, setting oneself on fire and jumping off cliffs were among the most popular. Whatever the method, the aim was always the same: martyrdom, eternal glory in heaven and eternal fame on earth—or so it was hoped.

The group most famous for practicing this were known as circumcellions.* As the academic Brent D. Shaw has argued, as itinerant farm workers, circumcellions were near the bottom of an extremely hierarchical empire. Their lives were difficult, precarious and grim. Commit suicide, however, and they would become not only a member of the most worshipped people on earth but be sped to a prize seat in heaven.

On the anniversaries of martyrs' deaths, circumcellions celebrated the deceased with long riotous bouts of drinking and dancing. The celebrations on the day of an actual death were, allegedly, even greater, and lurid rumors spread of the orgiastic celebrations and sex and hard drinking that went on after one of their number committed suicide. As Augustine wrote, these people lived "as bandits, die as circumcellions, and are honoured as martyrs."[16] "Drink up! Live long!" declared the inscription put up to one martyr, apparently without irony.

Others—Christians and non-Christians alike—watched such behavior with revulsion. The circumcellions "seduce others whom they can, of either sex, to join them in this mad behaviour," wrote Augustine.[17] To the alarm of many, this behavior seemed to be contagious. The fanatical followers of one bishop barricaded themselves inside a basilica and threatened to commit mass suicide by setting themselves on fire.[18] Augustine's writings on these men (for they were mainly men) are

---

* The unwieldy name most probably came from their lifestyle: they were farm workers who had a habit of hanging "around" (*circum*) the "cellars" (*cella*) of farms.

scornful and belittling: he was engaged in as much a propaganda war as an ideological one, and he knew it. The circumcellions claimed suicide as a high calling; Augustine batted it away dismissively as a game. It was, he wrote, the "daily sport" of these people "to kill themselves, by throwing themselves over precipices, or into the water, or into the fire."[19] They were, wrote another bishop in disgust, little more than a "death sect."[20]

It was by no means only the circumcellions who celebrated martyrs. A certain glamour clung to these doomed figures. Moreover, the idea that all sins were wiped out at the point of bloody death had not been lost on some of the soon-to-be martyrs. Many made the most of their last few hours on earth with enthusiasm and the atmosphere in the cells could become quite carnival-like—to the consternation of watching bishops. One observed "with groans and sorrow" how he and others had witnessed "frauds, and fornications, and adulteries" among those condemned to death.[21]

Pliny the Younger's letters throw other martyrdom tropes into question. The climax of the first part of each martyr story is usually when the Roman official tries to tempt the Christians before him to sacrifice to the Roman gods. Martyr narratives present such attempts as proof of demonic possession: the Romans are trying to force Christians to "worship at the altars of devils."[22] And indeed Pliny did bring accused Christians before him and request them to make offerings to a statue of Trajan. He also asked each one if they were Christian. If they admitted it he—as happens in many martyr tales—asked them again, and again—and warned them of the punishments that awaited them as he did so. If they persisted in calling themselves Christian, he ordered them to be executed.

Superficially then, Pliny bears some resemblance to the governor of martyrology. But read his letter closely, and a different picture emerges. The reason Pliny was writing to Trajan at all was that the numbers involved in this charge were proliferat-

ing. The archetypal Roman governor would no doubt have
delighted in this ripe harvest of Christians: Pliny, by contrast,
is distressed. "I have therefore postponed any further examination and hastened to consult you," he writes. "The question
seems to me to be worthy of your consideration, especially in
view of the number of persons endangered; for a great many
individuals of every age and class, both men and women, are
being brought to trial."

The adjective he uses for the people in front of him is telling.
Pliny doesn't consider those Christians being dragged before
him as wicked, or wrong, or impious; he is not bellowing at
them or eyeing them salaciously or terrorizing them. He sees
them as "*periclitantium*," "in danger." He is of course the agent
of that peril and, if pushed, will put them to death. They are
disrupting the peace in his province and it is his job to restore
that peace. Nevertheless, the strong implication in the letter is
that Pliny, like Arrius Antoninus, would really rather not execute large numbers of people.

Look at the martyr stories without the distorting lens of
Christianity and the Romans in them start to look very different. True, officials do indeed repeatedly ask Christians to
sacrifice. But just for a moment disregard the Christian theory
—that this is because of demonic possession—and look instead at the reasons given by the officials themselves and it becomes clear that the Romans in these tales want the Christians
to sacrifice not because they want them to be damned in the
next life but because they want them to be saved in this one.
They simply do not want to execute.

In one tale a Roman prefect named Probus asks the Christian on trial before him no fewer than nine times to obey him
and escape execution. The prefect begs the Christian to think
of his weeping family, to spare himself pain, to go free. "Give
up this madness of yours, yield to [your family's] tears, think
of your youth, and offer sacrifice," he says. "Spare yourself
death." When the Christian refuses to budge, Probus tries one

more time: "At least offer sacrifice for the sake of your children!" When the Christian is unmoved, Probus issues a more explicit warning: "Take thought for yourself, young man. Offer sacrifice, so that I shall not put you to torture."[23] The Christian refuses, and dies—but not for want of trying on Probus's part. In another story, when a young girl called Eulalia presents herself before a governor he struggles to dissuade her. Think of your future marriage, he begs. "Think of the great joys you are cutting off . . . The family you are bereaving follows you with tears . . . you are dying in the bloom of youth . . . your rash conduct is breaking their hearts."[24] Eulalia too ignores him.

Some Roman officials in these tales tried—unsuccessfully—to jolly the would-be martyr out of it. "Cease this foolishness and be of good cheer with us," orders one.[25] Another "minister of Satan" asks what person with intelligence "would choose to relinquish this sweetest light and prefer death to it?"[26] It is a question that many a baffled Roman governor asks. "Don't you see the beauty of this pleasant weather?" exhorts another. "There will be no pleasure to come your way if you kill your own self. But listen to me and you will be saved." Perhaps, this governor suggested, the Christian before him needed a little more time, asking, dampeningly, if he wanted a few days to think about things. "I have been lenient with you," he tells the would-be martyr. "If you for your part will only be lenient with yourself . . . then I shall be all the more pleased."[27] In the trial of a veteran soldier named Julius, financial incentives are even proffered under the nose of a Christian by a prefect named Maximus. "You shall receive a generous bonus if you will take my advice and sacrifice to the gods," says Maximus, temptingly.[28]

Martyr stories cannot, of course, be taken as fact. But they can be taken as an indication of what Christians would believe —or even what they wanted to believe. They show that early Christians could accept the idea that Roman officials might seem keen—desperate, even—to stop them dying. Officials in these tales go to extraordinary lengths to try to find a form of sacrifice that would be at once agreeable to the emperor and acceptable to the Christians. Realizing that Christians found full meat sacrifices repellent, officials also tried to tempt them with smaller acts of obedience. Just put out your fingers, Eulalia's judge begs her, and just *touch* a little of that incense, and you will escape cruel suffering.[29] They also struggled to find verbal formulae that Christians would agree to say. In one tale a prefect tells a Christian: "I will not tell you: 'Sacrifice.' You need not do any such thing. Simply take a little incense, some wine, and a branch and say: 'Zeus all highest, protect this people.'"[30] Maximus, having offered that bribe to the soldier and soon-to-be martyr Julius and been rebuffed, then thinks again and comes up with an almost Jesuitical solution to the problem. "If you think [sacrifice] is a sin," he suggests, then "let me take the blame. I am the one who is forcing you, so that you may not give the impression of having consented voluntarily. Afterwards you can go home in peace, you will pick up your ten-year bonus and no one will ever trouble you again."[31]

History supports this reading. In the Decian persecution, Christians who refused to sacrifice were given repeated opportunities to comply and pre-announced dates gave ample opportunities to flee. In 303, Emperor Diocletian had allowed that clergy who sacrificed could be released. Other officials commuted sentences to avoid execution, condemning would-be martyrs not to death but to a spell in the mines, or banishment instead. It is likely that almost all Christians in times of persecution simply sacrificed and escaped death. In Africa, for example, no governor is known to have executed Christians until the year 180. The Christian martyrs number "hundreds, not thousands," according to the scholar W.H.C. Frend.[32]

The officials in the martyr tales were rarely thanked for their efforts to save or dissuade. The Christian who was advised to look at the sunny weather rebuffed his tempter by declaring:

"The death which is coming to me is more pleasant than the life which you would give me."[33] The prefect—or, as the narrative has it, "tyrant"—who tells the Christian to cheer up and cease his foolishness is bluntly informed that he is the "most impious of all men."[34] When Eulalia's governor offers her a compromise, she spits in his eye. The prefect Maximus, who had alternately attempted to bribe and then reason the veteran Julius into living, was told that the money he was offering was "the money of Satan" and that "neither it nor your crafty talk can deprive me of the eternal light." It is not without some sympathy that one reads the prefect's terse response: "If you do not respect the imperial decrees and offer sacrifice, I am going to cut your head off." Julius replies boldly but somewhat ungraciously that "to live with you would be death for me." He is beheaded.[35]

Non-Christians were alternately baffled and repelled by such excess. Pliny himself describes Christianity as nothing more than a "degenerate sort of cult carried to extravagant lengths."[36] For a long time, Romans struggled to understand why Christians couldn't simply add the worship of this new Christian god to the old ones. It was known that Christianity had sprung from Judaism and that even the Jews had offered prayer and sacrifice to Augustus and later emperors in their temple. If they had done so—and theirs was the more ancient religion—then why couldn't the Christians? Monotheism in the rigid Christian sense was all but unthinkable to polytheists. "If you have recognized Christ," as one official put it, "then recognize our gods too."[37] Not just unthinkable but, to many, unnecessary to the point of histrionic. As another prefect in another trial pithily put it: "What is so serious about offering some incense and going away?"[38] The emperor Marcus Aurelius disparaged martyrdom as mere "stage heroics."[39] Others saw it as simply deluded: Lucian scornfully described the Christians as those "poor wretches [who] have convinced themselves, first and foremost, that they are going to be immortal and live for all time, in consequence of which they despise death and even willingly give themselves into custody."[40]

What appears to irritate Pliny the Younger in those who remain firm is less the implicit disrespect to his gods than their actual disrespect to his authority. He has been explicitly sent to Bithynia to sort the province out. Now, because of Christianity, he is faced with a town teeming with informers and bristling with discontent—and with some rigidly intransigent witnesses who are refusing to honor the emperor. When Pliny puts them on trial, some recant while others remain firm. Those who do remain firm are, if Roman citizens, sent to Rome—at astonishing expense and bureaucratic bother—for trial. If they are not, they are executed. For, as Pliny put it, "whatever the nature of their admission, I am convinced that their stubbornness and unshakeable obstinacy ought not to go unpunished." To show *contumacia*—contempt or "obstinacy" before a magistrate—was in itself a punishable crime, and one that Christians frequently either committed explicitly or teetered upon the edge of.[41]

Romans often found the Christians offensively irritating in court—not without reason, if the acts of the martyrs are to be believed. The Christians spat, metaphorically and literally, in the face of Roman legal process. In one famous trial, a martyr named Sanctus responded to every question with "I am a Christian." A Christian author records the event with great approbation. "With such determination did he stand up to their onslaughts that he would not tell them his own name, race, and birthplace, or whether he was a slave or free; to every question he replied in Latin, 'I am a Christian.' This he proclaimed over and over again, instead of name, birthplace, nationality and everything else, and not another word did the heathen hear from him."[42] The "heathen" were less approving of this behavior and the presiding governor promptly had him tortured some more.

What should Pliny do with these odd people? Trajan's reply is brief and to the point. He doesn't get into theological or legal debates about the legal status of Christianity (to the disappointment of later scholars); nor does he (thus confounding the martyrdom tropes) fulminate against the Christians. He does agree with Pliny that those who are proved to be Christian "must be punished" — though for precisely what charge is unclear. He also adds that "in the case of anyone who denies that he is a Christian, and makes it clear that he is not by offering prayers to our gods, he is to be pardoned as a result of his repentance however suspect his past conduct may be." Roman emperors wanted obedience, not martyrs. They had absolutely no wish to open windows into men's souls or to control what went on there. That would be a Christian innovation.

Despite declaring bluntly that those who are Christian should be punished, Trajan then goes on to add a clause that would give considerable legal protection to all Christians in his empire for well over a century. For Trajan is absolutely adamant that those unpleasant denunciations that started all this off should not happen again. "Pamphlets circulated anonymously must play no part in any accusation," he writes. "They create the worst sort of precedent and are quite out of keeping with the spirit of our age." And nor should Pliny take it upon himself to root out Christians. In a line that should be far better known than it is, Trajan adds three simple but powerful words. "*Conquirendi non sunt*" — "These people *must not be hunted out.*"[43]

Many Romans didn't like the Christians. They found their reclusive behavior offensive, their teachings foolish, their fervor irritating and their refusal to sacrifice to the emperor insulting. But for the first 250 years after the birth of Christ, the imperial policy towards them was first to ignore them and then to declare that they must not be hounded.[44]

In the encounter between the Christians and the Romans it is the former who are almost without fail remembered as the oppressed and the latter as the oppressors. Yet, apart from

Nero, it was almost two and a half centuries before emperors became involved in prosecutions of Christians—and even then, as we have seen, these prosecutions were brief.

This was a grace and liberty that the Christians would decline to show to other religions when they finally gained control. A little over ten years after the newly Christian Constantine took power, it is said that laws began to be passed restricting "the pollutions of idolatry."[45] During Constantine's own reign it seems to have been decreed that "no one should presume to set up cult-objects, or practise divination or other occult arts, or even to sacrifice at all."[46] Less than fifty years after Constantine, the death penalty was announced for any who dared to sacrifice.[47] A little over a century later, in AD 423, the Christian government announced that any pagans who still survived were to be suppressed. Though, it added confidently —and ominously: "We now believe that there are none."[48]

TRIUMPHAL ARCH, PALMYRA, 1ST–2ND CENTURY AD Palmyra, at the edge of the Syrian desert, took its name from the feathered palm trees that grew around it. Its wealth and air of glamour came largely from the diaphanous silks that were traded there.

ATHENA, 2ND CENTURY AD In the fourth century this colossal statue was decapitated by Christians because it was considered idolatrous. The arms were also chopped off. This photo shows the statue after reconstruction by archaeologists. In 2016 photos were released showing that the stature had again been decapitated and mutilated, this time by ISIS.

THE TRIUMPH OF CHRISTIANITY, C. 1585 A god has been knocked from its pedestal by a triumphant cross and now lies broken. The bases of destroyed Greco-Roman statues were frequently used, once the old statues had been removed, to mount Christian crosses.

TEMPTATION OF ST. ANTHONY, C. 1512–16
It was said that demons might appear to humans in any form: as wicked thoughts or wild animals, as corpses or even as officious bureaucrats. According to his biographer, St. Anthony was attacked by demonic lions, wolves, serpents, leopards and bears.

FUNERARY STELE, ROME, EARLY 3RD CENTURY AD One of the earliest Christian inscriptions. Above the fish symbols is a dedication to the "DM" — the Dis Manibus, Roman gods of the underworld.

BELIAL AND THE DEMONS, MANUSCRIPT, 1450 According to early Christian texts, mankind was under perpetual attack by Satan and his fearsome foot soldiers, the demons. Their aim was to drag all humans to damnation.

EPICURUS The Greek philosopher
Epicurus argued that the world and
everything in it was made not by God
but by the collision and combination
of atoms. Epicureans hoped this idea
would free people from irrational fear
of divine powers. Augustine disliked
the theory for much the same reason,
and celebrated the fact that, by his time,
this philosophy had been successfully
suppressed.

LUCRETIUS In his great philosophical poem "On the Nature of Things," Lucretius transformed Epicurus's ideas into poetry — successfully, according to Virgil: "Fortunate was he who was able to know the causes of things and crushed beneath his feet all fears and inexorable fate and the gaping grave."

EMPEROR CONSTANTINE, THE COUNCIL OF NICAEA, AND THE BURNING OF ARIAN BOOKS, 9TH CENTURY AD In the fourth century Constantine announced that the works of Porphyry, a formidable critic of Christianity, had been destroyed. Not a single book by Porphyry has survived to the modern era.

THE RAISING OF LAZARUS, 4TH CENTURY AD In early images Christ was sometimes portrayed with a sorcerer's wand. Skeptical pagans said that what Christians saw as miracles were no different from the tricks performed by hucksters in Egyptian marketplaces.

TRIUMPH OF FAITH — CHRISTIAN MARTYRS IN THE TIME OF NERO Historians now think that the actual number of Christians killed in persecutions should be numbered in the hundreds rather than the thousands.

COLOSSAL HEAD OF CONSTANTINE, 4TH CENTURY BC According to his biographer, Emperor Constantine converted after he saw a flaming cross in the sky, though at another time in his life Constantine was said to have seen a vision of the god Apollo.

EMPEROR THEODOSIUS AT THE COUNCIL OF CONSTANTINOPLE, 9TH CENTURY Under the fiercely Christian Theodosius I, a series of formidable laws was issued against pagans.

1158.—Second Temple of Diana at Ephesus.

TEMPLE OF DIANA, 19TH CENTURY The temple of Artemis (Diana, in Latin) at Ephesus was one of the Seven Wonders of the Ancient World. It had several incarnations, but according to the apocryphal Acts of John, its final end came when John the Apostle entered the temple and began praying. At that moment, the altar shattered to pieces and "half of the temple fell down, so that the priest was slain at one blow."

GERMANICUS CAESAR Germanicus's nose has been mutilated and a cross has been carved in his forehead—perhaps an attempt to "baptize" Germanicus and so neutralize any possible demons within.

CHAPTER SIX

The Most Magnificent Building in the World

He that sacrificeth unto any god, save unto the Lord only, he shall be utterly destroyed.

—Exodus 22:20

AT THE END OF the first century of Christian rule, the Colosseum still dominated Rome and the Parthenon towered above Athens. Yet when writers of this period discuss architecture, these aren't the buildings that impress them. Instead, their admiration is drawn by another structure in Egypt. This building was so fabulous that writers in the ancient world struggled to find ways to convey its beauty. "Its splendour is such that mere words can only do it an injustice," wrote the historian Ammianus Marcellinus.[1] It was, another writer thought, "one of the most unique and uncommon sights in the world. For nowhere else on earth can one find such a building."[2] Its great halls, its columns, its astonishing statues and its art all made it, outside Rome, "the most magnificent building in the whole world."[3] Everyone had heard of it.

No one has heard of it now. While tourists still toil up to the Parthenon, or look in awe at the Colosseum, outside academia few people know of the temple of Serapis. That is because in AD 392 a bishop, supported by a band of fanatical Christians, reduced it to rubble.

It is easy to see why this temple would have attracted the Christians' attention. Standing at the top of a hundred or more marble steps, it had once towered over the startling white marble streets below, an object to incite not only wonder but envy. While Christians of the time crammed into insufficient numbers of small, cramped churches, this was a vast—and vastly superior—monument to the old gods. It was one of the first buildings you noticed as you sailed towards Alexandria, its roof looming above the others, and one that you were unlikely to forget. No mean feat. One of several "Alexandrias" founded by Alexander the Great (a man rarely accused of modesty) this Alexandria was an admirably elegant city. Under the scorching Egyptian sun, its wide boulevards were laid out on an elegant grid designed to allow the fresh sea breeze to pass through them, cooling them. Its landmarks have become landmarks in the history of culture and architecture: the Great Lighthouse of Alexandria, one of the wonders of the ancient world, was here; as too was the Musaeum, most literally a shrine to the Muses but also, with its walkways, lecture hall, dining room and resident academics, a forerunner of the modern university; here too was the Great Library of Alexandria. It has been said that Julius Caesar was so impressed by the city that he had returned home determined to improve Rome. And above all of these buildings, and more beautiful than any, was the temple of Serapis.

By AD 392, some of what Caesar had admired had gone—done for by war and fire—but Serapis still stood, and still awed all who came. To reach it a visitor would have to climb up that grand flight of steps to the shrine's citadel-like walls. Once inside, you would have found yourself in a generous courtyard, edged about by shady porticoes. Your eye might have been caught by the much-admired statues—so realistic, it was said, that it looked as though they might at any moment take a breath. And beyond them, dazzling in the bright Mediterranean sunlight, rose the marble columns of the temple itself.

Walk on and, just behind the porticoes of the inner court, you would have found yourself in a vast library—the remnants of the Great Library of Alexandria itself. The library's collection was now stored here, within the temple precinct, for safekeeping. This had been the world's first public library, and its holdings had, at its height, been staggering, running into hundreds of thousands of volumes. Like the city itself, the collection had taken several knocks over the years, but extensive collections remained. The spirit of the original institution remained here too and anyone in the city who wished to could come and read these books. Excavations in the 1940s uncovered nineteen uniform rooms where, it is thought, the books were shelved: thousands of volumes, on every topic from religion to mathematics, were sitting on those shelves as the year 392 opened.

So Serapis was rich, then, in intellectual wealth. But go on, past the library, past the lecture rooms that surrounded it and into the temple itself, then you would have seen a more literal sort of richness. Enter through its great doors and, once your eyes adjusted to the frankincense-heavy dimness within, you would have seen a room of almost brash opulence, in which oil lamps glimmered on walls plated with gold and overlaid with silver. And in the center was the most brilliant object of all: a vast statue of the god Serapis. Like the Greco-Egyptian city he sat above, this god was an international hybrid. Look at his handsome bearded profile and you might think you were looking at Jupiter himself, though he was Egyptian enough that others called him "Osiris." An immortal amalgam that, some said, had been intentionally created to bring harmony to the mixed races in the city below, causing them to pray rather than fight together. Nonsense, maybe—but Serapis had nonetheless acted as an extremely effective divine diplomat, helping to unite this famously argumentative people. In a city that, at night, glowed with countless flames in a thousand temples, this god was one of the most eagerly worshipped of all.

Like all statues this size, Serapis was made of a wooden structure overlaid with precious materials: the god's profile was made of glowing white ivory; his enormous limbs were draped in robes of metal—very probably with real gold. The statue was so huge that his great hands almost touched either side of the room in which he sat; if he'd stood up, he would have taken the roof off. Even the sun adored him: the temple had been built with a tiny window carefully positioned in its east wall so that once a year on the appointed day the dawn rays would come in and kiss the lips of the god.

To the new generation of Christian clerics, however, Serapis was not a wonder of art or a much-loved local god. Serapis was a demon. And, in AD 392, the city's bishop decided to act against this demon once and for all. Theophilus, the new Bishop of Alexandria, had been preparing for this moment for months — from birth, if one is to believe his biographer. When he was a mere child, it was said, the boy's nurse had taken him to a temple of Artemis and Apollo to pray. As she had entered the temple with Theophilus in her arms the statues of the gods had spontaneously crashed to the ground and broken into pieces. This, then, was a man destined for destruction. As an adult Theophilus was little more compromising. "The cross," he said in one less than milk-and-honey homily, "is that which closed the temples of the idols and opened the churches and crowns them. The cross is that which has confounded the demons and made them flee in terror."[4]

Fierce words — but Christians had been fulminating in this way for decades and polytheists had been able to ignore them. But the world was changing. It was now eighty years since a Christian had first sat on the throne of Rome and in the intervening decades the religion of the Lamb had taken an increasingly bullish attitude to all those who refused it. Since taking control in Alexandria, Theophilus had lived up to his early promise as a statue-smashing scourge. A little earlier, he had stolen the most sacred objects from two temples and paraded them through the streets for Christians to mock. The worshippers of the old gods were shocked and enraged: this was a gross and unprompted act of sacrilege and Christians afterwards were attacked and even killed by outraged worshippers.

Upsetting and unedifying though the incident was, it would be utterly eclipsed by what was about to follow.

One day, early in AD 392, a large crowd of Christians started to mass outside the temple, with Theophilus at its head. And then, to the distress of watching Alexandrians, this crowd had surged up the steps, into the sacred precinct, and burst into the most beautiful building in the world.

And then they began to destroy it.

Theophilus's righteous followers began to tear at those famous artworks, the lifelike statues and the gold-plated walls. There was a moment's hesitation when they came to the massive statue of the god: rumor had it that if Serapis was harmed then the sky would fall in. Theophilus ordered a soldier to take his axe and hit it. The soldier struck Serapis's face with a double-headed axe. The god's great ivory profile, blackened by centuries of smoke, shattered.

The watching Christians roared with delight and then, emboldened, surged round to complete the job. Serapis's head was wrenched from its neck; the feet and hands were chopped off with axes, dragged apart with ropes, then, for good measure, burned.

As one delighted Christian chronicler put it, the "decrepit dotard" Serapis "was burned to ashes before the eyes of the Alexandria which had worshipped him."[5] The giant torso of the god was saved for a more public humiliation: it was taken into the amphitheater and burned in front of a great crowd. "And that," as our chronicler notes with satisfaction, "was the end of the vain superstition and ancient error of Serapis."[6]

A little later, a church housing the relics of St. John the Baptist was built on the temple's ruins, a final insult to the god — and to architecture. It was, naturally, an inferior structure.

According to later Christian chronicles, this was a victory. According to a non-Christian account, it was a tragedy — and a farce. The Greek writer Eunapius felt the destruction was done less from reverence for the Lord than out of pure greed. In his account the Christians weren't virtuous warriors: they were hoodlums and thieves. The only thing that they didn't steal, he observed acidly, was the floor—and that was left "simply because of the weight of the stones which were not easy to move from their place." As he wrote with scorn, "these war-like and honourable men" had destroyed this beautiful temple out of "greed," yet once they had finished their vandalism they "boasted that they had overcome the gods, and reckoned their sacrilege and impiety a thing to glory in."[7] Nothing was left. Christians took apart the temple's very stones, toppling the immense marble columns, causing the walls themselves to collapse. The entire sanctuary was demolished with astonishing rapidity; the greatest building in the world was "scattered to the winds."[8]

The tens of thousands of books, the remnants of the greatest library in the world, were all lost, never to reappear. Perhaps they were burned. As the modern scholar Luciano Canfora observed: "the burning of books was part of the advent and imposition of Christianity." A war against pagan temples was also a war against the books that had all too often been stored inside them for safekeeping—a concept that from now on could only be recalled with irony. If they were burned then this was a significant moment in what Canfora has called "the melancholy experiences of the war waged by Christianity against the old culture and its sanctuaries: which meant, against the libraries."[9] Over a thousand years later, Edward Gibbon raged at the waste: "The appearance of the empty shelves excited the regret and indignation of every spectator, whose mind was not wholly darkened with religious prejudice."[10]

Far more than a temple had gone. As the news of the destruction spread across the empire, something of the spirit of the old culture died too. It was said that many Alexandrians, seeing what had happened to the temple, converted to Christianity instantly. This was a terrifying act of aggression. Philosophers and poets fled the city in horror. The sky had not, as the old superstition had threatened, fallen in. But something had gone. A terrible melancholy settled among those intellectuals who dared to remain. As one Greek professor wrote in despair: "The dead used to leave the city alive behind them, but we living now carry the city to her grave."[11]

CHAPTER SEVEN

———

To Despise the Temples

The weakness of paganism as a religion is manifest . . . it was bound in the end to give way to a higher creed.

—Gilbert Grindle, *The Destruction of Paganism in the Roman Empire,* 1892

THIS NEW CHRISTIAN ERA began with a vision, and a declaration of liberty.

In October AD 312, the emperor Constantine saw one of the most famous visions in the history of Europe. One day, so the story goes, not long before a forthcoming battle against his imperial rival Maxentius, Constantine happened to look up into the sky at noon while praying. What he claimed to see would blaze out across the centuries. For above the sun, Constantine saw a cross of light. And next to it were the words "Conquer by this."[1] Constantine and his army, aided by the religion of the Prince of Peace, went on to win the battle. Constantine's conversion to the faith — so it was said — was now assured.

Constantine moved quickly to promote his new religion. The following year, he said that the persecution of the Christians was over. Indeed the Edict of Milan was said to have promised much more than that. It announced that "every man may have complete toleration in the practice of whatever worship he has chosen."[2] This was a wonderful time, wrote the historian Eusebius. "Men had now lost all fear of their former oppressors . . . light was everywhere . . . They danced and sang in city and country alike."[3]

That wasn't quite true. Not everyone danced and sang. Christian history might recall Constantine as "pre-eminent in every virtue that true religion can confer," but non-Christians looked on him rather less fondly.[4] Many treated his sudden conversion to Christianity with profound suspicion and more than a little distaste. This man of "evil disposition" and "vicious inclinations" had converted, wrote one non-Christian historian, not because of any burning heavenly crosses but because, having recently murdered his wife (he had—allegedly—boiled her in a bath because of a suspected affair with his son), he had been overcome by guilt. Yet the priests of the old gods were intransigent: Constantine was far too polluted, they said, to be purified of these crimes. No rites could cleanse him. At this moment of personal crisis Constantine happened to fall into conversation with a man who assured him that "the Christian doctrine would teach him how to cleanse himself from all his offences, and that they who received it were immediately absolved from all their sins." Constantine, it was said, instantly believed.[5]

Or such was the story as told by the historian Zosimus—a starchy Roman traditionalist. The dates don't really work—Constantine had embraced Christianity long before he killed his wife—but the tale hints at how ill-disposed the ancient patrician families of Rome felt towards their suddenly Christian emperor. Even without his ostentatiously flourished new faith, there was much about Constantine that grated on aristocratic Roman sensibilities. In the glory days of Rome, real men had scorned luxury in their dress: merely wearing one's sleeves a little too long, as the infamously dapper Caesar had done, had been enough to raise eyebrows and suspicions. Proper Romans —or so the rhetoric ran—should wear simple tunics that were becomingly manly. Constantine, by contrast, favored such a profusion of jewels, diadems and silk robes that even his usually adoring biographer Eusebius was forced to defend him. Left to his own devices, Eusebius wrote, Constantine naturally preferred to clothe himself instead in the "knowledge of God" and the embroidery of "temperance, righteousness, piety, and all other virtues."[6] Alas, Constantine realized that his people, like children, enjoyed a bit of show and so he was forced to wear crasser threads, which often involved gold embroidery and flowers. Such are the sacrifices one makes for the glory of the faith.

It wasn't only Constantine's imperial person that was draped in gold. The Church, so recently persecuted, suddenly found itself the unexpected recipient of staggering amounts of money. One bishop was told that if he were to ask the emperor's finance officer for "any sum, he is to arrange for its transfer to you without question."[7] Tax relief was given to Church lands, clerics were exempted from public duties, bishops were lavished with gifts and banquets; annual allowances were given to widows, virgins and nuns . . . The expensive list went on. The vast churches Constantine built were astonishing. "The decorations really are too marvellous for words," wrote one awed pilgrim to the Church of the Holy Sepulchre. "All you can see is gold and jewels and silk . . . the magnificent building itself . . . was decorated with gold, mosaic, and precious marble." These buildings spoke volumes about where Constantine's allegiances now lay; they were "sermons in stone" as the modern historian Peter Brown has beautifully described them. This was about architecture—but it was also about intent.[8]

The funds for all this had to be found from somewhere. Now, Constantine turned to "those accursed and foul people" who had chosen to stubbornly "hold themselves back" from Christianity and continue visiting their "sanctuaries of falsehood"—in other words, those people who would soon be called "pagans."[9]

The means by which Constantine chose to take some of this wealth was simple—and humiliating: he demanded that the statues be taken from the temples. Christian officials, so it was said, traveled the empire, ordering the priests of the old religion to bring their statues out of the temples. From the 330s onwards some of the most sacred objects in the empire started to be removed. It is hard, today, to understand the enormity of Constantine's order. If Michelangelo's *Pietà* were taken from the Vatican and sold, it would be considered a terrible act of cultural vandalism—but it wouldn't be sacrilege as the statue is not in itself sacred. Statues in Roman temples were. To remove them was a gross violation, and Constantine knew it.

Indeed, the insult was part of the attraction. Many of Constantine's subjects still feared and venerated their "vain idols." Why wouldn't they? The history of Greco-Roman cult stretched back a millennium and more, long before the pages of Homer, into pre-history. The upstart Christianity had been around for a mere three centuries. Constantine had only taken up this "superstition" two decades before. The possibility that Jesus would triumph over all other gods would, at the time, have seemed almost preposterous. Constantine was faced with an intransigent population who insisted on worshipping idols at the expense of the risen Lord. He realized that conversion would be more "easily accomplished if he could get them to despise their temples and the images contained therein."[10] And what better way to teach wayward pagans the vanity of their gods than by cracking open their statues and showing that they were, quite literally, empty? Moreover, a religious system in which sacrifice was central would struggle to survive if there was nothing to sacrifice to. There was good biblical precedent for his actions. In Deuteronomy, God had commanded that His chosen people should overthrow altars, burn sacred groves and hew down the graven images of the gods.[11] If Constantine attacked the temples then he was not being a vandal. He was doing God's good work.

And so it began. The great Roman and Greek temples were —or so Eusebius said—broken open and their statues brought out, then mutilated. Officials "scraped off the material which seemed to be usable, purifying it by smelting with fire," then poured the precious metal into the public purse. The valueless remains were left for "the superstitious to keep as a souvenir of their shame."[12] The emperor, however, didn't stop there. The temples themselves were attacked: their doors were removed at his order; others had their roofs stripped, "others were neglected, allowed to fall into ruin, or destroyed."[13] One shrine was demolished; a temple at Cilicia was razed to the ground. According to Eusebius, Constantine's plan worked and "nations and citizens spontaneously renounced their former opinion."[14] The word "spontaneous" seems, in the context, a little tenuous.

Not all the temple statues were melted down. The "tyrant" Constantine also had an eye for art and many objects were shipped back as prize baubles for the emperor's new city, Constantinople (Constantine, like Alexander the Great, was not one for self-effacement). The Pythian Apollo was put up as "a contemptible spectacle" in one square; the sacred tripods of Delphi turned up in Constantinople's hippodrome, while the Muses of Helicon found themselves relocated to Constantine's palace. The capital looked wonderful. The temples looked — were — desecrated. As his biographer wrote with satisfaction, Constantine "confuted the superstitious error of the heathen in all sorts of ways."[15]

And yet despite the horror of what Constantine was asking his subjects to do there was little resistance. "To carry this project into execution he did not require military aid," records the chronicler Sozomen. "The people were induced to remain passive from the fear that, if they resisted these edicts, they, their children, and their wives, would be exposed to evil."[16] Constantine, as his nephew the "apostate" emperor, Julian, would scornfully say, was a "tyrant with the mind of a banker."[17] His destruction emboldened other Christians and the attacks spread. In many cities, people "spontaneously, without any command of the emperor, destroyed the adjacent temples and statues, and erected houses of prayer."[18]

Christianity could have been tolerant: it was not pre-ordained that it would take this path.[19] There were Christians who voiced hopes for tolerance, even ecumenicalism. But those hopes were dashed. For those who wish to be intolerant, monotheism provides very powerful weapons. There was

ample biblical justification for the persecution of non-believ-
ers. The Bible, as a generation of Christian authors declared,
is very clear on the matter of idolatry. As the Christian author
Firmicus Maternus reminded his rulers—perfectly correctly
—there lay upon emperors an "imperative necessity to casti-
gate and punish this evil." Their "severity should be visited in
every way on the crime." And what precisely did God advise as
a punishment for idolatry? Deuteronomy was clear: a person
indulging in this should be stoned to death. And if an entire
city fell into such sin? Again, the answer was clear: "destruction is decreed."[20]

The desecration continued for centuries. In the fifth century
AD, the colossal statue of Athena, the sacred centerpiece of
the Acropolis in Athens, and one of the most famous works
of art in the empire, was torn down from where she had stood
guard for almost a thousand years, and shipped off to Constantinople—a great coup for the Christian city and a great
insult to the "pagans." This act of imperial defilement haunted
the dreams of one Athenian philosopher: he had a nightmare
in which Athena, now homeless, came to him seeking shelter.
Other philosophers, who so loathed this aggressive new religion that they could not bring themselves even to say the word
"Christian," took to calling them the people "who move that
which should not be moved."[21]

A market in plundered art developed and Christians, braving
demonic reprisals, took to levering out and selling statues that
were particularly valuable. In their turn, polytheists, realizing
that a good artistic pedigree might save a statue from mutilation, started chiseling false attributions into statues' bases.
Many an underwhelming statue suddenly found its pediment
declaring, entirely untruthfully, that it was the work of one of
the great Greek sculptors—Polyclitus or Praxiteles—to save it
from Christian hammers. Some managed to joke about all this.
As the Greek poet Palladas archly observed, as he looked at a
fine array of gods in the house of one wealthy Christian, "the

inhabitants of Olympus, having become Christians, live here undisturbed: for here, at least, they will escape the cauldron that melts them down for petty change."[22]

Later, Christians liked to tell a story.[23] Many years ago, they said, there had been seven good Christian men who lived in the great Christian city of Ephesus. Those were terrible days to be a Christian: the emperor Decius was on the throne and he had announced (so the story goes) that all Christians must sacrifice to the gods, or be killed. Hearing this, the seven brothers were filled with sorrow but, being good Christians, they refused to sacrifice and hid instead in a cave in a nearby mountain, where they began to pray.

Decius, hearing of this, grew angry. He decided to starve the Christians to death and so had the mouth of the cave walled up. And there the brothers would have stayed, their bodies entombed, were it not for an extraordinary chance — or rather, for the will of the merciful Lord. For 362 years later* a group of masons were working nearby and they opened the mouth of the cave. The seven sleepers within were raised from their sleep by the noise; they greeted each other as usual, assuming that they had slept for one night only. They then decided to send one of their number, Malchus, to the city, to buy some bread.

Malchus walked out of the cave and down the hill until he came to the gates of the city of Ephesus, from where they had fled all those years ago. But when he came to the city gate, Malchus was utterly astonished, for he saw above it a great cross. Marveling, he turned and hurried to another gate, and saw the same: a second great cross above the entrance to the city. Wondering whether he was dreaming, Malchus walked into the city

---

* It is best not to press *The Golden Legend* too hard on dates: 362 years is the amount of time it gives for their slumber; 120 years would be closer to the true timespan between the two emperors mentioned whose reigns bookend the sleep of the seven men.

and heard men around him speaking about God. What is this? he asked. This could not be the city of Ephesus. Yesterday no one had dared to utter the name of Christ and yet today every man confessed him. And yet Ephesus it was.

When historians come to tell how an entire empire had turned so swiftly from sacrificing to Serapis to worshipping Christ, their narratives often carry more than a shade of the Seven Sleepers. When Malchus walks into Ephesus, he doesn't bump into any worshippers of Artemis disgruntled that Christian zealots have torn down her statues or erected crosses all over their city. No worshippers of Dionysus angrily complain that men now spend their time talking about Jesus. "Paganism" in this story has not so much been beaten as disappeared — and no one mourns its passing.

Later historians would go further and declare that the end of "paganism" was not suppression, but liberation. So far from being an imposition, so this narrative ran, the advent of Christianity was in fact a welcome relief. Polytheistic religion was so fundamentally foolish that even the polytheists were relieved to see it go. They had never really taken Zeus or Hera or Dionysus seriously anyway. Who could? "Human reason," as Gibbon put it, "had already obtained an easy triumph over the folly of Paganism."[24] Well into the twentieth century, distinguished scholars would declare that the "pagans" and the "heathens" had already given up on their own religious systems long before Christianity even appeared. As another academic concluded: "the weakness of paganism as a religion is manifest . . . it was bound in the end to give way to a higher creed." Any attempt to revive or preserve it was "foredoomed to failure."[25]

Roman religion was already moribund long before that cross had appeared in the sky. These old religions, it was said, were never going to work in a time of anxiety since the religious pluralism they involved had resulted in a "bewildering mass of alternatives."[26] Simply too many gods. The empire didn't resist this new religion; it had been waiting for it — it welcomed it with open arms. As the twentieth-century French author Jacques Lacarrière put it, Constantine, in announcing Christian freedom, "merely proclaimed an actual fact: the final establishment of Christianity in the *orbis romanus*."[27] Constantine did no more than give official recognition to what had long been the case on the ground. The hugely influential German academic Johannes Geffcken wrote that "no scholar of ancient history who is to be taken seriously . . . will now believe the dogma of earlier days, that there is a direct connection between the coming into existence and spread of Christianity on the one hand and the decline of paganism on the other."[28]

Other historians described — still do describe — the adoption of Christianity as a boon to a flagging empire. A recent popular book on manuscripts presents the transition to Christianity as a sort of pragmatic civic regeneration scheme, explaining that, under pressure from barbarian attack, Rome "saved its identity by reinventing itself as a Christian empire."[29] Christianity, in these accounts, was not a sudden imposition; it was a release, a relief, a salvation. Modern historians glibly refer to the moment of Constantine's conversion as the "End of Persecution." The phrase "triumph of Christianity" is used frequently, uncritically and with positive overtones.[30]

This is quite simply not true. Empires of tens of millions of people do not abandon religions that they have observed for over a millennium almost overnight without at least some disturbance. The Roman Empire was no different. Many did convert willingly and happily to Christianity (whatever "conversion" meant in this period). But many did not. At the moment when Constantine had supposedly seen that flaming cross, the vast majority of the empire was not Christian. Precise numbers are very hard to judge but Christians at that moment were very much in the minority. It has been estimated they made up as little as between seven and ten percent of the empire's total population. That means that only about four to six million people out of a population of roughly sixty million were Christian. That left over fifty million to be converted. The idea that everyone in the empire celebrated the fact that a Christian now wore the imperial purple is nonsense.[31]

Were these tens of millions of people singing and dancing in the streets and looking at each other with smiling faces and shining eyes as their temples were smashed? It seems unlikely. Yet historians have shown a magnificent indifference to their reactions. History is written by the winners and the Christian victory was absolute. The Church dominated European thought for more than a millennium. Until 1871 the University of Oxford required that all students were members of the Church of England, while in most cases to be given a fellowship in an Oxford college one had to be ordained.[32] Cambridge was a little freer — but not much. This was not an atmosphere conducive to criticism of Christianity and indeed, in English histories, there was little. For centuries, the vast majority of historians unquestioningly took up the Christian cause and routinely and derogatorily referred to non-Christians as "pagans," "heathens" and "idolaters." The practices and sufferings of these "pagans" were routinely belittled, trivialized or — more often — entirely ignored. As one modern scholar has observed: "The story of early Christian history has been told almost wholly on the basis of Christian sources."[33]

But look for a moment at the spread of Christianity from the other side and what emerges is a far less easy picture. It is neither triumphant, nor joyful. It is a story of forced conversion and government persecution. It is a story in which great works of art are destroyed, buildings are defaced and liberties are removed. It is a story in which those who refused to convert were outlawed and, as the persecution deepened, were hounded and even executed by zealous authorities. The brief and sporadic Roman persecutions of Christians would pale in comparison to what the Christians inflicted on others — not to mention on their own heretics. If this seems implausible, then consider one simple fact. In the world today, there are over two billion Christians. There is not one single, true "pagan." Roman persecutions left a Christianity vigorous enough not only to survive but to thrive and to take control of an empire. By contrast, by the time the Christian persecutions had finally finished, an entire religious system had been all but wiped from the face of the earth.[34]

———

CHAPTER EIGHT

How to Destroy a Demon

He completely demolished the temple belonging to the false religion and reduced all the altars and statues to dust.

—*Life of St. Martin*, 14.6

THE PAGES OF HISTORY might overlook this destruction, but stone is less forgetful. Go to Room 18 in the British Museum in London and you will find yourself in front of the Parthenon Marbles, taken from Greece by Lord Elgin in the nineteenth century. The astonishingly lifelike statues are, today, in a sorry state: many are mutilated or missing limbs. This, it is often assumed, was the fault of Lord Elgin's clumsy workmen or fighting during the Ottoman occupation. And indeed some of this was—but not all. Much was the work of zealous Christians who set about the temple with blunt instruments, attacking the "demonic" gods, mutilating some of the finest statuary Greece had ever produced.[1]

The East Pediment fared particularly badly. Hands, feet, even whole limbs have gone—almost certainly smashed off by Christians trying to incapacitate the demons within. The vast majority of the gods have been decapitated—again, almost certainly the work of Christians. The great central figures of the Pediment, that would have shown the birth of Athena, were the most sacred—and thus to the Christians the most demonic. They therefore suffered most: it is likely that they were pushed off the Pediment and smashed on the ground below, their fragmented remains ground down and used for mortar for a Christian church.

The same tale is told by objects in museums and archaeological sites across the world. Near the Marbles in the same museum is a basalt bust of Germanicus. Two blows have hacked off his nose and a cross has been cut in his forehead. In Athens, a larger-than-life statue of Aphrodite has been disfigured by a crude cross carved on her brow; her eyes have been defaced and her nose is missing.[2] In Cyrene, the eyes have been gouged out of a life-sized bust in a sanctuary of Demeter, and the nose removed; in Tuscany a slender statue of Bacchus has been decapitated. In the Sparta Archaeological Museum, a colossal statue of the goddess Hera looks blindly out, her eyes disfigured by crosses. A beautiful statue of Apollo from Salamis has been castrated and then struck, hard, in the face, shearing off the god's nose. Across his neck are scars indicating that Christians attempted to decapitate him but failed. In Palmyra Museum there stood, at least until the city's recent occupation by the Islamic State, the mutilated and reconstructed figure of the once-great Athena that had dominated a temple there. A huge dent in her once-handsome face was all that remained when her nose was smashed off. A recent book on the Christian destruction of statues focusing just on Egypt and the Near East runs to almost three hundred pages, dense with pictures of mutilation.[3]

But while some evidence remains, much has gone entirely. The point of destruction is, after all, that it destroys. If effective, it more than merely defaces something. It obliterates all evidence that the object ever existed. We will never know quite how much was wiped out. Many statues were pulverized, shattered, scattered, burned and melted into absence. Tiny piles of charred ivory and gold are all that remain of some. Others were so well disposed of that they will probably not be found: they were thrown into rivers, sewers and wells, never to be seen again. The destruction of other sacred objects is, because of the nature of the object, all but impossible to detect. The sacred groves of the old gods for example, those tranquil natural shrines like the one Pliny had so admired, were set about with axes and their ancient trees hacked down. Pictures, books, ribbons even, could be seen as the work of the devil and thus removed and destroyed. Certain sorts of musical instruments were censured and stopped: as one Christian preacher boasted, the Christians smashed the flutes of the "musicians of the demons" to pieces. Some of the demolition, such as that of the temple of Serapis, was so terrible that several authors recorded it. Other moments of vandalism were immortalized in glowing terms in Christian hagiographies. Though these are the exceptions. Far more violence was buried by silence.

Nevertheless, where written sources are silent, archaeology can speak volumes. In Egypt, countless chisel blows neatly defaced (in the most literal sense of the term) the images of the gods in the Dendera temple complex on the left bank of the Nile. Divine figures were attacked with tiny hack marks — usually several hundred for each figure. The archaeologist Eberhard Sauer, a specialist in the archaeology of religious hatred, has observed that the closeness of these cuts, and their regularity, hints at blows made with almost frantic rapidity. In Rome, he explains that the axe that mutilated a fresco of the god Mithras was swung with what must have been considerable force. The marks of the hammers, chisels and iron bars on these ancient statues can — a mute Morse — tell archaeologists a great deal. In Palmyra, what remains of the statue of Athena shows that one single, furious sword-blow had been enough to decapitate her. Though often one blow was not felt to be sufficient. In Germany, a statue of the goddess Minerva was smashed into six pieces. Her head has never been found. In France, a relief of Mithras was smashed into more than three hundred pieces.

Christian writers applauded such destruction — and egged their rulers on to greater acts of violence. One gleefully observed that the Christian emperors now "spit in the faces of dead idols, trample on the lawless rites of demons, and laugh at the old lies."[4] An infamous early text instructed emperors to wash away this "filth" and "take away, yes, calmly take away . . . the adornments of the temples. Let the fire of the mint or the blaze of the smelters melt them down."[5] This was nothing to be ashamed of. The first Commandment could not have been clearer. "Thou shalt not make unto thee any graven image," it said. "Thou shalt not bow down thyself to them," it continued, "nor serve them: for I the Lord thy God am a jealous God, visiting the iniquity of the fathers upon the children unto the third and fourth generation of them that hate me."[6] The Greek and Roman temples, no matter how ancient or beautiful, were the homes of false gods and they had to be destroyed. This was not vandalism: it was God's will. The good Christian had a duty to do nothing less.

The speed with which toleration slipped into intolerance and then downright suppression shocked non-Christian observers. Not long after Constantine had gained control of the whole empire in AD 324, it is said that he forbade any governors who were still pagan from sacrificing or from worshipping idols, thus disbarring non-Christians from moving into the plum positions in the imperial government. Then he went still further, and passed two new laws against what he called these "sanctuaries of falsehood."[7] One law "restricted the pollutions of idolatry . . . so that no one should presume to set up cult-objects, or practise divination or other occult arts, or even to sacrifice at all." The second law, assuming the success of the first, ordered mass building and extension of churches: "as if almost everybody would in future belong to God, once the obstacle of polytheistic madness had been removed."[8]

Over the course of the fourth century, in language that was at times hostile to the point of hysterical, legal pressure against the "pagans" increased. In AD 341, Constantine's son, Emperor Constantius, banned sacrifices. "Superstition," the law announced, "shall cease; the madness of sacrifices shall be abolished." Anyone who dared to disobey could look forward to an ominously vague "suitable punishment." A little later it was ordered that the temples were to be closed. It started to feel dangerous to even visit them. The emperor Julian later acerbically observed that while Constantine robbed the temples his sons overthrew them. In AD 356, it became illegal—on pain of death—to worship images.⁹ The law adopted a tone of hitherto unseen aggression. "Pagans" began to be described as "madmen" whose beliefs must be "completely eradicated," while sacrifice was a "sin" and anyone who performed such an evil would be "struck down with the avenging sword."¹⁰

This is not to say that, in the century that followed Constantine's conversion, there were not periods of quiet; there were. There were pauses, even reversals, in the persecution. Under the reigns of Valentinian I and his brother Valens in the middle of the century, state interference lessened. The reign of the emperor Julian—"the Apostate" as later Christian generations would disparagingly call this non-Christian ruler—was of course another. But Julian's reign was brief and, just half a century after Constantine, it was already too late to reverse the attrition that had begun. Julian, one Christian would tell his flock, was "but a cloud which will speedily be dispersed."¹¹ He was right.

By the time Theophilus attacked Serapis the laws were on his side. But many other Christians were so keen to attack the demonic temples that they didn't wait for legal approval. Decades before the laws of the land permitted them to, zealous Christians began to indulge in acts of violent vandalism against their "pagan" neighbors. The destruction in Syria was particularly savage. Syrian monks—fearless, rootless, fanatical—became infamous both for their intensity and for the violence with which they attacked temples, statues and monuments—and even, it was said, any priests who opposed them. Libanius, the Greek orator from Antioch, was revolted by the destruction that he witnessed. "These people," he wrote, "hasten to attack the temples with sticks and stones and bars of iron, and in some cases, disdaining these, with hands and feet. Then utter desolation follows, with the stripping of roofs, demolition of walls, the tearing down of statues, and the overthrow of

altars, and the priests must either keep quiet or die . . . So they
sweep across the countryside like rivers in spate."[12] Libanius
spoke elegiacally of a huge temple on the frontier with Persia, a magnificent building with a beautiful ceiling, in whose
cool shadows had stood numerous statues. Now, he said, "it
is vanished and gone, to the grief of those who had seen it"
—and the grief of those who now never would.[13] This temple
had been so striking, he said, that there were even those who
argued that it was as great as the temple of Serapis—which,
he added with an irony not lost on later historians, "I pray may
never suffer the same fate."[14]

Not only were the monks vulgar, stinking, ill-educated and
violent; they were also, said their critics, phonies. They pre-
tended to adopt lives of austere self-denial but actually they
were no better than drunken thugs, a black-robed tribe "who
eat more than elephants and, by the quantities of drink they
consume, weary those that accompany their drinking with the
singing of hymns." After going on their rampage these men
would then, he said, "hide these excesses under an artificially
contrived pallor" and pretend to be holy, self-denying monks
once again.[15] Drunks they might have been but, as Libanius
saw, they were ferociously effective. "After demolishing one
[temple], they scurry to another, and to a third, and trophy is
piled on trophy"—and all this "in contravention of the law."[16]

As the century drew to its close, the period of leniency ended.
In the 380s and 390s rulings started to be issued with increasing rapidity and ferocity against all non-Christian ritual. In AD
391, the fervently Christian emperor Theodosius passed a formidable law. "No person shall be granted the right to perform
sacrifices; no person shall go around the temples; no person
shall revere the shrines." Nor could anyone "with secret wickedness" venerate his household gods, or burn lights to them,
or put up wreaths to them, or burn incense to them.[17] Then, in
399, a new and more terrible law came. It was announced that
"if there should be any temples in the country districts, they

shall be torn down without disturbance or tumult. For when they are torn down and removed, the material basis for all superstition will be destroyed."[18]

It has been argued that the laws issued against "pagans" were mere noise: no imperial troops followed the words into the provinces and the sheer number of laws hints at their ineffectiveness. Like a teacher who has to repeatedly tell a class to be quiet, their frequency indicates their impotence—as indeed one law petulantly admits. "We have been impelled," it huffs, by the "madness of the pagans . . . to repeat the regulations which we have ordered." But repetition need not necessarily mean that a law was ineffectual; it might also mean that it required clarification.[19] These edicts were far more than just words and it is disingenuous to suggest otherwise. They gave carte blanche to Christians to cleanse the demons from the sinful pagans.

Many were ready and waiting for the chance to do just that. Not always as mindful of Mark 12:31 as they might have been, many Christians declined to love their polytheist neighbors and instead agitated to reduce their temples to rubble. Bishops badgered their rulers for new laws then used their congregations as de facto troops to carry out demolitions.

As the laws became increasingly shrill, the extent of the destruction increased, as too did the openness with which it was done. At some point, probably just before the attack on the temple of Serapis, a bishop named Marcellus became "the first of the bishops to put the edict in force and destroy the shrines in the city committed to his care."[20] Then, in 392, Serapis fell. Almost no event, with the exception of the Sack of Rome by the Visigoths in AD 410, would resound more loudly through literature of the time.[21] Its collapse would not be heard by later centuries: in the newly Christian world this was one tale, one of many, that would be quietly forgotten.

The attacks were hymned by hagiographies and histories. In fourth-century France, St. Martin, or so the *Life of St. Mar-*

tin proudly records, "set fire to a most ancient and famous shrine" before moving on to a different village and a different temple. Here, he "completely demolished the temple belonging to the false religion and reduced all the altars and statues to dust."[22] Martin was no anomaly. Flushed by his success at the temple of Serapis, Bishop Theophilus went on to demolish numerous shrines in Egypt. Hagiography records such attacks not as dismal or even embarrassing acts of vandalism but as proof of a saint's virtue. Some of the most famous saints in Western Christianity kicked off their careers—so the stories like to boast—demolishing shrines. Benedict of Nursia, the revered founder of Western monasticism, was also celebrated as a destroyer of antiquities. His first act upon arriving in Monte Cassino, just outside Rome, was to smash an ancient statue of Apollo and destroy the shrine's altar. He didn't stop there, but toured the area "pulling down the idols and destroying the groves on the mountain . . . and gave himself no rest until he had uprooted the last remnant of heathenism in those parts."[23] Of course hagiography is not history and one must read such accounts with, at best, caution. But even if they do not tell the whole truth, they certainly reveal a truth—namely that many Christians felt proud, even jubilant, about such destruction.

Farther south, the firebrand preacher John Chrysostom— John "Goldenmouth"—weighed in. This man was so charismatic that crowds of Christians would pack into Antioch's Great Church to hear him speak, his eyes flashing, then leave as soon as he was finished, "as if," he observed, with a distinct want of monkish humility, "I were a concert performance."[24] Chrysostom was nothing if not zealous. Hearing that Phoenicia was still "suffering from the madness of the demons' rites," he sent violent bands of monks, funded by the faithful women in his congregation, to destroy the shrines in the area. "Thus," concludes the historian Theodoret, "the remaining shrines of the demons were utterly destroyed."[25] A papyrus fragment shows Bishop Theophilus standing triumphantly over an image of Serapis, Bible in hand, while on the right-hand side monks can be seen attacking the temple. St. Benedict, St. Martin, St. John Chrysostom: the men leading these campaigns of violence were not embarrassing eccentrics but men at the very heart of the Church.

Augustine evidently assumed his congregants would be taking part in the violence—and implied that they were right to do so: throwing down temples, idols and groves was, he said, no less than "clear proof of our not honouring, but rather abhorring, these things."[26] Such destruction, he reminded his flock, was the express commandment of God. In AD 401, Augustine told Christians in Carthage to smash pagan objects because, he said, that was what God wanted and commanded. It has been said that sixty died in riots inflamed by this burst of oratorical fire.[27] A little earlier a congregation of Augustine's, eager to sack the temples of Carthage, had started reciting Psalm 83. "Let them be humiliated and be downcast forever," they chanted with grim significance. "Let them perish in disgrace."[28]

It is obvious that this violence was not only one's Christian duty; it was also, for many, a thoroughly enjoyable way to spend an afternoon. Those carrying out the attacks sang as they smashed the ancient marble and roared with laughter as they destroyed statues. In Alexandria, "idolatrous" images were taken from private houses and baths, then burned and mutilated in a jubilant public demonstration. Once the assault was complete, the Christians "all went off, praising God for the destruction of such error of demons and idolatry."[29] Broken statues themselves were another cause for hilarity, their fragmented remains an occasion for "laughter and scorn."[30] Chants appeared celebrating these attacks. Coptic pilgrims who visited the city of Hermopolis in Egypt could join with fellow faithful as they sang a local hymn to the destruction.[31] The humorously apposite insult was much enjoyed by God's warriors. In Carthage, there was an annual religious ceremony in which the beard of a statue of Hercules was ceremonially gilded; at the beginning of the fifth century some Christians mockingly "shaved" the statue's beard off. It was, for them, a moment of much hilarity. For the watching polytheists it was a desecration.

Statues, the very seat of the demons themselves, suffered some of the most vicious attacks. It was not enough merely to take a statue down; the demon within it had to be humiliated, disgraced, tortured, dismembered and thus neutralized. A Jewish tractate known as the *Avodah Zarah* provided detailed instructions on how to properly mistreat a statue. One can desecrate a statue, it advised, by "cutting off the tip of its ear or nose or finger, by battering it — even although its bulk be not diminished — it is desecrated." Merely taking the statue down, or spitting at it, or dragging it about, or throwing dirt upon it, was not, the treatise warned, sufficient — though the resourceful Christian might indulge in all of these as an added humiliation to the demon within.[32]

Sometimes, as was the case with the bust of Aphrodite in Athens, the statues appear to have been "baptized," with deep crosses gouged on their foreheads. If this was a "baptism" then it may have helped not only to neutralize the devil within, but also to vanquish any more personal demons that could arise when looking at such beautiful naked figures. A naked statue of Aphrodite was, wrote one Christian historian in disgust, "more shameless than that of any prostitute standing in front of a brothel"[33] — and, like a prostitute, Aphrodite and her plump bottom and naked breasts might incite the demon of lust in the viewer. Far less easy to feel desire for a statue who has had a cross gouged in her head, her eyes blinded and her nose sliced from her face. Erotically appealing statues suffered more than chastely clothed ones. We can still see the consequences of this rhetoric. Today, a once-handsome Apollo missing a nose stands in a museum; a statue of Venus that stood in a bathhouse has had her nipples and mons pubis chiseled away; a statue of Dionysus has had his nose mutilated and his genitalia removed.

These attacks may have been beneficial for God—but they were not unhelpful to local Christians, either. People built themselves houses from the stones of the demolished temples. Look closely at the buildings in the east of the Roman Empire and you can see the remains of the classical tradition in the new Christian architecture: a pair of cut-off legs here, the top of a handsome Grecian column there. One law announced that the stones from demolished temples should be used to repair roads, bridges and aqueducts.[34] In Constantinople, a former temple of Aphrodite was used to store a bureaucrat's chariots.[35] Christian writers reveled in such little humiliations. As one exulted, "your statues, your busts, the instruments of your cult have all been overturned—they lie on the ground and everyone laughs at your deceptions."[36]

"Sinful" pagans who suddenly found themselves beset by raging mobs of Christians often felt themselves to be more sinned against than sinning and, objecting to the destruction of their sacred monuments, fought back. The violent, temple-destroying Bishop Marcellus was seized and burned alive by outraged polytheists.[37] In the 420s, in Carthage, the temple of the Roman goddess Caelestis and all nearby sanctuaries were leveled. This was no mean feat: the shrine of Caelestis was a mile long. Pagans protested vocally—and impotently. "No craftsman will ever again make the idols that Christ has smashed," gloated Augustine. "Consider what power this Caelestis used to enjoy here at Carthage. But where is the kingdom of this Caelestis now?"[38] Fights could ensue during destruction and, in the process, Christians were sometimes killed—not necessarily a bad thing to some Christian minds, of course: a martyr's crown awaited those who died in this way. Encouraged by this tempting incentive, some went further and intentionally provocative attacks were launched by Christians wishing less to destroy than to be destroyed—and win martyrdom in the process. It was a process that seems to have gotten out of hand. As early as the start of the fourth century some Spanish bishops were moved to declare that "if anyone breaks idols and is killed on the spot" they would not after all be awarded the martyr's crown.[39]

The destruction did not stop at public property. Later, bands of Christians began to enter houses and bathhouses, and remove suspect statues from them which, when found, would be publicly burned. Sometimes, according to the Christian chronicles, such vandalism happened without the need for human hand: the mere presence of godliness was enough to cause statues to autodestruct. As the (somewhat dubious) hagiography of a bishop in Gaza records, when he approached a statue with a cross "the demon that dwelt in the statue . . . came forth out of the marble with great confusion and cast down the statue itself and brake it into many pieces." Miraculous enough in itself, but this good deed also had some advantageous collateral damage. As our hagiographer records with satisfaction, "two men of the idolators were standing beside the base on which the statue stood, and when it fell, it clave the head of the one in twain, and of the other it brake the shoulder and the wrist. For they were both standing and mocking at the holy multitude."[40]

Christian accounts revel in such fortuitous accidents. The apocryphal (and similarly dubious) *Acts of John* tells what happened when the apostle John traveled to Ephesus and to the famous temple of Artemis, one of the seven wonders of the ancient world. John arrived on a feast day, so while all the locals were wearing white and celebrating, John, dressed in black, entered the temple and started to preach against their godless ways. Then, with divine help, he caused the altar to splinter into many pieces, all dedications in the temple to fall and the images of the gods to topple. As if that weren't enough, then "half of the temple fell down so that the priest was slain at one blow by the falling of the [roof]." After this satisfactory display the Ephesians, with due rending of garments and weeping, promptly came to heel and started worshipping the one true God.[41]

Like martyrdom, this holy and important work required no special knowledge or skills. While it might take months of effort, years of training and centuries of accumulated knowledge to build a Greek temple, it took little more than zeal and patience to destroy one. At the end of the fourth century, as the laws against pagans were building to an aggressive crescendo, the bishop Marcellus was said to have destroyed the vast and still hugely popular temple of Zeus at Apamea with prayers and the help of a man who was "no builder, or mason, or artificer of any kind." Today, Marcellus is worshipped as a saint in the Orthodox Church.[42]

Though even Christian accounts often present these divine destroyers as incompetent bunglers: Marcellus launched numerous failed attempts on that ancient temple before finally getting it to collapse (it transpired that a "black demon" had been thwarting his purpose).[43] The efforts of St. Martin in France also teetered on disaster. While burning down one ancient temple his triumph nearly rebounded on him when, mid-conflagration, the flames flared out of control and almost set alight a nearby house; Martin just managed to prevent this PR disaster by climbing "up on to the roof of the house, throwing himself in the path of the flames as they came towards him."[44] The idea of such incompetence fits with some of the archaeological evidence. Some of the Parthenon frieze, for example, may well have been saved because it was so high and the slope beneath the temple was so steep that its offensive figures were hard to see.

Today, histories of this period, if they mention such destruction at all, hesitate to condemn it outright. The 1965 edition of *The Penguin Dictionary of Saints* records with little more than amused indulgence that Martin of Tours "was not averse to the forcible destruction of heathen shrines."[45] In modern histories those carrying out and encouraging the attacks are rarely

described as violent, or vicious, or thuggish: they are merely
"zealous," "pious," "enthusiastic" or, at worst, "over-zealous."
As the academic John Pollini puts it: "modern scholarship,
influenced by a Judeo-Christian cultural bias," has frequently
overlooked or downplayed such attacks and even at times
"sought to present Christian desecration in a positive light."[46]
The attacks themselves are diminished in importance, both
implicitly by the lack of attention they are given, and at times
even explicitly. We should not make too much of these events,
one influential academic has argued; we should not "amplify
them unduly" as such desecrations "may have been the work
of a determined few, briskly performed."[47]

The events may have been briskly performed. But the effects of such acts were deep and long-lasting. As indeed the
Christians intended them to be: that was the point. Again and
again, it is recorded that the violent destruction of a temple resulted in almost instantaneous conversion among locals. In Alexandria, after the destruction of the temple of Serapis, many,
"having condemned this error and realised its wickedness, embraced the faith of Christ and the true religion." According
to this Christian source, the Alexandrians converted merely
because their eyes had been opened. It is easy to see another
reading of their conversion: they were terrified. In Gaza, after
watching a statue smash into pieces at the appearance of the
cross, it was said that thirty-two men and seven women converted instantly.[48] When Marcellus destroyed the great temple
of Zeus in Apamea, it fell with a crash that was loud enough
to bring all the townspeople running. Sure enough, "no sooner
did the multitude hear of the flight of the hostile demon than
they broke out into a hymn of praise to God."[49]

Educated non-Christians balked at the violence. Libanius,
who would go down in history as the last of the great "pagan" orators, protested vividly. The Church might declare that
it was winning converts through these attacks but this, said
Libanius, was bunk: "they speak of conversions apparent, not

real. Their 'converts' have not really been changed — they only say they have." In which case, he went on, "what advantage have they won when adherence to their doctrine is a matter of words and the reality is absent? Persuasion is required in such matters, not constraint."[50] Some of the greatest orators in the ancient world stepped forward to defend the empire's long tradition of religious pluralism — and, yes, tolerance.*[51] Another orator named Themistius echoed Libanius's arguments closely in a speech delivered in AD 364. People had always, he said, worshipped different gods and there was nothing wrong with that. On the contrary, the divine law sets "free each person's soul for the path of religious devotion which they think best. No confiscation of property, no punishment, no burning has ever overcome this law; it may happen that the body is broken and dead, but the soul will depart carrying with it the knowledge of the law of freedom, even if its expression has been constrained."[52]

Christians disagreed and took pride in conversions made after a show of force. In Carthage, two imperial officials destroyed the temples of the "false gods" and broke their statues. This little burst of thuggishness had, in Christian eyes, a pleasingly invigorating effect on the locals. As Augustine observed contentedly, "almost thirty years have gone by since that day and anyone can see how Christianity has grown, especially by the conversion of those who were held back from the faith."[53] In Gaul, after watching St. Martin pulverize their ancient temple in silence, it is said that the local villagers "realised that the

---

* The question of whether Romans were "tolerant" is a vexed one. It is possible to argue that they were not, since true tolerance implies first disagreeing with what someone is doing, then allowing them to do it anyway. Voltaire's stance on freedom of speech — "I disapprove of what you say but I will defend to the death your right to say it" — is a perfect example of such true toleration. Therefore, it is argued that while the Romans were infinitely more tolerant of other religions than the Christians were, they did not, by this yardstick, show true "toleration": it had simply not occurred to them to be intolerant. However, to say that what matters is the intention and not the deed feels an anachronistically Christian — even Augustinian — way to look at Roman toleration.

divine will had rendered them speechless and panic-stricken to stop them resisting the bishop, and as a result almost all of them converted to the Lord Jesus." St. Martin, encouraged, set off to destroy yet another temple in yet another village. Martin's good efforts exerted a doubly beneficial effect on the unbelievers of Gaul "for in those places where he had destroyed the pagan shrines, he immediately built either churches or monasteries."[54] Quite probably using the same stones. One might dismiss the hagiography of Martin as mere fiction—but archaeology supports its general theme: Gaul started to become ever more Christianized at around the time of Martin's episcopate.

The destruction of temples, the vandalizing of statues, the terrorizing of citizens. It is all a long way from the peaceful fiction of the Seven Sleepers story. To understand what really went on in this period, imagine for a moment a parallel tale—a tale to which the archaeology of Ephesus can even add a little hard fact. Imagine for a moment that there was another sleeper, an eighth man who, like the Christians, slipped into a divine stupor on that day in AD 250. Imagine that he, too, wakes, perhaps a century later, and that he too walks into the city that he had once known.

Almost immediately, this worshipper of the old gods would, like Malchus, have known that something fundamental had changed. Had he walked through one of the city's great gates he would not merely have noticed the triumphant cross. He would almost certainly have also noticed that the handsome relief on the side of the gate had been violently mutilated. As he walked on, he would have seen more to make him feel uneasy: that the doors of the temples, some of which had been founded almost a thousand years before, had been stripped and vandalized; that many of the statues which had once stood in the temples' niches were missing. Had our sleeper then paid a visit to the town's bathhouse in the harbor, he would have noticed even more desecration: in one street an image of Artemis had been defaced; in the baths Artemis's very name had been erased from a plinth where she had once stood. Everywhere, he would have seen numerous figures that had been viciously attacked. Even a statue of the emperor Augustus himself had not escaped: Augustus, his nose sliced off, now wore a Christian cross on his forehead.

And if our imaginary sleeper had walked on, he would have been confronted with a final image which would have pointed to the source of all of this destruction. For there, right in the center of the city of Ephesus, was a large wooden cross. If he had peered at its base, he would have seen large, crudely gouged Greek letters. There, beneath the cross, was an inscription made by a local man named Demeas. "Having destroyed a deceitful image of demonic Artemis," it announced in emphatic capitals, "Demeas set up this sign of truth, honouring both God the driver-away of idols, and the cross, that victory-bringing, immortal symbol of Christ."[55]

At the end of the fourth century, the orator Libanius looked out and described in despair what he observed. He and other worshippers of the old gods saw, he said, their temples "in ruins, their ritual banned, their altars overturned, their sacrifices suppressed, their priests sent packing and their property divided up between a crew of rascals."[56]

They are powerful words, and it is a powerful image. Yet in the Christian histories, men like Libanius barely exist. The voices of the worshippers of the old gods are rarely, if ever, recorded. But they were there. Some voices, such as his, have come down to us. Far more must have expressed such feelings. It is thought that when Constantine had come to the throne, ten percent of the empire, at most, were Christian. That is not to say that the rest were fervent worshippers of Isis or Jupiter — the popularity of different gods waxed and waned over time and the spectrum of classical belief ran from firm believer to utter skeptic. But what is more certain is that probably around

ninety percent were *not* Christian. By the end of that first, tu-
multuous century of Christian rule, estimates suggest that this
figure had been reversed: between seventy and ninety percent
of the empire *were* now Christian.[57] One law from around that
time declared, entirely untruthfully, that there were no more
"pagans." None. The aggression of the claim is remarkable.
Christians were writing the wicked "pagans" out of existence.
In the crowing words of one triumphalist account: "The pagan
faith, made dominant for so many years, by such pains, such
expenditure of wealth, such feats of arms, has vanished from
the earth."[58]

It had not. Nevertheless, it is clear that a staggering reversal
had taken place. Tens of millions of people had converted—or
were said to have converted—to a new and alien religion, in
under a century. Religions that had lasted for centuries were
dying with remarkable rapidity. And if some of these millions
were converting not out of love of Christ but out of fear of his
enforcers? No matter, argued Christian preachers. Better to be
scared in this life than burn in the next.

The worshippers of the old gods pleaded eloquently with
the Christian elite for toleration. One of the most famous requests was sparked by a dispute over an altar. The Altar of Victory had stood in the Senate House in Rome for centuries, and
for centuries Roman senators had made offerings at it before
meetings of the Senate. It was an ancient custom, dating back
to Augustus, and a revered one. But Christians began to find
it increasingly intolerable that they had to share the Senate
with idols and breathe what they saw as the polluting demonic
smoke. After decades of to-ing and fro-ing, in AD 382 the Christian emperor Gratian ordered the altar out.

Rome's senators—at any rate those who were still worshippers of the old gods—were dismayed. Not only was this a
gross break with tradition, it was a serious insult to the gods.
The brilliant orator Symmachus wrote an appeal. First, he
begged the emperor to allow religious difference among his

subjects. Echoing Herodotus, Celsus, Themistius and many another before him, he observed that "each person has their own custom, each their own religious rite" and that mankind was ill-equipped to judge which of these was best, "since all reasoning is shrouded in ambiguity." He doesn't ask for any curbing of Christianity. It was, he said, "not possible to attain to so sublime a mystery by one route alone." One can dismiss this as mere pragmatism and politics — and true, Symmachus was hardly in a position to ask for more. But that is too cynical: whether the Greco-Roman polytheism was truly "tolerant" or not, there is no doubt that the old ways were fundamentally liberal and generous. Men such as Symmachus had no wish to change that. Or, as he put it to his intolerant Christian rulers: "We offer you now prayers, not a battle."[59]

Symmachus might not have wanted a battle but a battle was precisely what the Christians saw themselves as fighting. For a Christian, reasoning was not shrouded in ambiguity: it was explicitly laid out in the Bible. And the Bible, on this point, was clear. As those thundering words of Deuteronomy had it, toleration of other religions and their altars was not what was required. Instead, the faithful were required to raze them to the ground.[60] No Christian could agree with the relativistic quibbles of Symmachus. To a Christian there were not different but equally valid views. There were angels and there were demons. As the academic Ramsay MacMullen has put it, "there could be no compromise with the Devil."[61] And, as Christians made clear in a thousand hectoring sermons and a hundred fierce laws, objects associated with other religions belonged to the Dark Lord. "The Devil's worship," fulminated one Christian, "consists of prayers in the temples of idols, honours paid to lifeless idols, the lighting of lamps or burning of incense."[62] Symmachus lost. His plea was ignored.

Then, some twenty years later, in AD 408, came one of the fiercest pronouncements yet. "If any images stand even now in the temples and shrines," this new law said, "they shall be

torn from their foundations . . . The buildings themselves of
the temples which are situated in cities or towns or outside
the towns shall be vindicated to public use. Altars shall be destroyed in all places."[63]

Rome's ancient cults were collapsing. And yet though Symmachus lost—perhaps because he lost—his words still have a
terrible power. "We request peace for the gods of our forefa-
thers," he had begged. "Whatever each person worships, it is
reasonable to think of them as one. We see the same stars, the
sky is shared by all, the same world surrounds us. What does
it matter what wisdom a person uses to seek for the truth?"[64]

CHAPTER NINE

The Reckless Ones

For the wisdom of this world is foolishness with God.

—1 Corinthians 3:19

THEY CALLED THEM THE *"parabalani"*—"the reckless ones."[1]
At first, the name had been a compliment. Under the scorching
heat of the Alexandrian sun, in this city at the crossroads of
busy trading routes, someone needed to carry away the bodies
of the sick and the weak—not to mention the merely unsa-
vory poor—and do so swiftly, to protect everyone else.

This was a city that knew how devastating a plague could
be. A hundred and fifty years before, a new disease had arrived
in Alexandria, then fanned out into the rest of the empire,
killing millions. Then, a hundred or so years later, the Plague
of Justinian struck. Its symptoms were even more abhorrent:
buboes appeared, followed variously by coma, delirium, agonizing pain, "black pustules about as large as a lentil," the vomiting of blood and, finally, death.[2] The plague was more devastating than the last: twenty-five million people died.

To deal with the dead and the dying in an ancient city was
therefore an essential job and, like most essential jobs, a despised one. In fifth-century Alexandria, the men who stepped
forward to do this work were the *parabalani,* the "reckless"
young Christians brave enough to act as stretcher bearers in
this medicine-free world.[3] These men were in many ways at
the bottom of society: they were not wealthy, or educated,
or even literate, but they had muscle, they had faith—and
they had strength in numbers.[4] By the beginning of the fifth
century there were an estimated eight hundred members of

the *parabalani* in Alexandria alone: an army—and the word is used advisedly—of young men, devoted to the service of God.[5]

Or more precisely, to the service of His representatives on earth: the bishops. As the scholar Peter Brown has pointed out, in cities across the empire at this time, powerful clerics were beginning to marshal huge followings of young men, strong believers, in both senses of the word. In Rome, those who flocked behind the bishop were the *"fossores,"* the diggers who mined out the city's famous catacombs. In Antioch, it was the pallbearers who surrounded their patriarch. These men had all initially been gathered to do good Christian deeds—but they could and would be deployed to do terrible ones. The control that many bishops had over their flocks was firm to the point of unyielding. They were the gatekeepers of heaven and could shut those gates in the faces of those who displeased them. In the fourth and fifth centuries, bishops controlled de facto militaries of the faithful—and they were not afraid to use them. In Rome, the diggers upset an episcopal election with the use of "alarming" violence. As one bishop somewhat smugly observed, bishops were "the calmers of disturbances, and anxious for peace, except when even they are moved by some offence against God, or insult to the Church," as Brown has observed.[6]

Except. Brown has rightly drawn attention to that word. Peace could only be had at the Church's say-so. The Lamb of God was now flanked by lions. The diggers in Rome were fearsome enough, but it was the *parabalani* in Alexandria who became infamous. Cross the bishop of Alexandria and, as locals knew to their cost, he might send some of the eight hundred *parabalani* to visit you. Argument incarnate, they massed outside the town hall, the theater and the law courts. Their mere presence was enough to bully opponents into submission. They have been described as a "terrorist charity"—a strange oxymoron, but a good one. These men did, at times, do good deeds but they also sowed fear. "Terror" is the word used in Roman legal documents about them.[7]

One spring day in AD 415, the *parabalani* would go much further than merely threatening violence. On that day, they committed one of the most infamous murders in early Christianity.[8]

Hypatia of Alexandria was born in the same city as the *parabalani* and yet a world away from them. While they spent their days toiling among the filthy and the dying, this aristocratic intellectual spent her days working with abstract mathematical theories and astrolabes. Hypatia was not only a philosopher; she was also a brilliant astronomer and the greatest mathematician of her generation. The Victorians, who became much taken with her, granted her other graces posthumously. One famous painting shows her draped naked against an altar, her nubile body shielded by little more than her tumbling tawny locks. A novel about her by the Reverend Charles Kingsley, author of the children's novel *The Water Babies*, is rich in such breathless phrases as "the severest and grandest type of old Greek beauty" and in musings on her "curved lips" and the "glorious grace and beauty of every line."[9]

This, alas, is romantic bunk. Hypatia was, without doubt, a beauty—but far from draping herself and her tumbling curls over altars, she always dressed in the austere and concealing uniform of a philosopher's cloak. She was devoted to the life of the mind rather than of the flesh and remained a virgin. Any man bold enough to attempt to sway her from this resolve met with a bracing response. It is said that one of her students fell in love with her and, "not being able to control his passion," confessed his feelings. Hypatia responded briskly. "She brought some of her sanitary towels and threw them before him, and said, 'You love this, young man, and there is nothing beautiful about it.'"[10] The relationship, understandably, went no further.

By the early fifth century AD, Hypatia had become something of a local celebrity. Alexandria was a city that had, for hundreds of years, been in thrall to its intellectuals. Almost as soon as there had been a city in that spot, there had been a library; and almost as soon as there was a library, stories about the library, and particularly about its foundation, had started to accumulate. According to one story, Ptolemy II, the ruler of Alexandria, had written a letter to every king and ruler on earth begging them to send his library works by all kinds of authors, "poets and prose-writers, rhetoricians and sophists, doctors and soothsayers, historians and all the others too."[11] Not just in Greek, either, but in every language. Men, too, were sought and experts enlisted from every nation to act as translators. "Each group of scholars was allocated the appropriate texts, and so a Greek translation of every text was made."[12]

Nothing was to be left out of this ambitious new collection —not even religion. Indeed, particularly not religion. It had been Alexander's firmly held belief that to govern a people you needed to understand them—and who could hope to understand a people unless you knew what they worshipped? Understand *that* and you understood their souls; understand a nation's soul and you could control it. Vast efforts were made with religious texts: two million lines of verse, said to be by the ancient Iranian prophet Zoroaster, were translated. The very first translation of the Hebrew Bible into Greek was, according to legend, made here in the third century BC.

This was intellectual conquest as much as academic inquiry and it could, at times, feel invasive. If you had docked in the city's handsome port in the third century BC then your ship would have been boarded by the officials of King Ptolemy III Euergetes. These officers would then have conducted a brisk search of your ship, hunting not for contraband but for something that was, here, considered far more valuable: books.

If any were found, they would be confiscated, taken off and copied. The copies—the librarians, well aware of the fallibility of scribes, preferred originals—would then be returned to the ships while the originals were labeled "from the ships" and taken to the Great Library itself.

The Athenian government was written to and their official copies of the great tragedies of Aeschylus, Sophocles and Euripides—believed to be the most accurate in existence—were requested. The Athenians, naturally, refused. Ptolemy III pressed them. He would pay a vast deposit, he said, fifteen talents, as proof of his good faith. Finally, the Athenians were persuaded and they sent their tragedies. The faithless Ptolemy made magnificent copies, on the finest writing materials—then sent these back across the sea. Athens got the money and the handsome new copies, but Alexandria had the best.

It was a library of awesome ambition—and size. The number of scrolls that it held is contested, but estimates of the collection give an idea of its extent—and they are astonishing. One puts the library's holdings at an implausibly high 700,000 volumes by the first century BC. Nonsense, probably, but there were perhaps as many as 500,000 scrolls by the third century BC. Certainly there were so many that, for the first time, a system of categorizing the scrolls had to be invented to keep track of them all.

This was easily the greatest library that the world had ever seen—or that it would see for centuries. The famous later monastic libraries were paltry by comparison: the earlier ones usually held around only twenty books, and even the major libraries of the twelfth century contained no more than five hundred or so—and naturally such collections were heavily weighted towards Christian texts. It took well over a millennium for any other collection to come close to what Alexandria had achieved in terms of volume, and longer still before any other library demonstrated such intellectual omnivorousness. By 1338, the library of the Sorbonne in Paris, the richest in the Christian world, offered a theoretical 1,728 works for loan — 300 of which, as its registers noted, it had already managed to lose.[13]

It wasn't only books that Alexandria collected, but intellectuals. Scholars here were treated with reverence and to some marvelous facilities. Together, the Great Library and the Musaeum provided them with a charming existence: there were covered walkways to stroll through, gardens in which to rest and a hall to lecture in. Almost every need was catered for: academics were also given a stipend from public funds, board and lodging, and meals in an elegant, domed-roof dining hall. There may also have been, somewhat incongruously, a zoo.

The intention of all this was to lure the empire's intellectuals here — and it worked. Some of the most brilliant minds of the classical period flocked there to write, read, study, eat those free meals and, of course, to bicker. "In populous Egypt," one vinegary observer wrote, "many cloistered bookworms are fed, arguing endlessly in the chicken-coop of the Muses."[14] The brilliant mathematician and physicist Archimedes, who famously stepped in a bath, noticed its water move and announced "Eureka!," had studied here.[15] So too did Euclid, whose mathematical textbook remained the basis of math education until the twentieth century. Eratosthenes, who worked out the circumference of the earth to an accuracy of 80 kilometers using little more than a stick and a camel, was also here, as too were the poet Callimachus; Aristarchus of Samos, who proposed the first heliocentric model of the solar system; the astronomer Hipparchus; Galen . . . The catalogue of Alexandria's intellectuals is as remarkable as that of its books.

Hypatia's own father, Theon, had studied here. He was a mathematician of astonishing perspicacity, not to mention longevity: the commentaries he produced on Euclid were so authoritative that they form the foundation of modern editions of his texts. Read Euclid today, and you are reading, in part, the work of Hypatia's father.

Nothing lasts forever. As she stepped out on her daily ride through Alexandria in her chariot, Hypatia would have passed through a very different city to the one enjoyed by her forebears. As the fourth century opened, even its horizon had changed: the great temple of Serapis that had once dominated the city's skyline had now gone; passing through the city she would have seen other desecrations—smaller but still shocking. After razing Serapis the Christians had gone on a victorious rampage through the city and its 2,500 shrines, temples and religious sites.[16] Busts of Serapis that had (much like the Virgin Mary in Italian villages today) previously stood in streets, wall niches and above doorways had been removed—"cleansed." The Christians had "so cut and filed [them] away that not even a trace or mention of [Serapis] or any other demon remained anywhere. In their place everyone painted the sign of the Lord's cross on doorposts, entrances, walls and columns."[17] Later, with bolder finality, crosses were carved in.

The city's intellectual life had suffered. The final remnants of the Great Library had gone, vanishing along with the temple. Many of Alexandria's intellectuals had gone too, fleeing to Rome, or elsewhere in Italy, or anywhere they could to get away from this frightening city.[18]

Nevertheless, though much had gone, much remained. At the beginning of the fifth century, Alexandria still exerted a pull on the intellectuals of the empire and Hypatia moved in a gilded circle. It was said that anyone who wanted to study philosophy traveled vast distances to get to her, coming from as far afield as Rome, Libya and Syria. Some of Alexandria's leading citizens petitioned her for advice which, it seems, she doled out with alarming frankness.[19] Whenever anyone new and notable visited Alexandria, one of the first things they did was to pay Hypatia a visit. Orestes, the aristocratic governor of Alexandria and one of the most important men in the city, had become a confidant, friend and a powerful ally—and, as it would turn out, a dangerous one.[20]

In a world that was becoming increasingly riven along sectarian lines, Hypatia remained determinedly non-partisan in her behavior, treating non-Christian and Christian with meticulous equality. Orestes himself was a Christian. People of all faiths crowded in to hear her lecture and flocked to her house to hear her speak. Devotees gathered round her at all times. Those who were taught by her grew almost queasily rhapsodic in their praise: they were "fortune's darlings" to be able to sit at the feet of this "luminous child of reason."[21] Many of Hypatia's pupils had other, more concrete reasons to consider themselves blessed: they were some of the wealthiest and best-educated young men in the empire. When away from Alexandria, they wrote each other fondly affectionate letters from their country villas, extolling the virtues of simple rural life with the enthusiasm of those who have never had to do any simple rural work. When one student wished to show his affection for another, he bought him a horse. Now in her late middle age, Hypatia had established herself as one of the most respected figures in Alexandria. The entire city, as one later admirer gushed, "naturally loved her and held her in exceptional esteem."[22]

It was not true. In the spring of the year 415, relations between Christians and non-Christians in Alexandria were tense. The sky above the city might have been darkened by only a few scudding white clouds but in its streets the atmosphere —always quarrelsome—was more precarious than ever. To make matters worse the city had a new bishop, Cyril. After the zealot Theophilus, many Alexandrians must have hoped that their next cleric would be more conciliatory. He was not. But then his breeding hinted at as much—he was, after all, Theophilus's nephew. And, true to family form, he was a thug. Cyril had not been in power long before he showed himself to be, if anything, more vicious than his uncle. Even Christians had reservations about this brutal and ambitious man: he was, as one council of bishops put it, "a monster, born and educated for the destruction of the Church." And within a few years of his coming to power his violence had begun.

The Jews were among the first to suffer. The population of Jews in Alexandria was large and, according to the legend, had itself benefited from the city's bibliomania. Ptolemy II—or so the charming story goes—had been desperate to find scholars who could translate the mysterious but highly respected Jewish writings for him so that they could be added to the library's collection. However, no Greek could fathom the script in which they were written. So Ptolemy had asked the Jewish leaders for help. They had agreed to send him some elders as translators—but there were terms. In return, they wanted the 100,000 or so Jewish prisoners of war held in the city to be set free. It was a vast number. Ptolemy thought for a moment, then agreed. He got his translators—seventy or so of them; the Jewish prisoners gained their liberty; and the Great Library got its translation—which became known, in the translators' honor, as the Septuagint.[23]

There was little interest in Hebrew writings by now. According to the hectoring sermons being preached by a new generation of intolerant Christian clerics, the Jews were not a people with an ancient wisdom to be learned from: they were instead, like the pagans, the hated enemies of the Church. A few years earlier, the preacher John Chrysostom had said that "the synagogue is not only a brothel . . . it also is a den of robbers and a lodging for wild beasts . . . a dwelling of demons . . . a place of idolatry."[24] St. John Chrysostom's writings would later be reprinted with enthusiasm in Nazi Germany.

At that moment in Alexandria, the smoldering Christian dislike of Jews burst into outright violence. A Christian attempt to regulate the dancing and theatrical displays—apparently much enjoyed by the city's Jewish population—started a complicated chain of reprisals that climaxed in a Jewish attack on some Christians. Some were killed in the attack—and Cyril was provided with the pretext he needed. Mustering together a mob of the *parabalani,* as well as some of the merely brutal and enthusiastic, Cyril set out. He "marched in wrath to the synagogues of the Jews and took possession of them, and purified them and converted them into churches." "Purified" in such texts is often a euphemism for stole, self-righteously. The Christians then completed their work by purifying the Jewish "assassins" of their possessions: stripping them of all they owned, including their homes, they turned them out of the city into the desert.[25]

Orestes looked on in horror. He was an educated man, and one who—much like his good friend Hypatia—refused to live his own life along sectarian lines, despite the increasingly hysterical atmosphere of the time. Ostensibly the most powerful man in the city, he was nonetheless unable to stop this uprising: a mere governor's retinue was no match for eight hundred marauding, muscular *parabalani.* Moreover, Orestes knew well how determined Cyril could be: the bishop had previously tried to set his spies on Orestes, ordering them to follow the governor as he went about his business around the city—and presumably as he called on Hypatia, too. Surrounded by informers, powerless to retaliate, Orestes took the only action he could in the face of Cyril's aggression: he wrote to the emperor to complain about it.

Cyril, in turn, went to see Orestes. If Orestes had expected an apology from this belligerent man, he was to be disappointed. What he received instead was piety. When he approached the governor, Cyril held out a copy of the gospels towards him, "believing"—or so the chronicle says—"that respect for religion would induce him to lay aside his resentment." It was an infuriatingly ostentatious act and, unsurprisingly, did little to end the quarrel.[26]

The atmosphere in the city darkened; the numbers of Cyril's

militia swelled. Around five hundred monks descended from their shacks and caves in the nearby hills, determined to fight for their bishop. Unwashed, uneducated, unbending in their faith, they were, as even the Christian writer Socrates admits, men of "a very fiery disposition."[27] One day, as Orestes rode in his chariot through the city, these monks in their dark and foul-smelling robes suddenly surrounded him. They began to insult him, accusing him of being a "pagan idolater."[28] He protested that, on the contrary, he was a baptized Christian. It made no difference. One of the monks threw a rock and it struck Orestes on his head. The wound started pouring with blood. Most of his guards, seeing what they were up against, scattered, plunging into the crowd to get away from the monks.

Orestes was left almost entirely alone, his robes covered in blood. The monks drew closer, forming a black crowd around him. He was outnumbered, and almost certainly afraid; yet he refused to give in. Helped by some locals who rushed to his aid, he got away. Once again, intimidation only seems to have made him more determined, as his next act was to capture then torture to death the monk who had hurled the rock. Everything about this episode would have been abhorrent to a cultured citizen like Orestes: cities should not be dictated to by the whims of bishops or terrorized by lynch mobs. They should be ruled by the law of the government that was administered by imperial officials. Anything less was the behavior of savages. Many of the city's aristocrats, perhaps repelled by the Christians' violence, supported him in his defiant stance towards Cyril. So too, crucially, did Hypatia.[29]

And then the whispering began. It was Hypatia's fault, said the Christians, that the governor was being so stubborn. It was she, they murmured, who was standing between Orestes and Cyril, preventing them from reconciling. Fanned by the *parabalani*, the rumors started to catch, and flame. Hypatia was not merely a difficult woman, they said. Hadn't everyone seen her use symbols in her work, and astrolabes? The illiterate *para-*

balani ("bestial men — truly abominable" as one philosopher would later call them) knew what these instruments were. They were not the tools of mathematics and philosophy, no: they were the work of the Devil. Hypatia was not a philosopher: she was a creature of hell. It was she who was turning the entire city against God with her trickery and her spells. She was "atheizing" Alexandria. Naturally, she seemed appealing enough — but that was how the Evil One worked. Hypatia, they said, had "beguiled many people through satanic wiles."[30] Worst of all, she had even beguiled Orestes. Hadn't he stopped going to church? It was clear: she had "beguiled him through her magic."[31] This could not be allowed to continue.

One day in March AD 415, Hypatia set out from her home to go for her daily ride through the city. Suddenly, she found her way blocked by a "multitude of believers in God."[32] They ordered her to get down from her chariot. Knowing what had recently happened to her friend Orestes, she must have realized as she climbed down that her situation was a serious one. She cannot possibly have realized quite how serious.

As soon as she stood on the street, the *parabalani*, under the guidance of a Church magistrate called Peter — "a perfect believer in all respects in Jesus Christ"[33] — surged round and seized "the pagan woman." They then dragged Alexandria's greatest living mathematician through the streets to a church. Once inside, they ripped the clothes from her body and, using broken pieces of pottery as blades, flayed her skin from her flesh. Some say that, while she still gasped for breath, they gouged out her eyes. Once she was dead, they tore her body into pieces and threw what was left of the "luminous child of reason" onto a pyre and burned her.[34]

CHAPTER TEN

To Drink from the Cup of Devils

We, if wise, shall take from heathen books whatever befits us and is allied to the truth, and shall pass over the rest.

—St. Basil, *Address*, IV

NEAR THE BEGINNING of Umberto Eco's novel *The Name of the Rose*, an erudite medieval abbot turns to a monk who has just arrived in his monastery in Italy. "*Monasterium sine libris,*" he declaims, in Latin, naturally, "*est sicut ... hortus sine herbis, pratum sine floribus, arbor sine foliis.*" A monastery without books is like a garden without herbs, a meadow without flowers, a tree without leaves. The abbot continues this explanation (or, less charitably, exposition) of monastic life in the vernacular. His order of monks, the Benedictines, he explains, "growing up under the double command of work and prayer, was light to the whole known world, depository of knowledge, salvation of an ancient learning that threatened to disappear in fires, sacks, earthquakes, forge of new writing and increase of the ancient."[1]

It is a powerful image, this: Christianity as the inheritor and valiant protector of the classical tradition—and it is an image that persists. This is the Christianity of ancient monastic libraries, of the beauty of illuminated manuscripts, of the Venerable Bede. It is the Christianity that built august Oxford colleges, their names a litany of learnedness—Corpus Christi, Jesus, Magdalen. This is the Christianity that stocked medieval libraries, created the *Très Riches Heures du Duc de Berry,* the *Hours of Jeanne de Navarre* and the sumptuous gold illustrations of the Copenhagen Psalter. This is the religion that, inside the walls of the Vatican, even now keeps Latin going as a living language, translating such words as "computer," "video game" and "heavy metal" into Latin, over a millennium after the language ought to have died a natural death.

And indeed all that is true. Christianity at its best did do all of that, and more. But there is another side to this Christian story, one that is worlds away from the bookish monks and careful copyists of legend. It is a far less glorious tale of how some philosophers were beaten, tortured, interrogated and exiled and their beliefs forbidden; it is a story of how intellectuals set light to their own libraries in fear. And it is above all a story that is told by absences: of how literature lost its liberty; how certain topics dropped from philosophical debate—and then started to vanish from the pages of history. It is a story of silence.

The intellectual world was changing. Some years before Hypatia's murder, an elderly Christian bishop named Basil wrote an anxious address to young men advising them on "The Right Use of Greek Literature."[2] It was a brisk and starchy work intended to show youthful readers which classical authors made for acceptable reading material—and which did not. As Basil warned, young readers should not "surrender to these men once for all the rudders of your mind . . . and follow them whithersoever they lead; rather, accepting from them only that which is useful, you should know that which ought to be overlooked."[3]

In Basil's eyes there was a lot to overlook. Today, in a world in which the very word "classical" hints at something revered to the point of dullness, it is hard to understand quite how alarming many of these works were to the Christians. But to Christian eyes the classical canon had the power to horrify. It was replete with sins of every kind. Open Homer's *Iliad* and you might find your eyes falling on a passage about how the god Ares seduced golden Aphrodite—and how they were both then caught in flagrante delicto. Open *Oedipus the King* and you might find a declaration that "the power of the gods is perishing." Even works by the most stuffily august of authors were not without danger: open a work by the tediously virtuous Virgil, and you might find Dido and Aeneas up to no good in a cave in a rainstorm.[4] Idolatry, blasphemy, lust, murder, vanity —every sin was there. That was what made them so enjoyable and, to the Christians, so damnable.

Callow Christians, then, could not be allowed to make their way through the classical canon unrestrained. It was far too dangerous, lest, as Basil warned, a soul "through our love for letters . . . receive some contamination unawares, as men drink in poison with honey."[5] The classical writers should also be ignored, he felt, whenever they wrote too rapturously about the pleasures of great banquets, or when they enjoyed a wanton song. Even to speak such works out loud was to pollute oneself. The famously learned St. Jerome, himself an inveterate reader, weighed in advising against "adultery of the tongue." Do not pollute yourself by reading out such words. How could one recite such filth and then go on to read Christian works? "How can Horace go with the psalter, Virgil with the gospels, Cicero with the apostle?" One should not, he said, warming to emphatic climax, "drink the cup of Christ, and, at the same time, the cup of devils."[6]

For every classical work that sat comfortably with Christian minds and morals, there was another that grated unbearably on them. "Carmen 16" by the poet Catullus was a particular thorn. This poem opens with the infamously bracing line: "I will bugger you and I will fuck your mouths" —hardly the sort of thing to gladden the heart of Basil.[7]

"Epigram 1.90" of Martial was little better: this little verse attacks a woman for having affairs with other women. Or, as Martial put it:

> *You improvised, by rubbing cunts together,*
> *And using that bionic clit of yours*
> *To counterfeit the thrusting of a male.*[8]

Open a work by Ovid and the trembling young reader might find the poet explaining how to seduce a married woman over dinner by writing secret messages in spilled wine. Dip into a later poem and they might read an account of Ovid's lunchtime lovemaking ("Oh, how the shape of her breasts demanded that I caress them!"), and a detailed description of his lover's body: her flat belly beneath those breasts, her youthful thighs . . .[9]

Enough, said Basil. Good Christians, he advised, should entirely omit the bawdier classical works. If by chance your eye alighted on a classical passage that portrayed depraved men, then, said Basil, you "must flee from them and stop up your ears."[10] The Christian reader should, he warned, always be on guard against Ovidian naughtiness. "We shall not," he wrote sternly, "praise the poets . . . when they represent fornicators and winebibbers."[11] Not all classical writers were so dangerously lusty — the Stoic emperor Marcus Aurelius, for example, had treated sex with the sort of disdain of which a Christian might approve. But even his language was a little too precise for Christian comfort. Where Christian writers frequently resorted to the safety of abstract nouns ("lust," "desire," "wantonness" and similar) to describe the demon of sexual desire, Marcus Aurelius, with queasy precision, described sexual intercourse as "the friction of a piece of gut and, following a sort of convulsion, the expulsion of some mucus."[12] In an extended simile that would have been at home in that heathen Homer, Basil therefore advocated caution. Young men should read classics much in the manner that bees visit flowers, "for the bees do not visit all the flowers without discrimination . . . rather, having taken so much as is adapted to their needs, they let the rest go."[13]

Most of all, though, it was felt that Greek and Roman authors should be ignored when they talked about their gods "and especially when they represent them as being many" — which was basically all the time.[14] Almost everything about these gods caused Christian readers to shift anxiously in their seats. Not only were they demons, but their behavior was deplorable. Unlike the Christian God, these gods did not merely traverse the more dignified divine emotions of wrath, pity and love. They ran the gamut of all the lesser ones too, indulging every feeling from lust to wantonness to jealousy—and then back to lust again. These gods were, one Christian writer felt, an "utter absurdity."[15] Far from being a distant, omniscient presence, they were shamefully and disagreeably human: they squabbled, they wept, had sex, got drunk and behaved badly to everyone, even—perhaps especially—their own family.

In the Greco-Roman pantheon, not only did brother fight against brother but, worse, brother sometimes did quite unmentionable things with sister. Or with anyone else they could get their hands on. Zeus was infamous among Christian authors as he had lusted "with a disgraceful passion for his sister."[16] Indeed he was so badly behaved that Basil was unable to bring himself to describe what "the one they call Zeus" had got up to; it was impossible to speak of Zeus's adulteries "without blushing."[17] Such things, wrote the Christian apologist Tertullian, "should not have been invented by god-fearing people." Classical comedies, in which everyone, including the gods, had flapped about in phalluses, were even worse: "Is not the majesty of your gods insulted and their godhead defiled by your applause?"[18]

Classical literature not only questioned the reality of divine beings, it frequently laughed at them too. The works of Greek and Roman philosophy were full of punchy one-liners poking fun at religion. In one famous story, the Greek philosopher Diogenes finds himself standing next to a wall covered in temple inscriptions left by grateful sailors saved at sea. Noticing a man marveling at the inscriptions, Diogenes remarks: "There would have been far more, if those who were not saved had set up offerings."[19] In another story, Diogenes is watching some temple officials arrest a man who has stolen items from a temple treasury. Look, he says: "The great thieves are leading away

the little thief."[20] In yet another yarn—one whose punch line
hit even closer to the mark—a philosopher named Antisthenes finds himself listening to a priest of Orphism, a Greek cult
that believed in an afterlife. The priest explains at length how
initiates to his religion would enjoy great advantages in the
afterlife. Why then, asks Antisthenes bluntly, "don't you die?"[21]

Better, Basil wrote, to avoid dangerous works altogether.
"Just as in culling roses we avoid the thorns, from such writings
as these we will gather everything useful, and guard against
the noxious."[22] As Basil explained, such ecclesiastical censorship was not illiberal; it was loving. Just as Augustine advocated
the beating of heretics with rods out of fatherly care, so Basil
advocated the removal of great tracts of the classical canon as
an act of "great care" to ensure the soul was safely guarded.
Sometimes this editing process might be even more intrusive
and scribes were asked to report suspicious works to the authorities so they could be censored. In Alexandria, Cyril conducted house searches to hunt out works by the loathed pagan
emperor Julian "the Apostate."[23]

The influence of Basil's essay on Western education was profound. It was read, reread and copied fervently for centuries.
It would have affected what was read, studied—and crucially,
what was preserved—in schools in Byzantium.[24] And what
was not. It was so important that this was—somewhat ironically—one of the first works translated from Greek during
the Renaissance. The Jesuits placed it on their international syl-
labus, the *Ratio Studiorum*, where it would have had an influence on Jesuit education worldwide.[25] Later generations would
present Basil as a liberal intellectual. One twentieth-century
edition of this essay described Basil's attitude to pagan literature as "that of an understanding friend, not blind to its worst
qualities, but by no means condemning the whole."[26] Another
twentieth-century edition of Basil's *Address* explains that this
was "not the anxious admonition of a bigoted ecclesiastic, ap-
prehensive for the supremacy of the Sacred Writings. Rather,

it is the educational theory of a cultured man."[27] That is non-sense. Supremacy was precisely what Basil wanted—and he got it. However honeyed the words, however beguiling the simile, this was censorship.

It wasn't just Basil. The editing of the classical canon would continue for a millennium and more. Open an 1875 edition of the Latin poet Martial and many of his more explicit poems will have been translated not into English but into Italian—evidently considered a suitable language for sexual deviancy.[28] Elsewhere poems were omitted entirely, or glossed in Greek, a language that not only looked erudite and respectable but that had the benefit of being understood by even fewer people than Latin. The opening lines of Catullus's "Carmen 16" were, as the academic Walter Kendrick has pointed out, still causing trouble well into the twentieth century: they were left out of a 1904 Cambridge University Press edition of his *Collected Poems* altogether. Discreetly sparing the readers' blushes (or perhaps their interest) the poem was described as merely "a fragment."[29] Open the 1966 Penguin edition and you will find that the first line has, equally discreetly, been left in the original Latin. "*Pedicabo et irrumabo,*" it declares, percussively but impenetrably.[30] "Carmen 16" would have to wait until almost the end of the twentieth century to find a translation that rendered it correctly—though such was the richness of Latin sexual slang that five English words were needed for that single Latin verb *irrumabo*.[31]

In this new, ever-watchful Christian era, the tone of what was being written began to change. Polytheist literature had discussed and mocked anything and everything, from the question of whether mankind can have free will in an atomic universe, to the over-credulity of the Christians, to the use of urine to clean one's teeth (a process that was considered effective, but revolting). After Christianity, what was seen as worth recording on the pages of parchment changed. Unlike the centuries before Constantine, the centuries afterwards produce no rambunctious satires or lucidly frank love poetry. The giants of fourth- and fifth-century literature are instead St. Augustine, St. Jerome and St. John Chrysostom. All are Christian. None are easily confused with Catullus.

The writings of John Chrysostom provide a rich taste of the tone of this new literature. "Let there be no fornication," he declared in one of his many fiery speeches on the topic of lust.[32] A beautiful woman was, he warned, a terrible snare. A (non-exhaustive) list of other snares that the work of this revered speaker warned against includes laughter ("often gives birth to foul discourse"); banter ("the root of subsequent evils"); dice ("introduces into our life an infinite host of miseries"); horse-racing (as above); and the theater, which could lead to a wide variety of evils including "fornication, intemperance, and every kind of impurity."[33] The index of a collection of his sermons gives a taste of the whole. Under the word "Fear" one is offered:

> *needful to holy men, 334;*
> *a chastisement for carelessness, 347;*
> *of the Lord true riches, 351;*
> *a punishment, 355;*
> *awakens conscience, 363;*
> *of harm from man ignoble, 366;*
> *a good man firm against, 369;*
> *without the fear of hell death terrible, 374;*
> *of hell profitable . . .*

And so on, for twenty-five references, before ending in the nicely conclusive: "purifies like a furnace." Look under "Happiness" and the eager reader would be greeted with rather scant offerings. Here, one is merely offered:

> *in God alone, 460*[34]

This was a new literary world and a newly serious one. "The extent to which this new Christian story both displaced and substituted for all others is breathtaking," writes the modern academic Brent D. Shaw. "The power of this Christian talk was produced by many things, among them a remorseless hortatory pedagogy, a hectoring moralising of the individual, and a ceaseless management of the minutiae of everyday life. Above all, it was a form of speech marked by an absence of humour. It was a morose and a deadly serious world. The joke, the humorous kick, the hilarious satires, the funny cut-them-down-to-size jibe, have vanished."[35] And in the place of humor came fear. Christian congregations found themselves rained on by oratorical fire and brimstone. For their own good, of course. As Chrysostom observed with pleasure: "in our churches we hear countless discourses on eternal punishments, on rivers of fire, on the venomous worm, on bonds that cannot be burst, on exterior darkness."[36]

But however threatening Christian preachers might have found the easy classical talk about sex, abortions, buggery and the clitoris, there was another aspect of classical literature that presented an even more alarming prospect: philosophy. The competing clamor of Greek and Roman philosophical schools provided a panoply of possible beliefs. Classical philosophers had variously argued that there were countless gods; that there was one god; that there were no gods at all; or that you simply couldn't be sure. The philosopher Protagoras had neatly summed up this attitude to divine beings: "I cannot know either that they exist or that they do not exist."[37]

Even philosophers like Plato, whose writings fit better with Christian thought—his single form of "the good" could, with some contortions, be squeezed into a Christian framework—were still threatening. Perhaps even more so: Plato would continue to (sporadically) alarm the Church for centuries. In the eleventh century, a new clause was inserted into the Lenten liturgy censuring those who believed in Platonic forms. "Anathema on those," it declared, "who devote themselves to Greek studies and instead of merely making them a part of their education, adopt the foolish doctrines of the ancients and accept them as the truth."[38]

For many hard-line Christian clerics, the entire edifice of academic learning was considered dubious. In some ways there was a noble egalitarianism in this: with Christianity, the humblest fisherman could touch the face of God without having his hand stayed by quibbling scholars. But there was a more aggressive and sinister side to it, too. St. Paul had succinctly and influentially said that "the wisdom of this world is foolishness with God."[39] This was an attitude that persisted. Later Christians scorned those who tried to be too clever in their interpretation of the scriptures. One writer railed furiously at those who "put aside the sacred word of God, and devote themselves to geometry . . . Some of them give all their energies to the study of Euclidean geometry, and treat Aristotle . . . with reverent awe; to some of them Galen is almost an object of worship."[40]

In Christian eyes, Galen was not to be worshipped, God was. Gnosticism, a highly intellectual second-century movement (the word "gnostic" comes from the Greek word for "knowledge") that was later declared heretical, didn't help. Heretics were intellectual, therefore intellectuals were, if not heretical, then certainly suspect. So ran the syllogism. Intellectual simplicity or, to put a less flattering name on it, ignorance was widely celebrated. The biography of St. Antony records with approval that he "refused to learn to read and write or to join in the silly games of the other little children." Education and silly games are here bracketed together, and both are put in opposition to holiness. Instead of this, we learn, Antony "burned with the desire for God."[41] That this wasn't quite true—Antony's letters reveal a much more careful thinker than this implies—didn't much matter: it appealed to a powerful ideal. No need to read: give up both books and bread and you will win God's favor. Even intellectuals were susceptible to this pretty picture: it was hearing about how the simple, unlettered Antony had inspired so many to turn to Christ that led Augustine to start striking himself on the head, tearing his hair and asking, "What is wrong with us?"[42] Ignorance was power.

Some Christians, evidently deciding that the project of assimilation was impossible, simply shut their Homer and Plato and never opened them again. One Christian author sold all his books of literature and philosophy upon conversion: poverty was a virtue and books were expensive. Besides, the true Christian had no need of philosophy anymore: they had God. As the Christian orator Tertullian put it: "What indeed has Athens to do with Jerusalem?" He went on: "What concord is there between the Academy and the Church? . . . Away with all attempts to produce a mottled Christianity of Stoic, Platonic, and dialectic composition! We want no . . . inquisition after enjoying the gospel! With our faith, we desire no further belief."[43] No need for knowledge, for the philosophy of the Stoics, or the Platonists or indeed anything else. One had faith; that was enough.

Out of all this exuberant illiteracy there arose a problem, however. While storming the gates of heaven might be achieved with no education at all, storming the gates of the elite villas of Rome required a little more sophistication. Educated Romans and Greeks such as Celsus and Porphyry had long looked at the literature of Christianity with the utmost disdain—and writers such as Augustine and Jerome knew it. Part of the problem was the Bible: not only what it said but the way in which it said it. Today, robed in the glowing English of the King James Version, it is hard to imagine the language of the Bible ever causing problems. In the fourth century it had no such antique grandeur. The gospels of the old Latin Bible were written in a distinctly demotic style, rich in grammatical solecisms and the sort of words that grated on educated ears.[44]

The loss of meaning was negligible—the ancient equivalent of saying "serviette" rather than "napkin." The loss of status was intolerable. If this was the word of God, then God seemed to speak with a distinctly common accent.

And this society had an acute ear for accents. Augustine grew up knowing that grammatical error was more frowned on than moral error and that one might be more despised for saying "'uman being" than one would for being the sort of human being who judged another on his accent.[45] Aitches in Latin, as in Victorian England (and indeed modern Britain), were often a giveaway of class, and the ability to know where to put them was the mark of a gentleman. The upper-class Catullus had sneered mercilessly at a man who, anxious to sound more aristocratic than he was, managed to misplace his aitch.[46] In this aspirational world the language of the Bible was deeply embarrassing.

Augustine, well aware of this, launched into a defense of the Bible's register: what did it matter, he asked hotly, if one used the wrong word or the incorrect grammatical case? Everyone understood what was being said anyway, whatever words or cases it was said with. What did it matter, when you were beseeching God to pardon your sins, "whether the word *ignoscere* (to pardon) should be pronounced with the third syllable long or short?"[47] God might pardon such grammatical sins: Roman aristocrats would not. The simplicity of Christian texts repelled many who might otherwise have considered converting, and shamed many who already had. To convert was, in the words of that telling Augustine phrase, to enter the intellectual world less of a Plato or a Pythagoras than of your concierge. The upper classes simply weren't going to countenance that; and as long as they stood firm against Christianity then many below them would too. This disdainful elite was, Augustine said, the "ramparts of a city that does not believe, a city of denial."[48]

Christianity was caught in an impossible situation. Greek and Roman literature was a sump of the sinful and the satanic and so it could not be embraced. But nor could it entirely be ignored either. It was painfully obvious to educated Christians that the intellectual achievements of the "insane" pagans were vastly superior to their own. For all their declarations on the wickedness of pagan learning, few educated Christians could bring themselves to discard it completely. Augustine, despite disdaining those who cared about correct pronunciation, leaves us in no doubt that he himself knows how to pronounce everything perfectly. In countless passages, both implicitly and explicitly, his knowledge is displayed. He was a Christian, but a Christian with classical dash, and he deployed his classical knowledge in the service of Christianity. The great biblical scholar Jerome, who described the style of sections of the Bible as "rude and repellent,"[49] never freed himself from his love of classical literature and suffered from nightmares in which he was accused of being a "Ciceronian, not a Christian."[50]

And so, in part from self-interest, in part from actual interest, Christianity started to absorb the literature of the "heathens" into itself. Cicero soon sat alongside the psalters after all. Many of those who felt most awkward about their classical learning made best use of it. The Christian writer Tertullian might have disdained classical learning in asking what Athens had to do with Jerusalem—but he did so in high classical style with the metonymy of "Athens" standing in for "philosophy" and that prodding rhetorical question. Cicero himself would have approved. Everywhere, Christian intellectuals struggled to fuse together the classical and the Christian. Bishop Ambrose dressed Cicero's Stoic principles in Christian clothes; while Augustine adapted Roman oratory for Christian ends. The philosophical terms of the Greeks—the "logos" of the Stoics—started to make their way into Christian philosophy.[51]

Not all attempts at assimilation were so successful. One poet rewrote the Gospel of John in the style of a Homeric epic. Another scholar, during the reign of Julian the Apostate—who forbade anyone who didn't believe in the old gods to teach works such as Homer that contained them—redrafted the entirety of biblical history in twenty-four books of Homeric hexameter and recast the Epistles and the gospels into the form of Socratic dialogues. Fanciful intellectual genealogies were invented to defend Christianity's favorite philosophers. Long-dead thinkers who happened to have any resemblances to Christianity in their writings found themselves adopted as unwitting ancestors in the tradition. The whiff of Christianity hung around Plato? Ah, that was because he had visited Egypt and, while there, he had perhaps read a copy of the first five books of the Bible that Moses had, conveniently, left behind. He was, really, one of us. Socrates was a Christian before Christ.[52]

Classical scholars had been reading Homer allegorically for centuries; now better-read Christians started to do the same with the Bible—much to the disgust of non-Christian critics who felt that this was a cowardly intellectual cheat. As Celsus observed with irritation, the "more reasonable Jews and Christians are ashamed of these things and try somehow to allegorise them."[53] Some Christians would remain suspicious of the habit. Another writer raged at those Christians who "avail themselves of the arts of unbelievers" to smooth over scriptural bumps.[54]

Less than a hundred years after the first Christian emperor, the intellectual landscape was changing. In the third century, there had been twenty-eight public libraries in Rome and many private ones.[55] By the end of the fourth they were, as the historian Ammianus Marcellinus observed with sorrow, "like tombs, permanently shut."[56] Was Christianity's rise cause or mere correlation in this? Christian emperors would later struggle to increase literacy to ensure that the state even had enough literate functionaries. Certain fields of inquiry started to become not only off-limits but illegal. As a law of AD 388 announced: "There shall be no opportunity for any man to go out to the public and to argue about religion or to discuss it or to give any counsel." If anyone with "damnable audacity" attempted to then, the law announced with a threat no less ominous for being vague, "he shall be restrained with a due penalty and proper punishment."[57]

Philosophers who wished their works and careers to survive in this Christian world had to curb their teachings. Philosophies that treated the old gods with too much reverence eventually became unacceptable. Any philosophies that dabbled in predicting the future were cracked down on. Any theories that stated that the world was eternal — for that contradicted the idea of Creation — were, as the academic Dirk Rohmann has pointed out, also suppressed. Philosophers who didn't cut their cloth to the new shapes allowed by Christianity felt the consequences. In Athens, some decades after Hypatia's death, a resolutely pagan philosopher found himself exiled for a year.

The stated aims of historians started to change too. When the Greek author Herodotus, the "father of history," sat down to write the first history he declared that his aim was to make "inquiries" — *historias*, in Greek — into the relations between the Greeks and the Persians. He did so with such even-handedness that he was accused of tipping over into treachery, of over-praising the Greeks' enemies and being a *philobarbaros* — a "barbarian lover," a viciously insulting word.[58] Not all historians were so even-handed, but impartiality was an aim that endured. The last of the pagan historians, Ammianus Marcellinus, struggled to achieve it: posterity, he wrote, ought to be an "impartial judge of the past."[59]

Christian historians took a different view. As the influential Christian writer Eusebius — the "father of Church history" — wrote, the job of the historian was not to record everything but instead only those things that would do a Christian good to read. Uncomfortable truths, such as the awkward fact that many Christian clerics, rather than leaping onto the Great Persecution's pyres, had instead scuttled away from them with undignified haste, were not to be dwelt on. Instead, he crisply announced, "I am determined therefore to say nothing even about those . . . I shall include in my overall account only those things by which first we ourselves, then later generations, may benefit."[60] Herodotus had seen history as an inquiry. The father of Church history saw it as a parable.

What was not "of profit" could easily fade from view. The shocking death of Hypatia ought to have merited a good deal of attention in the histories of the period. Instead it is treated lightly and obliquely, if at all. In history, as in life, no one in Alexandria was punished for her murder. There was a cover-up.[61] Some writers were highly critical—even to fervent Christian eyes this was an appalling act. But not all: as one Christian bishop later recorded with admiration, once the satanic woman had been destroyed, then all the people surrounded Cyril in acclamation for he had "destroyed the last remains of idolatry in the city."[62] The affected myopia of Christian historians could be magnificent: as the historian Ramsay MacMullen has put it, "Hostile writings and discarded views were not recopied or passed on, or they were actively suppressed." The Church acted as a great and, at times, fierce filter on all written material, the centuries of its control as "a differentially permeable membrane" that "allowed the writings of Christianity to pass through but not of Christianity's enemies."[63]

CHAPTER ELEVEN

To Cleanse the Error of Demons

Stay clear of all pagan books!

—*Apostolic Constitutions*, 1.6.1

IN ALEXANDRIA, TOWARDS THE END of the fifth century, a Christian chronicler named Zachariah of Mytilene entered the house of a man and found that he was "sweating and depressed." Zachariah instantly knew what was wrong: this man was struggling with demons. Zachariah knew too where these demons were coming from: the man had some documents containing pagan spells in his house. "If you want to get rid of the anxiety," the man was now told, "burn these papers." And so he did. He took his works and, in front of Zachariah, set light to them. The encounter concludes with a homily being read to the man who had now been cleansed of his "demons" —not to mention of part of his library.[1] As the pious Zachariah makes very clear, he did not consider that he had harmed this man by forcing him to burn his papers. He had not bullied him, or acted cruelly towards him. Quite the reverse: he had saved him.

This was not a unique event. During the years and decades following Constantine's conversion, in towns and cities across the empire, zealous officials again and again "saved" the souls of the erring from the dangers posed to them by books. Constantine had set the precedent early and emphatically for all of this when he had ordered the works of the heretic Arius to be burned and had condemned to death all who hid the heretic's books. Works suspected of "heretical" or "magical" practices —whatever those terms meant—went up in smoke in public bonfires.

In Alexandria, Antioch and Rome, bonfires of books blazed and Christian officials looked on in satisfaction. Book-burning was approved of, even recommended, by Church authorities. "Search out the books of the heretics . . . in every place," advised the fifth-century Syrian bishop Rabbula, and "wherever you can, either bring them to us or burn them in the fire."[2] In Egypt at around the same time, a fearsome monk and saint named Shenoute entered the house of a man suspected of being a pagan and removed all his books.[3] The Christian habit of book-burning went on to enjoy a long history. A millennium later, the Italian preacher Savonarola wanted the works of the Latin love poets Catullus, Tibullus and Ovid to be banned while another preacher said that all of these "shameful books" should be let go, "because if you are Christians you are obliged to burn them."[4]

Books had been burned under non-Christian emperors — the controlling Augustus alone had ordered the burning of over two thousand books of prophetic writings, and had exiled the misbehaving poet Ovid — but now it grew in scope and ambition. There is little evidence that Christians intentionally destroyed entire libraries; the damage that Christianity inflicted on books was achieved by subtler — but no less effective — means of censorship, intellectual hostility and pure fear. The existence of a sacred text, it was argued, demanded this. Before, there had been competing philosophical schools, all equally valid, all equally arguable. Now, for the first time, there was right — and there was wrong. Now, there was what the Bible said — and there was everything else. And from now on any belief that was "wrong" could, in the right circumstances, put you in grave danger.

As Dirk Rohmann has highlighted, Augustine said that works that opposed Christian doctrine had no place in Christian society and had scant time for much of Greek philosophy. The Greeks, Augustine said dismissively, "have no ground for boasting of their wisdom."[5] The Church's authors were greater, and more ancient. Besides, he wrote with disapproval, ancient philosophers had disagreed all the time. Rohmann has drawn attention to a passage in which Augustine complains that no senate or power of "the impious city has ever taken care to judge between all [these] dissensions of the philosophers, approving and accepting some, and disapproving and rejecting others."[6] That philosophers should clamorously disagree with each other had been axiomatic to the Greeks: that was precisely how intellectual progress was made, by argumentation and competition. The very idea was anathema to Augustine. John Chrysostom went far further. He described pagan philosophy as a madness, the mother of evils and a disease.[7]

Classical literature was filled with the incorrect and demonic and it came under repeated and vicious attack from the Church fathers. Atheism, science and philosophy were all targeted. The very idea that mankind could explain everything through science was, as Rohmann has shown, disparaged as folly. "Stay clear of all pagan books!" the *Apostolic Constitutions* advised Christians bluntly. "For what do you have to do with such foreign discourses, or laws, or false prophets, which subvert the faith of the unstable?" If you wish to read about history, it continued, "you have the Books of Kings; if philosophy and poetry, you have the Prophets, the Book of Job and the Proverbs, in which you will find greater depth of sagacity than in all of the pagan poets and philosophers because this is the voice of the Lord . . . Do therefore always stay clear of all such strange and diabolical books!"[8]

Neoplatonic works—which were studied by the philosopher Damascius—enraged Christians for centuries. Neoplatonism was a philosophical school that, to modern eyes, is decidedly odd. Yes, Damascius and his fellow Athenian philosophers studied Plato's *Timaeus* and Aristotle's *Physics*—and some of these philosophers were very close to what we would call scientists. One colleague of Damascius, an excellent mathematician, was an early experimentalist, and spent his time trying to understand the properties of different dyes.[9] Yet other Neoplatonists moved on from mathematics and physics into the realm of the metaphysical, blending astronomy with astrology and philosophy with theurgy.

Damascius himself is—to modern eyes—just such an odd combination. On the one hand, he is a highly trained rational scientist, an expert in mathematics who directs the school away from its more ritualistic leanings to hard philosophy. On the other, he is a man who lovingly retells fantastical tales in which human heads the size of a pea roar with the sound of a thousand men.[10] The whiff—and more—of the supernatural in his work was enough to contaminate the whole in the eyes of many Christians. Plato, Edward Gibbon later sniffed, would have blushed to acknowledge these men.[11] Perhaps worst of all, in Christian eyes, they dabbled in prophecy—an art that was particularly loathed by emperors who feared it might be used to prophesy their successors and hence sow dissent. Christianity would later absorb some of this philosophy—but it also turned on it with violence.

An accusation of "magic" was frequently the prelude to a spate of burnings. In Beirut, at the turn of the sixth century, a bishop ordered Christians, in the company of civil servants, to examine the books of those suspected of this. Searches were made, books were seized from suspects and then brought to the center of the city and placed in a pyre. A crowd was ordered to come and watch as the Christians lit this bonfire in front of the church of the Virgin Mary. The demonic deceptions and "barbarous and atheistic arrogance" of these books were condemned as "everybody" watched "the magic books and the demonic signs burn."*[12]

---

* In 2017, in London, a pamphlet by Jehovah's Witnesses advocated similar caution. Under the heading "Intrigued by the Supernatural!" this issue asked whether films and books about witches, wizards and vampires were merely harmless fun. Quoting Deuteronomy ("There should not be found in you . . . anyone who employs divination, anyone practicing magic" because "whoever does these things is detestable to Jehovah"), the article con-

As with the destruction of temples, there was no shame in this. This was God's good work and Christian hagiography hymned its virtue. The life of the sixth-century saint Simeon Stylites the Younger records what happened when an important official named Amantius arrived in Antioch. His appearance was much anticipated: on his way, as proof of his Christian determination, he had searched out, tortured and executed large numbers of local "idolaters."

Once this alarming man was inside the city, St. Simeon then received a vision. "A decision," Simeon reported, "has been made by God against the pagans and the heterodox that this chief shall search out the error concerning idolatry, to collect all their books and to burn these in the fire." After hearing this, Amantius was overcome by zeal and promptly "conducted an inquisition [and] found that the majority of the first citizens of the city and many of its inhabitants had been involved in paganism, Manicheaism, astrology, [Epicureanism], and other gruesome heresies. These he had detained, thrown in prison, and having brought together all of their books, which were a great many, he had these burnt in the middle of the stadium."[13]

What did the books burned on such occasions really contain? Doubtless some did contain "magic"—such practices were popular prior to Christianity and certainly didn't disappear with its arrival. But they were not all. The list given in the life of St. Simeon clearly refers to the destruction of books of Epicureanism, the philosophy that advocated the theory of atomism. "Paganism" appears to have been a charge in itself —and while it could mean outlawed practices it could, at a stretch, refer to almost any antique text that contained the

---

cluded that it was not, before telling the story of Michael. Michael was a teenager who was once an enthusiastic reader of fantasy novels and who then went on to read books about magic and satanic rituals. However, after studying the Bible in depth, Michael realized his error. "I drew up a list of everything that had a link with spiritism and got rid of it all," he says. "I learned an important lesson."

gods. Christians were rarely good chroniclers of what they burned.

Sometimes, clues to the texts remain. In Beirut, just before the bonfire of the books, pious Christians had gone to the house of a man suspected of owning books that were "hateful to God." The Christians told him that they "wanted the salvation and recovery of his soul"; they wanted "liberation." These Christians then entered his home, inspected his books and searched each room. Nothing was found — until the man was betrayed by his slave. Forbidden books were discovered in a secret compartment in a chair. The man whose house it was — clearly well aware of what such "liberation" might involve — "fell to the ground and begged us, in tears, not to hand him over to the law." He was spared the law but forced to burn his books. As our chronicler Zachariah records with pleasure, "when the fire was lit he threw the books of magic into it with his own hands, and said that he thanked God who had granted him with his visit and liberated him from the slavery and error of demons."[14] One of the books removed from the house in Beirut is mentioned: it is very possible it was not magic but a history by a disapproved-of Egyptian historian.

Divination and prophecy were often used as pretexts to attack a city's elite. One of the most infamous assaults on books and thinkers took place in Antioch. Here, at the end of the fourth century, an accusation of treasonous divination led to a full-scale purge that targeted the city's intellectuals. By sheer chance, Ammianus Marcellinus, a non-Christian and one of the finest historians of the era, happened to be in the city, a wonderful piece of luck for later historians and wretched luck for the man himself, who was horrified. As Ammianus describes it, "the racks were set up, and leaden weights, cords, and scourges put in readiness. The air was filled with the appalling yells of savage voices mixed with the clanking of chains, as the torturers in the execution of their grim task shouted: 'Hold, bind, tighten, more yet.'"[15] A noble of "remarkable literary attainments" was one of the first to be arrested and tortured; he was followed by a clutch of philosophers who were variously tortured, burned alive and beheaded.[16] Educated men in the city who had considered themselves fortunate now, Damocles-like, realized the fragility of their fortune. Looking up, it was as if they saw "swords hung over their heads suspended by horse-hairs from the ceiling."[17]

And, once again, there was the burning of books as bonfires of volumes were used as post hoc justification for the slaughter. Ammianus Marcellinus writes with distaste that "innumerable books and whole heaps of documents, which had been routed out from various houses, were piled up and burnt under the eyes of the judges. They were treated as forbidden texts to allay the indignation caused by the executions, though most of them were treatises on various liberal arts and on jurisprudence."[18] Many intellectuals started to pre-empt the persecutors and set light to their own books. The destruction was extensive and "throughout the eastern provinces whole libraries were burnt by their owners for fear of a similar fate; such was the terror which seized all hearts."[19] Ammianus wasn't the only intellectual to be scared in these decades. The orator Libanius burned a huge number of his own works. The Alexandrian poet Palladas, the writer who had described himself and other "pagans" as being reduced to ashes, burned what he called his "worrisome book-scrolls."[20]

Even Christians in Antioch lived in fear that winter. One day, at the height of the terror, a young man named John happened to be walking through the city near the river with a friend. Suddenly, his friend noticed something floating in the water. "He thought it was a piece of cloth," John remembered, "but on coming closer he saw it was a book and went down to fish it out . . . He opened it and saw magic signs. At the same time a soldier came by. My friend put the book in his cloak and moved away, petrified with fear. For who would believe that we had found that book in the river and pulled it out, when everybody was being arrested, even the least suspicious? We did not dare throw it away for fear of being seen, and were equally afraid to tear it up." This John was John Chrysostom, a man who would go on to become one of the most important of all figures in the early Church, and a saint. Yet, at that moment, merely being near such a book petrified him.[21] He got away — "God," he concluded, had delivered him. Many others were not so lucky.

Just as houses were combed for unacceptable books, so during this period literature was combed for unacceptable phrases. One aggressively disapproving Christian asked St. Jerome why he chose to constantly "quote examples from secular literature and thus defile the whiteness of the church with the foulness of heathenism?" Jerome, ever the scholar, replied that he had good literary precedent for doing so: St. Paul had done the same. Besides, he added, he was not being conquered by the foulness of the heathens: on the contrary, he was conquering them. Like David, he was wrenching the sword from the enemy's hand and using it to attack them.

Jerome concluded this letter with one of the most unappealing metaphors in the entire debate. Had not the Lord commanded in Deuteronomy that "when a captive woman had had her head shaved, her eyebrows and all her hair cut off, and her nails pared, she might then be taken to wife?" Well then, said Jerome, "Is it surprising that I too, admiring the fairness of her form and the grace of her eloquence, desire to make that secular wisdom which is my captive and my handmaid, a matron of the true Israel? Or that shaving off and cutting away all in her that is dead whether this be idolatry, pleasure, error, or lust, I take her to myself clean and pure and beget by her servants for the Lord of Sabaoth?"[22] A Christian might take the defeated prisoner, enjoy them, rape them — so long as they mutilated them first. Their ornaments were to be pared away, ostensibly to allow the prisoner to "mourn" for what they had lost, but it was a clear humiliation, too.

The Great Library of Alexandria might have attempted to

collect books on every topic, but Christianity was going to be considerably more selective. It had little interest in copying out the writings of philosophers who contradicted them, in poets who described "perverted" acts or in rambunctious satires on the gods.

Far from wishing to protect classical texts, many within the Church were violently hostile to their "foulness" and actively wished them destroyed.[23] Some "obscene" erotic works were simply not copied out. One surviving Byzantine manuscript of Ovid has been scarred by a series of ridiculous redactions — even the word "girl" seems to have been considered too racy to remain.[24] In the seventeenth and eighteenth centuries, Jesuits were still censoring and bowdlerizing their editions of the classics.[25] Individual abbots, far from Umberto Eco's avenging intellectual ideal, sometimes censored their own libraries. At some point in the fifteenth century, a note was left in a mutilated manuscript in Vienna. "At this point in the book," it records, "there were thirteen leaves containing works by the apostate Julian; the abbot of the monastery . . . read them and realised that they were dangerous, so he threw them into the sea."[26]

Much classical literature was preserved by Christians. Far more was not. To survive, manuscripts needed to be cared for, recopied. Classical ones were not. Medieval monks, at a time when parchment was expensive and classical learning held cheap, simply took pumice stones and scrubbed the last copies of classical works from the page. Rohmann has pointed out that there is even evidence to suggest that in some cases "whole groups of classical works were deliberately selected to be deleted and overwritten in around AD 700, often with texts authored by [the fathers of the Church or by] legal texts that criticised or banned pagan literature."[27] Pliny, Plautus, Cicero, Seneca, Virgil, Ovid, Lucan, Livy and many, many more: all were scrubbed away by the hands of believers.[28]

The evidence from surviving manuscripts is clear: at some

point, a hundred or so years after Christianity comes to power,
the transcription of the classical texts collapses. From AD 550 to
750 the numbers copied plummeted. This is not, to be clear, an
absolute collapse in copying: monasteries are still producing
reams and reams of religious books. Bible after Bible, copy after copy of Augustine is made. And these works are vast. This
was not about an absolute shortage of parchment; it was about
a lack of interest verging on outright disgust for the ideas of a
now-despised canon. The texts that suffer in this period are the
texts of the wicked and sinful pagans. From the entirety of the
sixth century only "scraps" of two manuscripts by the satirical
Roman poet Juvenal survive and mere "remnants" of two others, one by the Elder and one by the Younger Pliny. From the
next century there survives nothing save a single fragment of
the poet Lucan.[29] From the start of the next century: nothing
at all.

Far from mourning the loss, Christians delighted in it. As
John Chrysostom crowed, the writings "of the Greeks have
all perished and are obliterated."[30] He warmed to the theme
in another sermon: "Where is Plato? Nowhere! Where Paul?
In the mouths of all!"[31] The fifth-century writer Theodoret of
Cyrrhus observed the decline of Greek literature with similar
enthusiasm. "Those elaborately decorated fables have been utterly banned," he gloated. "Who is today's head of the Stoic
heresy? Who is safeguarding the teachings of the Peripatet-
ics?"[32] No one, evidently, for Theodoret concludes this homily
with the observation that "the whole earth under the sun has
been filled with sermons." Augustine contentedly observed the
rapid decline of the atomist philosophy in the first century of
Christian rule. By his time, he recorded, Epicurean and Stoic
philosophy had been "suppressed" — the word is his. The opin-
ions of such philosophers "have been so completely eradicated
and suppressed . . . that if any school of error now emerged
against the truth, that is, against the Church of Christ, it would

not dare to step forth for battle if it were not covered under the Christian name."[33]

A slow but devastating edit of classical literature was taking place. It is true that the appalling losses of knowledge that followed were not usually the result of dramatic, discrete actions—the burning of this library, the fury of that particular abbot—though these played their part. Instead, what ensured the near-total destruction of all Latin and Greek literature was a combination of ignorance, fear and idiocy. These weapons have less narrative heft, perhaps, but when left unchecked they can achieve a great deal.

Much was preserved. Much, much more was destroyed. It has been estimated that less than ten percent of all classical literature has survived into the modern era.[34] For Latin, the figure is even worse: it is estimated that only one hundredth of all Latin literature remains.[35] If this was "preservation"—as it is often claimed to be—then it was astonishingly incompetent. If it was censorship, it was brilliantly effective.

The ebullient, argumentative classical world was, quite literally, being erased.

CHAPTER TWELVE

———

Carpe Diem

Let the girl with a pretty face lie supine, let the lady
Who boasts a good back be viewed
From behind . . . The petite should ride horse.

> —the Roman poet Ovid advises on
> positions for lovemaking, *Ars Amatoria*, 3

"*Imperium sine fine.*" Empire without end.[1] That, so the poet had said, had been Rome's aim as it had sought to push itself forwards, outwards, onwards into new countries, new continents and new worlds. But the Christianity that had taken it over was, according to its preachers, no less ambitious. As the world's first century of Christian rule drew to a close and the fifth century opened, the effects of this conquest were everywhere to be seen. In Italy, Gaul, Greece, Spain, Syria and Egypt, temples that had stood for centuries were falling, shutting, crumbling. Brambles began to grow across disused ruins, as the mutilated faces of gods looked on silently.

An entire way of life was dying. Writers in the ancient world who had held out against the Christian religion struggled to put their feelings into words. In a bleak epigram Palladas asked, "Is it not true that we are dead and only seem to live, we Greeks . . . Or are we alive and is life dead?"[2] Their old society was being swept away. The banner of the cross, in Gibbon's resonant phrase, was being erected on the ruins of the Capitol in Rome.[3]

But, according to some of the most famous preachers of the time, even this was not enough to satisfy the Christian God. Christians may have taken control of the empire's landmarks and temples but their God, they told their congregations, wanted more. He was not satisfied by mere buildings. Nor was He content with the appearance of piety only. The old Roman gods might have been fooled by a mere show of obedience to their rites—just *touch* the incense, as Roman governors had pleaded with Christians—but this god would not be so easily duped. He didn't want ritual observance or temples or stones; He wanted souls. He wanted—He demanded—the hearts and minds of every single person within the empire.

And, these clerics threatened, He would know if He didn't get them. As preachers in the fourth century started to warn their congregations, God's all-seeing gaze followed you everywhere. He didn't only see you in church; you were also watched by Him as you went out through the church doors; as you went out into the streets and as you walked round the marketplace or sat in the hippodrome or the theater. His gaze also followed you into your home and even into your bedroom—and you should be in no doubt that He watched what you did there, too. That was not the least of it. This new god saw into your very soul. "Man looketh on the face, but God on the heart," thundered Cyprian, the Bishop of Carthage. "Nothing that is done is hidden from God."[4] There was, congregations across the empire were warned, no escape: "Nothing, whether actually done or only intended, can escape the knowledge of God"—or His "everlasting punishment of fire."[5]

Many Roman and Greek intellectuals had shown profound distaste for such an involved deity. The idea that a divine being was watching every move of every human being was, to these observers, not a sign of great love but a "monstrous" absurdity. The Christian God in their writings was frequently described as a prurient busybody, a peculiar "nuisance" who was "restless, shamelessly curious, being present at man's every act."[6] Why was He so interested in the every doing of mere mortals? Even before Christianity, sophisticated Roman thinkers had poured scorn on such an idea. As Pliny the Elder had put it: "that [a] supreme being, whate'er it be, pays heed to man's affairs is a ridiculous notion. Can we believe that it would not be defied by so gloomy and so multifarious a duty?"[7] Didn't a god have better things to do?

No, declared the Christian clerics. He did not. His attention was a sign of His great love for man. As too was His punishment. For make no mistake, God was not merely a disinterested observer of men's souls; He would judge them — and He would punish them. Horribly. A very particular kind of fear starts to appear. As Peter Brown has pointed out, this is the perpetual anxiety of people who believed that not only their every deed, nor even their every word, but their every thought was now being watched. One Christian had a vision in which he could, quite literally, see stains upon his heart. They were there, he realized, because he had not made up "at once" a quarrel that he had had with another Christian.[8]

Such were the words and the threats of the bishops and the Christian elite. But did the people listen to these diatribes? Did most of them even hear them? The words of preachers such as John Chrysostom and Augustine may have resounded in the ears of their listeners and in the literature of the age, but the vast majority of the empire — perhaps eighty to ninety percent of men, and a higher percentage of women — was illiterate.[9] Did such people also absorb the message that they were now Fallen and had to be redeemed? In short, in the pithy words of the academic E. A. Judge: "what difference [did it make] to Rome to have been converted?"[10]

The short answer is: we cannot know for certain. Late antiquity offers a frustratingly thin web of texts with which to answer this question. Of the tiny percentage of the empire who were literate, far fewer would have been confident writers. The vast majority of the empire lived and died leaving almost no traces for future historians to analyze.

Faced with such uncertainty, scholars have had the freedom to offer widely differing responses — and have done so. For centuries, their obedient answer was to say that the spread of Christianity had made all the difference in the world — or rather, in heaven. Before Christianity, Europe was damned, its religions and much of its behavior primitive and damnable. After Christianity, it was saved. In the modern era, scholars—less likely to be quite so obedient to ecclesiastical authority—have taken a more robust, even iconoclastic approach. What difference did Christianity make? No difference at all, came the provoking reply from the twentieth-century scholar A.H.M. Jones. None. He instead argued that "Christian belief, if anything, led to a lowering of moral standards in the community."[11]

The truth, as always, lies somewhere between these extremes. For without a doubt, something, certainly, did change.

In the mid-eighteenth century, some workmen happened to be digging in an Italian hillside known tantalizingly as "la Cività"—the city. These Neapolitan laborers started to clear the pumice and ash that Pliny the Younger had watched falling seventeen centuries before. The effect was a cultural cataclysm. Figures of unimaginable sexual frankness started to be unearthed. Even to modern eyes, Pompeii offers a bracing spectacle. Whether it is the image of Priapus, in which the god is weighing his enormous phallus in some scales; or the frescoes of couples having sex; or the infamous statue of the god Pan, his lip jutting forward as he enters a goat, the erotic is everywhere.

The phallus is a staple of home decoration: it appears on walls, on statues and in frescoes, and is carved into the very paving stones of the city. One bar was lit by a pretty bronze lamp in the form of a small figure with a vast penis, bells hanging down from its enormous shaft. Some images were astonishingly vivid. On the walls of a brothel there was a fresco that now survives only in a nineteenth-century reproduction. It depicts a man and a woman; he stands behind her and they are drinking what must be wine from what looks like two pint glasses. The man is holding his glass up, as if for inspection. They might, to judge from their serene expressions, be discussing the provenance of their drinks. However their minds are evidently on other things: the man is pushing his large erection into her.

Pompeii was a revelation. In some ways, it shouldn't have been. For those willing and able to read it, Latin literature had contained numerous hints that all in the pre-Christian world was not as chaste as St. Basil might have liked. The infamous "Carmen 16" of Catullus was an obvious one. Few could read the line "I will bugger you and I will fuck your mouths" and think that the author was being chastely pure—but then few could read it.[12] By the time Pompeii was rediscovered, Latin had become an increasingly rare accomplishment.

By contrast, anyone with eyes could see the images that were being pulled from the Pompeian soil. No one could begin to pretend that the god Pan was doing anything other than entering the goat; or that the people in those frescoes were doing anything other than having enthusiastic sex. Even more disquieting, these paintings couldn't be dismissed as the reprehensible habits of the poor, the immoral or the uneducated, as these images were not just found in brothels; they were found everywhere, even—especially—in some of the most opulent villas in the town. The Pompeians had not simply put up images of naked people; they had done so openly and without shame. No one in these images was struggling to hide their modesty with their hands or with fig leaves.

For centuries, Christian Europe had, as effective as any Vesuvius, been carefully obscuring the sexuality of the classical world, scraping nipples from statues, suppressing lewd frescoes and obscene poems. Now, a world untouched by the hand of Christianity was coming to light. It is just conceivable that there had been Christians in Pompeii when Vesuvius had erupted in AD 79, but if there were they would not have been in a position of power, and would not have been able to do anything to its art. No zealous Christians had attacked the Pompeian frescoes with hammers; no squads of the godly had chiseled away at the herms that stood on almost every street corner. The people in these images in Pompeii were not just naked; they were unashamedly naked. This was a world that had, quite literally, seen no Fall.

The site's excavators, who knew not only the Fall but also the Catholic Church, were appalled. Some excavators simply reburied works that were considered too lewd. Others buried these objects in silence, and early guidebooks glided over the racier objects. There was no illustration of the penis lamp in the first published collection of the finds. The first English guide by Sir William Gell, published in 1824, neglected to mention a single object that might raise the polite eyebrows of his readers. As the scholar Walter Kendrick put it, "Gell managed to get through two thick, heavily illustrated volumes without once letting on that anything untoward was to be found."[13]

Nevertheless, word eventually got out and the world was shocked—or at any rate professed itself to be—and remained so for decades. One nineteenth-century author described the frescoes as being the sort of thing that would "be seized in any modern country by the police."[14] Those Pompeian guidebooks that did mention sexual objects strenuously draped them in disapproval. One visitor was pained by their "moral degradation."[15] One privately printed guide to some of the ruder objects was typically prim. "The customs to which the women of antiquity devoted themselves were dissolute and scandalous," wrote its author. "The nudities of that epoch, and the impure writings of its authors, are unchallengeable witnesses to the libertinism which then prevailed in all classes. It was a time when men did not blush to make known to the world that they had obtained the favours of a fair youth, when women honoured themselves with the name of [lesbians]." The force of its disapproval was somewhat undermined by its lip-smacking title (*The Royal Museum at Naples, Being Some Account of the Erotic Paintings, Bronzes and Statues Contained in that Famous "Cabinet Secret"*) and the fact that its front page advertised that it came with "Sixty Full Page Illustrations."[16]

Lewder objects were smothered—the goat was considered "not lawful to show" and put in a cellar.[17] Such objects were eventually gathered together in a single collection and the "Secret Cabinet," as the museum became known, was created in 1819. Access to it was limited and monitored. The precise population of this collection varied over time; fascination with it remained constant.[18] As one 1871 guide recalled, entrance was "forbidden to women and children [and] only granted to men of mature age by means of special permission from the minister of the king's household."[19] One can only begin to imagine the embarrassment of making this request. The famous art historian Johann Winckelmann visited Naples at a time when a special license was needed that was "signed by his majesty" to see such objects. He decided not to bother: "I thought it did not become me to be the first to apply."[20] Women were not allowed access to the Secret Cabinet until the 1980s.[21]

It wasn't just in Pompeii. In museums all over Europe, classical statues that had been harvested during so many Grand Tours were shut away. Lacking the confidence of their early Christian forebears, later museum curators did with editing and discreet storage what earlier centuries had done with chisels. The result was the same: sexually explicit objects vanished, once again, from view. Other statues found their sexual organs disappearing under a new lush canopy of fig leaves that were fashioned by chaste curators then applied to the shamefully naked classical statues. The vivid images on Greek pots were tamped down. An exuberant satyr who had balanced a cup on his huge erection found his phallus painted out by an appalled curator, leaving the cup balancing in mid-air. Even classicizing statues were covered up. In 1857, Queen Victoria was given a cast of Michelangelo's *David* as a present. It is said that when the queen saw the massive statue for the first time in the Victoria and Albert Museum, she was so shocked by David's nakedness that a fig leaf was commissioned. A half-meter-high plaster cast of the leaf was thereafter kept at the ready for royal visits, whereupon it would be hung on the offending area with two hooks, saving the blushes of her Britannic majesty.

Eve's shame was being applied to the classical world. The eruption of Vesuvius was seen by pious Victorians as the just deserts of a wanton people. As that 1871 guide to the erotic paintings and statues of Pompeii piously concluded, "Eternal glory to the religion which, overturning these impure idols into the mire, and unrolling the code of chastity before our eyes, has made our sensations purer and our pleasures keener."[22] Then, perhaps less conscious of the code of chastity than it might have been, it printed one of those "Full Page Illustrations" of the satyr and the goat.

To say that the Roman world was pre-Fall is not to say that it had been without shame. It had not. There existed intricate and keenly felt distinctions between what was and what was not acceptable sexual practice. As the academic Paul Veyne has put it, "Actually, the pagans were paralysed by prohibitions."[23] Veyne is exaggerating: there were rules, but this was not paralysis. Sex was accepted, and expected to be enjoyable. That was a great difference. There were limits—and as always the main one was one of privilege. What was acceptable for a rich man was unacceptable for a poor one; what was acceptable for men was unacceptable for women; slaves had almost no rights at all and were de facto prostitutes peopling the houses of the free. Within the Roman Empire the atmosphere in the east was, as a general rule, more conservative than in the west.

Even wealthy men had to comply with certain rules: homosexuality was considered unremarkable, so long as one was not in the passive, "effeminate" role of being penetrated. An accusation that a man might have been could be enough to end a political career. As always there were exceptions: Julius Caesar was mockingly called "the Queen of Bithynia" for his alleged relationship with King Nicomedes. He survived, though it was, the biographer Suetonius writes, "always a dark stain on his reputation, and frequently quoted by his enemies."[24] Making love with the lights on was another, rather teenage-sounding, prohibition. To do so was considered dissolute. Roman poets, as poets tend to, liked to play with these rules: in one memorable poem, Ovid describes making love in the afternoon as light filtered into the bedroom through a half-open shutter—more than enough light for him to be able to see and describe every part of his lover's body in one of the most erotic poems he ever wrote.[25]

Above all, it was said that a man—and these texts were written by and largely for men—should govern his sexual urges rather than being governed by them. To fall abjectly in love with a woman was unacceptable. Poets who wrote that they were the "slave" of their woman set traditionalist teeth on edge. One should keep within certain limits: Ovid would be exiled for "carmen et error"—for a sexually rude poem and for personally overstepping the bounds of Augustus's crackdown on immorality.[26] In sex, as in everything else, the words carved into the temple at Delphi were to be followed: nothing in excess. Too much sex and you were boorish; but equally, to have too little—or rather, to go on about how little you had—was to be boring. "Do not," advised one writer, "make yourself offensive or censorious to those who so indulge, and do not make frequent mentions of the fact that you yourself do not indulge."[27]

Sex then ought to be contained—but it was not denied. In the writings of the Roman elite, like any other appetite it was, as Peter Brown has observed, something to be admitted and managed rather than something to be ashamed of. The feast of the Liberalia was on March 17, a now sadly forgotten festival at which Roman citizens celebrated a boy's first ejaculation. In Roman medical manuals, ejaculation had been readily and openly discussed by classical doctors who advised it for health and getting rid of the seed that might otherwise cause headaches. It was thought that if athletes could abstain from sex they would be stronger. Orgasms and sex were even recommended for women's health.[28]

Sex, sexual desire and the consequences of sex were frankly discussed. Poets chastised their lovers when they had abortions, less for the abortion than for endangering their own health. Ovid professed himself furious with his lover Corinna for rashly attempting one—but less because she had committed this act than because she had taken "that risk, and she never told me!"[29] Others followed more laborious methods of avoiding pregnancy. When Julia, the famously racy and beautiful daughter of the emperor Augustus, was asked how, given her many lovers, her children all resembled her husband, she replied that she would "take on a passenger only when the ship's hold is full."[30]

Why not have sex? Life was short and one didn't know what was coming next. Live now, proclaimed countless mosaics, paintings and poems in the old Roman world. For who knows what tomorrow might bring? In a recently discovered mosaic in Antioch, a skeleton reclines, a cup in his hand, and an amphora of wine nearby. Over his head, in clear Greek lettering, the mosaic gave an instruction to those diners above: "Be cheerful," it reads. "Enjoy your life."[31] The injunction to enjoy yourself is written in stone. One of the most famous of all classical poems had put this ideal into rather more elegant lines. "*Quam minimum credula postero*"—trust as little as possible in tomorrow—advised the poet Horace, and instead "*carpe diem.*" Seize the day.[32]

One of the most famous of all Roman poems had been a version of the ancient self-help book by the poet Ovid on the art of seduction. "Should anyone here in Rome lack finesse at love-making," Ovid announced in its opening lines, "let him / Try me—read my book, and results are guaranteed!"[33] Witty, erudite and egotistical, Ovid became one of the most famous poets in Rome which, one suspects, was no less than he felt

he deserved. "Wherever Rome's power extends over the conquered world," he gloated in another poem, "I shall have mention on men's lips, and . . . through all the ages shall I live in
fame."[34] Somewhat infuriatingly, he has so far been proved correct, and part of what assured him of this fame was the *Art of
Love*—a poem that, after it had advised on almost everything
else, also found time to advise on particular sexual positions.
"If you're built like a fashion model, with willowy figure, /
Then kneel on the bed, your neck / A little arched . . ."[35] And
so on.

But then something, slowly, had changed. A little over two
centuries after Pompeii experienced its cataclysm, the Roman
elite experienced a convulsion of their own when Constantine
converted. The effects reverberated throughout the fourth
century as temples were torn down, statues smashed and laws
passed outlawing the old "pagan" ways. The number of Christian converts—willing or otherwise—increased rapidly during
this period. And as they did so, literature started to change, too.
The old bawdy ways started to fade from the pages of poetry.
The sermon and the homily—stern, judgmental and often aggressive—bloomed in their stead. This literature alternately
threatened and instructed readers in minute detail on how to
behave in almost every aspect of life. Christianity was not the
sole cause of this—an increasingly moralizing tone had been
noticeable in literature already. Indeed, the rise in Christianity
might even have in part been a symptom of such moralizing.
But Christianity nevertheless embraced, amplified and promul-
gated this hectoring to a far greater extent than ever before.

Christian authors of this period were not charmed by the
sexual frankness that had been expressed by Roman authors
and paintings. They were repelled by it. St. Paul had set the
tone early. He had felt that the "pagans" were so far gone as to
be all but beyond redemption. Due in part to their idol worship,
God had "abandoned them to do whatever shameful things
their hearts desired. As a result, they did vile and degrading

things with each other's bodies."[36] Not only did they have sex, worse still they had homosexual sex. "Even the women turned against the natural way to have sex and instead indulged in sex with each other. And the men, instead of having normal sexual relations with women, burned with lust for each other. Men did shameful things with other men."[37] Still, Paul reassured his readers, these sinners would have their comeuppance. "Or do you not know that wrongdoers will not inherit the kingdom of God? Do not be deceived: neither the sexually immoral nor idolaters nor adulterers nor men who have sex with men."[38] Later centuries would follow suit. In the sixth century, during the reign of the repressive emperor Justinian, laws started to outlaw homosexuality with a viciousness never seen before.

For St. Paul and other Christian preachers, the body and its urges were not to be celebrated but smothered. In tortuous and embarrassed circumlocutions, Paul raged at "this body of death."[39] The rewards of a virgin in heaven were said to be sixty times greater. Christian writers in this period recorded the stirrings of their sexuality with great distaste—perhaps none more influentially than Augustine. Sex was, he felt, permissible if children resulted from the union but even then the action itself was lustful, evil and "bestial," while erections were "unseemly." The West would reap a bitter harvest of sexual shame from the disgusted writings of these two men. In the earliest days of the religion, some Christians went further, arguing that there was no need for sex anymore at all. A new form of creation, in the form of a great conflagration and rebirth of the godly, was imminent. What need for awkward, messy, inexact human reproduction? Eternal life rendered reproduction redundant.

If the most famous non-Christian manual had been Ovid's, then one of the most famous manuals by a Christian writer was a third-century tract by the theologian Clement of Alexandria. It is called the *Paedagogus*—the instructor—and its stated aim was to "compendiously describe what the man who is called a Christian ought to be during the whole of his life."[40] Clement then added some frank reminders of what lay in wait for those who strayed from his precepts and God's, namely the teeth of wild beasts and the rage of serpents. As Clement wrote, the Lord himself had said that "I will sharpen my sword ... and I will render justice to mine enemies, and requite those who hate me. I will make mine arrows drunk with blood, and my sword shall devour flesh from the blood of the wounded." This was not a mark of God's cruelty but of love. "Censure," the author reassured his reader, "is a mark of good-will, not of ill-will."[41]

Clement, in precise and authoritative paragraphs, peppered with frequent quotations and not infrequent threats from the scriptures, advised the faithful on every aspect of their day, from what they were allowed to eat and drink to what they could wear and put on their feet; from how they could style their hair to even what they were allowed to do in bed. In the three volumes of his guide he censured almost every human activity. "Unblushing pleasure," he wrote, "must be cut out by the roots."[42] He began with eating, opening with the reminder that we are all ultimately dust, before turning his attention on particular dishes. In starchy and unforgiving sentences, unseasoned by even a dash of humor, the extravagant dinner was deplored. As too was almost everything eaten at it. Overuse of the pestle and mortar was frowned upon. Condiments were considered unacceptable, as too were white bread ("emasculated") and sweetmeats, honey cakes, sugar plums, dried figs ... One should not, Clement warned, be like the gourmands who source their lampreys from Sicily, their turbots in Attica, their thrushes in Daphnis ...[43] The list went on.

Though, like those post–Second World War novels, the Bonds and *Bridesheads*, that were written in a period of austerity yet salivate over detailed descriptions of food, Clement's abstemious pen seemed to linger a little too long over these forbidden fruits.* Clement himself would have rejected the thought: people who enjoyed fine dining were, he wrote, nothing less than "beasts in human shape after the image of their father, the voracious beast."[44] Satan lurked among the sweetmeats. Then there was the wine—which in Clement's eyes was even more pernicious than food. This warming liquid, he wrote, would heat up the overheated bodies of the young adding "fire to fire. For hence wild impulses and burning lusts and fiery habits are kindled . . . and shameless pulsations follow abundance." Clement fulminated furiously against those "miserable wretches" whose life was nothing but "revel, debauchery, baths, excess . . . idleness, drink" and, intriguingly, "urinals."[45]

In the writings of preacher after Christian preacher, it was made clear that almost everything about a dinner was suspect. If one went out to dinner one might find oneself smitten with pernicious envy for another man's house and come home more discontented than when setting out. John Chrysostom advised avoiding them altogether in favor of funerals. "Is it better," he thundered at his congregation, "to go where there is weeping, lamentation, and groans, and anguish, and so much sadness, than where there is the dance, the cymbals, and laughter, and luxury, and full eating and drinking?"[46] One doesn't need to be too familiar with Chrysostom's oeuvre to know that the expected answer to this rhetorical question was a hearty "Yea, verily!" In a house of happiness one might envy a neighbor's well-appointed atrium, or his charming dining room. In a house of mourning one would, said Chrysostom, be more

---

* The Catholic Waugh would later disparage *Brideshead Revisited* (1945), declaring that it was written in "a bleak period of present privation and threatening disaster—the period of soya beans and Basic English—and in consequence the book is infused with a kind of gluttony, for food and wine, for the splendours of the recent past, and for rhetorical and ornamental language which now, with a full stomach I find distasteful." Clement would have approved.

likely to declare: "We are nothing, and our wickedness is inexpressible!"[47]

The breadth of Clement's self-help manual wasn't entirely new. Centuries before God's enforcers had started to prod at every corner of life, Ovid had bossily advised his gentle reader in similar detail to Clement how one should behave at dinner, though his aims were rather different. As he explained:

> Banquets, too, give you an entrée, offer
> More to the palate than wine:
> There flushed Love has often clasped
>   the horns of reclining
> Bacchus in a seductive embrace.[48]

Ovid, like Clement, spent some time on the topic of wine which, he agreed, should be drunk in moderation. Though once again, for different reasons: get too drunk and, Ovid warned, you'd lose your man: "The girl / Who's passed out drunk is the most disgusting object."[49]

He had also issued lengthy instructions on appearance and personal grooming. He advised men, for example, to take care of their appearance; to be fragrant; to ensure that their nails were clean and pared; and to monitor their nose hair:

> Don't let those long hairs sprout
> In your nostrils, make sure your breath
>   is never offensive,
> Avoid the rank male stench
> That wrinkles noses.[50]

One should not, he added, go much further than this: "Don't torture your hair, though, with curling-irons," he warned men. "Don't pumice / Your legs into smoothness." To do this was, he said, the behavior of "wanton women—or any half-man who wants to attract men."[51]

Women had received stringent instruction from Ovid too. Their hair should not be neglected; those with a plump face should pile their hair up; those with a long face should go for a plain central parting. Though he also recommended a careful dishevelment: "the Neglected Look suits many girls: quite often / You'd think it untouched since yesterday, though in fact it's fresh-combed."[52]

White clothes, he wrote, suited dark-skinned women; the pale looked becoming in gray; everyone should avoid purple and flounces. Personal hygiene should be attended to in women too: teeth should be clean and unstained; "rank goatish armpits" were, fairly enough, warned against.[53] Make-up, in moderation, was advised: "with powder, add rouge to a bloodless face, / Skilfully block in the crude outline of an eyebrow," and so on. The effect should be natural, since "the best / Make-up remains unobtrusive." On a similar note, Ovid was uncharacteristically strict on one point: you should not let your partner see you applying cosmetics:

> *Leave us to imagine*
> *You're asleep while you're at your toilet: only emerge*
> *When the public picture's complete.*
>   *I don't want to know how*
> *That complexion's built up.*

And, above all, Ovid advised: never let your partner see you cleaning your teeth: "The result may be attractive, but the process is sickening."[54]

Christian tracts took a similar stance to Ovid on many topics —Clement also disliked done-up women and over-groomed men—but the tone here was very different. Everything was laid down, from how to treat the hairs on the top of the head (which should not be dyed, plucked, or falsely curled—all "wicked arts") to the soles of the feet (which should be shod in plain sandals). Makeup was abhorred as a sign of a diseased soul.[55] Golden, silver and jeweled cups were inveighed against, as too were purple bedsheets—"proofs of tasteless luxury, cunning devices of envy and effeminacy."[56] The wearing of gold jewelry was deplored as a terrible habit through which women would "disfigure God's gifts, emulating the art of the evil one." So too was the wearing of diaphanous fabrics ("proof of a weak mind").[57] The odium heaped on women was, however, mild when compared to the disapproval reserved for men who depilated. Had not the Lord said that "the very hairs of your head are all numbered"? Well, then, said Clement, with nimble scriptural footwork, that settled it. "There must be therefore no plucking out, contrary to God's appointment, which has counted them in according to His will."[58]

Ovid had offered his opinion in the spirit of a connoisseur advising a novice. In Ovid's writings, if you get your dress wrong or drink too much at dinner, you will suffer the consequences in this life: you won't get your man, or people will think you uncouth. In the writings of the new Christian texts, it was not the taste of any man—even an expert—that mattered. It was the taste of God. "Man is the measure of all things," Protagoras had said. No longer. Now God was, and He was not only weighing and measuring man, He would, if he was found wanting, punish him.

Christian preachers expressed none of Horace's uncertainty about what tomorrow might bring. On the contrary, they knew precisely what was coming: death and judgment. Followed by heaven for the fortunate few—and hell for everyone else. One should therefore be perpetually mindful of the dangers threatened by the next life—and constantly watchful of one's behavior in this one. Eating, drinking and making love were, they warned, the last things that one must do. Merrymaking in this life would not win eternal bliss in the next. "You are too greedy of enjoyment, my brother," warned the Christian scholar Jerome, "if you wish to rejoice with the world here, and to reign with Christ hereafter."[59]

CHAPTER THIRTEEN

They That Forsake the Way of God

Then will the tragic actors be worth hearing, more vocal in their own catastrophe; then the comic actors will be worth watching, much lither of limb in the fire; then the charioteer will be worth seeing, red all over on his fiery wheel; then the athletes will be worth observing, not in their gymnasiums, but thrown about by fire.

—Tertullian reflects on the pleasures of Judgment Day,
De Spectaculis, 30.5

THE FLAMES OF DAMNATION began to lick at Roman daily life. In literature of a newly sadistic strain, Christian writers outlined in graphic detail what awaited those who did not comply with the edicts of this all-seeing God.[1] The punishments for sinners were, according to Christian texts, atrocious. Now regarded as apocryphal, but for a time widely read in Rome, the *Apocalypse of Peter* reveled in verse after stomach-churning verse on what happened in hell. In it, the reader is taken on an infernal safari in which the retributions for various misdeeds are pointed out with relish. This hell is a terrible place; its punishments are grimly apposite. Blasphemers, for example, are found hanging suspended by their tongues, or "gnawing their lips."[2] Adulterers are hung by their "feet" — a punishment that doesn't sound too bad until you realize that in these texts "feet" was a euphemism for "testicles."[3] Those who trusted in their riches are turned on a spit over a fire.[4] Even children don't escape. At the edge of a lake filled with the "discharge and the stench" of those who were tortured are babies that are "born before time" — a blameless crime one might have thought, but not so here. These babies will cry for eternity, alone.[5]

The censorious gaze of God's enforcers now went far beyond personal appearance. Theater was abhorred as a repository of blasphemous filth. The Roman Empire had never been wholly sure of the theater itself — plays were seen as sufficiently immoral that it was only in the first century BC that a stone theater had been built in the capital, allowing this dubious art form a permanent home.

But equally it had been acceptable for intellectuals to praise drama with sincere admiration—and for ordinary citizens to enjoy it. The orator Libanius celebrated, with unashamed delight, the fact that his hometown of Antioch resounded with "contests of pipes, lyre, and voice and the manifold delights of the stage."[6] The beauty of the dancers, he argued, in a work that defended them against long-standing slurs, even improved the soul: a man would be "more gentle both to his wife and his slaves when he takes his dinner after such a sight."[7] Pliny the Younger had disliked actors, particularly those who popped up and started to bore him with recitations after dinner parties; nevertheless, he counseled moderation when someone else complained about them. "Let us then be tolerant of other people's pleasures so as to win indulgence for our own." Please, he wrote, "don't be for ever frowning."[8]

Zealous and controlling Christian preachers begged to differ. Frowning was one of the few things that the new rhetoric did allow in excess. The theater, they hectored their congregations, was filth. Sinful, demonic filth. What the Greeks had considered civilized—even civilizing—the Christian preachers reviled as "depravity," a "deformity," a "disease" and a "wanton madness."[9]

Certainly there was much to trouble the chaste on the Roman stage. Farces were rich in sexual innuendo; while during the Roman festival of the goddess Flora real courtesans came on stage and performed in the nude—much to the delight of the audience.[10] In the fourth century, a new fashion for water theaters arrived in Antioch. In sparkling pools beneath the eastern sun, people gathered to watch the gleaming naked bodies of "nymphs" as they splashed and—the word is almost impossible to avoid—frolicked in pools before the eager eyes of the audience.

Christian preachers professed themselves horrified. Everything about the theater was, they said, from the Devil: the whole thing a foul idolatry contrived by demons "in order to turn the human race from the Lord and bind it to their glorification." The theater itself was a place of lust and drunkenness, a "citadel of all vile practices."[11] The abominations that happened on stage, meanwhile, were a "lawless corruption" designed to pollute the ears and eyes of the audience.[12] Theater stood between oneself and the divine. How could one worship God with the same hands with which one had just applauded an actor? One could not. One might not, if the Lord was watching, even get the chance. In one instructive little parable, a Christian writer noted that one woman who had dared to attend the theater dropped dead five days later.

Alas the theater did not have such a bracing effect on all viewers and Christian apologists were obliged to step in. Churches across the empire resounded with disapproval of the dramatic: tragedies were bloody, comedies were wanton; both would spawn impious behavior. Actors were little better than whores—no, they actually *were* whores: Christians regularly substituted the words "actor" and "dancer" with the word "prostitute"; the theater itself was "the temple of lust for prostitution."[13] The dangers of attending a performance were outlined in another vivid sermon by John Chrysostom that, like so many of them, revealed rather more about the speaker than the listener. "If someone puts coals in his lap, won't he burn his clothes?" Well, it is just the same with the man who goes to the theater. "Even if you aren't intimate with the prostitute, you've copulated with her by desire and have committed the sin in your thoughts."[14] Actual thunderbolts were threatened and oratorical ones delivered to those who went to watch the naked women in the water theaters. Spectators here were going, Chrysostom warned, "unto the fountain of the Devil, to see a harlot swim, and to suffer shipwreck of the soul. For that water is a sea of lasciviousness . . . And whereas she swims with naked body, thou beholding, are sunk into the deep of lasciviousness."[15] The stain of such visions would remain in one's eyes long after the performance had ended for who, as another asked, "can bathe in mud without being soiled?"[16]

Almost every kind of display was, Christian preachers argued, stained with satanism. Acrobats who contorted their bodies were in the Devil's service, as too were those who juggled with knives and cartwheeled. The music that these people danced to was considered perilous, for music might take away men's senses and mesmerize them, whipping them into a frenzy of lust and ungodliness. Was it for this, asked another preacher, rising in a disapproving crescendo, that God had created humans? So that they could "practise singing and piping; that they should swell out their cheeks in blowing the flute; that they should take the lead in singing impure songs, and . . . abandon themselves to clumsy motions, to dance and sing, form rings of dancers, and finally, raising their haunches and hips, float along with a tremulous motion of the loins?"[17]

In anxious, threatening sermons, other pastimes came under attack. Public shows were feared as much for the public as for the entertainment. What might go on in the anonymous hurly-burly of a crowd? The Roman erotic poets had known perfectly well what might happen—indeed they had celebrated it. As Ovid had gleefully explained, when one goes to watch the races, "the spacious Circus offers / Chances galore." A trip to the Roman hippodrome was rich in possibilities for the ardent and not-too-scrupulous suitor. "Often it happens that dust may fall on the blouse of the lady," Ovid advised in his seduction manual:

> If such dust should fall, carefully brush it away.
> Even if there's no dust, brush off whatever there isn't.
> Any excuse will do: why do you think you have hands?[18]

"Not for that," declared the new generation of clerics. Going to the races was frittering away your time "idly and in evil." God had not given us lives so that we could have fun.[19]

The bathhouses were also deplored as sinks of immorality. To Roman emperors and their subjects, bathing had been a mark of civilization. The irretrievably barbarian Britons had, it was felt, only finally begun to become civilized when they started to embrace bathing and banquets. Even the Roman philosopher and orator Cicero, in one of his more man-of-the-people moments, had said that the noise of the gong that opened the baths was a sweeter sound than the voices of the philosophers in their schools. The buildings themselves were astonishing: the cathedrals of paganism as they have been called. It is not an excessive analogy. Often the most imposing buildings in any city, they were wonders of architectural genius, soaking up vast amounts of money and nudging innovation forwards to meet their demands. The citizens of the empire went to the baths as regularly as churchgoers—indeed far more so, as most went every day. Once inside the great hallways of these grand edifices, they passed through the marbled rooms in a routine as ancient as any liturgy: *apodyterium, tepidarium, caldarium, frigidarium* . . .

Going to the baths was not merely a functional event of cleansing—which was just as well, given that the baths lacked chlorination, filtration or regular changing of the water. Modern research has concluded that they must have been absolutely filthy—something that ancient poets knew long ago. "Zoilus," Martial wrote, "you spoil the bathtub washing your arse. To make it filthier, Zoilus, stick your head in it."[20]

Zoilus aside, a trip to the baths was a sensuous delight: writers wax lyrical about the light that fell through the windows into the gleaming marble halls. As one famous proverb advised: "Bathing, wine and Venus wear out the body but are the real stuff of life."[21] On fortunate occasions, if the frescoes are to be believed, all the pleasures might be celebrated in one go. Bathhouses were crammed with art: jewel-bright mosa-

ics, statues of nymphs and Nereids, and countless statues
of Aphrodite, her cool marble skin perspiring slightly in the
steam. These buildings were less like modern swimming pools
—machines for exercising in as Iris Murdoch disparagingly
called them—and more like town squares with water. Everything—business, pleasure, eating, drinking, pissing and, in the
darker rooms, sex—went on in them. The philosopher Seneca
lived above some baths for a while and described (not entirely
contentedly) how they resounded with the noises of "the cake-
seller with his varied cries, the sausageman, the confectioner,
and all the vendors of food hawking their wares, each with his
own distinctive intonation." These sounds competed with the
grunting gym obsessives, the slap of a masseur and the shriek
of the skinny armpit-hair plucker, advertising his business, a
man who never stops shouting "except when he is plucking the
armpits and making his victim yell instead."[22]

In Seneca's day, at the height of the empire, bathing was
done naked and not usually segregated by sex. People went to
the baths to see—and be seen—all over by men and women
alike. The reliably smutty Martial describes how men would
gather round and applaud whenever they saw one particularly
well-endowed bather. Occasionally this caused embarrassment.
Young men didn't go to the baths with their fathers for fear of
the unexpected erection; even for liberal Romans, it seems that
seeing one's son's hard-on was felt to be a bit much. Shyness
struck elsewhere: one woman was so embarrassed about her
body odor that she covered her nakedness in depilatory creams
and layers of bean unguent. She still smelled anyway. Or so the
scurrilous Martial said.[23]

Christian moralists professed themselves scandalized. In the
writings of the early Christian clerics, the baths were reviled
as the haunts of demons and of those who lead a "soft, effeminate, and dissolute life."[24] Their very structure was to be abhorred: those statues, wrote another Christian moralist, were
nothing more than demonic idols—proof that "Satan and his

angels have filled the whole world."[25] Even the exercises done outside the baths were suspect: wrestling was deplored as "the Devil's trade . . . the very movements of the wrestler have a snakelike quality."[26] What went on in them was far worse. The water seemed to wash away what little modesty these sinners had left. Christian preachers pronounced it intolerable that men and women alike stripped naked—and that women then allowed every inch of their bodies to be manhandled by a "crouching menial." Dangerous behavior, all this nudity, "for from looking, men get to loving."[27] Statues in bathhouses suffered particularly vicious attacks as these buildings were targeted by mobs of Christians keener on the cleansing of the soul than the body.

Christians could, their preachers told them, wash for simple utility as long as they didn't enjoy it too much. The good Christian should certainly not wallow in the sensual pleasures of the baths. Some defied such pious grubbiness: Augustine openly claimed bathing to be one of the pleasures of life. Others took a more robust approach to washing. Ascetics celebrated the ideal of being *"alousia"*—unwashed. As one writer asked, what need did a Christian have to wash at all? Even if one's skin becomes rough and scaly from lack of cleaning, he had no need, since "he that is once washed in Christ need not to wash again."[28] An intellectual change had taken place. Filth was moving from something that was found outside a man to something that stained his soul. A clean body was no longer one that was free from dirt: it was one that was unsoiled by sexual activity—and particularly by "deviant" sexual activity, which started to be precisely defined then deplored in newly fierce and censorious terms.

Male homosexuality was denounced, and then outlawed. By the sixth century, those who were, as one chronicler put it, "afflicted with homosexual lust" started to live in fear. And with good reason. When a bishop called Alexander was accused of having a homosexual relationship, he and his partner were "in

accordance with a sacred ordinance . . . brought to Constantinople and were examined and condemned by Victor the city
prefect, who punished them: he tortured Isaiah severely and
exiled him and he amputated Alexander's genitals and paraded
him around on a litter. The emperor immediately decreed that
those detected in pederasty should have their genitals amputated. At that time many homosexuals were arrested and died
after having their genitals amputated."[29]

Sex between a husband and wife was allowed but it should
not, preachers said, be enjoyed. The old merry marriage ceremonies, in which people had eaten, drunk and sung profane
songs about sex, were bluntly deplored as the Devil's dungheap.
Admiring stories of married couples who never slept with each
other but spent their nights wearing hair shirts proliferated.

What difference did Christianity make? In some ways none.
The people of empire, resistant to the clerics' diatribes, continued going to the baths and the theater, still enjoyed the horse
races. They still had sex; one might even dare to say that they
enjoyed it. The theater still opened; plays were still shown.
The fervently Christian emperor Theodosius, for one, supplied
players during a theater festival. Ovid's racy manuals were copied and read—presumably with enthusiasm—throughout the
medieval period.

But some things did change. In the glare of Christian disapproval the once-loved art of pantomime dance withered and
died. Sexually explicit—and sexually joyful—poetry stopped
being openly written. There were no new Ovids. There were
certainly no more Catulluses.[30] Desire started to be called "lust"
—and it became something shameful that was to be feared, despised, smothered and—if homosexual—punished, horribly.
What was celebrated at holy days and festivals also underwent
a transformation. On March 17, Roman citizens had celebrated
the Liberalia. On March 17, the Christian Church celebrated
instead the saint's day of Ambrose of Alexandria—a pupil of
Origen, the man who (allegedly) had castrated himself for the

sake of heaven. What was acceptable in terms of sexuality narrowed. It would be well over a thousand years before Western civilization could come to see homosexuality as anything other than a perversion and a crime. Throughout the empire, statues were brought out of the bathhouses, their bodies mutilated, and burned as jeering crowds looked on in delight. Nipples were smashed from one naked figure of Aphrodite; Aphrodite herself was beheaded and left in the dirt.

Something more was lost, too. Many of those who disobeyed the furiously moralizing preachers and went to the races, or to the theater, or to look at "nymphs" cavorting in the sun, now did so in the knowledge that they were sinners. And they would, too, have known what awaited sinners in the kingdom that was to come. As the Christian writer Tertullian joyfully explained, when that moment came, all of these miscreants would be consumed in the avenging fires of the Lord—and he and his fellow obedient Christians would be there, enjoying the sight. What need for the theater or the hippodrome now? he asked. Because for the Christian faithful there are "other spectacles to come—that day of the Last Judgement, when the hoary age of the world and all its generations will be consumed in one fire."[31]

———

CHAPTER FOURTEEN

To Obliterate the Tyranny of Joy

For the eye of God always sees the works of a man and nothing
escapes him.

—*The Sayings of the Desert Fathers*, Gelasius, 6

IF YOU HAD TRAVELED to the great cities in the eastern empire, to Alexandria and to Antioch, in the fourth and fifth centuries, then long before you came to a city itself you would have seen them. At dawn, they emerged from caves in the hills and holes in the ground, their dark robes flapping, their faces gaunt and pale from hunger, their eyes hollow from lack of sleep. As the cocks began to crow, while the city beyond was still slumbering, they gathered in the monasteries and hills beyond and, "forming themselves into a holy choir, they stand, and lifting up their hands all at once sing the sacred hymns."[1] An impressive sight—and an eerie one, their filthy, emaciated figures a living rebuke to the opulence and bustle of urban life below: a new, and newly strange, power in the world.

This was the great age of the monk. Ever since Antony had set out to the desert to do battle with demons, men had flocked after him in imitation. These men were the ideal Christians, the perfect renouncers of all those sinful pleasures of the flesh. And their way of life was thriving: so many had gone out since Antony that the desert was described as a city.[2] And what a strange city this was. You wouldn't find bathhouses and banquets and theaters here. The habits of these men were infamously ascetic. In Syria, St. Simeon Stylites ("of the pillar") stood on a stone column for decades, until his feet burst open from the continual pressure.[3] Other monks lived in caves, or holes, or hollows or shacks. In the eighteenth century, a traveler to Egypt had looked up into the cliffs above the Nile and

seen thousands of cells in the rock above. It was in these bur-
rows, he realized, that monks had lived out lives of unimaginable austerity, surviving on almost no food and only able to
drink by letting down buckets on ropes to draw water from the
river when it was in flood.[4]

What was a monk at this time? In the fourth and fifth centuries, the now-ancient tradition of monasticism was only in its
infancy and its ways were still being formed. In this odd and
as yet uncodified existence, monks turned to the wisdom of
their famous predecessors to know how to live. Collections of
monkish sayings proliferated. Self-help guides of a sort—but
a world away from Ovid. What is a monk? "He is a monk,"
wrote one, "who does violence to himself in everything."[5] A
monk was toil, said another. All toil. How should a monk live?
"Eat straw, wear straw, sleep on straw," advised another revered
saying. "Despise everything."[6] Athletes of austerity, these men
mortified their flesh in a hundred ways on a thousand days.
One monk, it was said, had stood upright in thorn bushes for
a fortnight. Another lived with a stone in his mouth for three
years, to teach himself to be silent. Some, nostalgic for the
tortures of past persecutions, draped themselves in chains and
clanked round in them for years.

This monkish "city" was a living rebuke to the Roman way
of life. If you can judge an empire by its adjectives, then the
Roman Empire had been one that adored the urban. In Latin,
urbanus meant, at its most basic, to be someone who lived in
the town. But much more than that, like its English descen-
dant, it meant to be cultivated, courteous, witty, *urbane*. The
noun *urbanitas* meant "refinement."[7] Men of the empire were
hugely proud of their cities: one wealthy citizen of Antioch
felt so enthusiastic about his that he covered the floor of his
house with a large mosaic depicting his hometown's great
public buildings. A second-century manual on public speaking
advised how to structure a funeral oration. In the list of for-
ty-odd workmanlike points that one should mention about the

deceased, the very second (point I.B.1) should be his native city. This should be closely followed by mention of his fellow citizens (point I.B.2) and then, a little lower, his "public service." Such virtues as "wisdom" and "temperance" languished far below, at points III.A.1 and III.A.2 respectively. Piety came in even lower, at III.A.5[8]: a tertiary-league virtue, if that.*

The affluent competed to lavish money on their towns, pave their roads, raise the stone stages of theaters and cover the heads of gods in ever-grander temples. "Philanthropy" is the term that later ages would give to such behavior. The Roman Empire was not so mealy-mouthed: as the plaques on such buildings frankly announced, their benefactors had paid for them because of their *philotimia:* their "love of honor." The great stones of a theater or an aqueduct, engraved with your name, were a far more impressive monument than any tombstone — and frankly a far more socially useful one.

It is hardly surprising, therefore, that many of the empire's urban, urbane men found this new breed of men who shunned the civilized life baffling to the point of repellent. To the Greek orator Libanius, monks were madmen, "that crew who pack themselves tight into the caves" and who then "claim to converse with the creator of the universe in the mountains."[9] Their fasts were fiction, he said. These men weren't starving themselves: they didn't not eat; they just didn't grow or buy their own food. When no one was looking, he said, they scuttled into the temples of the loathed pagans, stole those sinful sacrifices and ate them instead. Far from being ascetics they were "models of sobriety, only as far as their dress is concerned."[10] Their vicious and thuggish attacks on the temples weren't done out of piety, said Libanius. They committed them out of pure greed. "They claim to be attacking the temples but these

---

* The whole list makes for fascinating reading. Particularly pleasing is point "II.D" where, under the subheading "Bodily Excellences," the author advises praising the "bubbling vitality and capacity for deep feeling of the deceased." And, no doubt, the deep feeling of the speaker, too.

attacks are a source of income" because after raiding not only shrines but also local peasant homes, "the invaders depart with the loot from the places they have stormed."[11]

There may have been more than a touch of snobbishness in such disdain as many of those who set out for the hills were poor and illiterate. Some were even slaves—much to the irritation of their Christian superiors. Nietzsche and Engels would later equate Christianity and its values with slaves and slave morality—but if that is true, then no one had told the most powerful Christians in this period. They had no truck with such dangerously revolutionary ideas as the emancipation of slaves. Far from encouraging the escape of Christian slaves, senior clerics cracked down hard on any who attempted to escape their mortal bondage by disappearing into the desert for a more heavenly servitude. When one bishop advised slaves to desert their masters and become ascetics, the Church was appalled and promptly excommunicated him. "We shall never," stated a canon of the Holy Apostles, "allow such a thing, which brings sorrow to the masters to whom the slaves belong and which is a disrupting influence."[12] The heavenly realm weighed in to help too. In the fourth century, St. Theodore appeared: a saint whose specialty was finding missing slaves. Sleep on St. Theodore's tomb and, it was said, he would appear in your dream and show you where your recalcitrant slave was hiding.

Monks needed to be in the desert for here, they knew, was where the demons swarmed and gathered. Here, where the city petered out and the empty spaces began, was where Satan's minions swooped and slithered and struck. A monk out of the desert, Antony had said, was like a fish out of water.[13] The monkish battle with Satan was not a pitched battle but a duel, and so monks shunned the distracting company of others. "I will not meet anyone this year," resolved one.[14] Such resolutions were not always easy to keep. In the endless solitude of desert life monks flailed and struggled and gasped. Loneliness gnawed like hunger. Their own desert places often had the power to scare these men far more thoroughly than any natural wilderness might. One monk was said to have wept so continuously that his tears, like a stream, had worn a hollow in his chest. Proof of his virtue, said admiring fellow monks. The modern mind would tend towards a more clinical (albeit anachronistic) conclusion: many of these men must have been profoundly depressed.

Starvation was one of the most popular of monkish mortifications—no special equipment was required—but it was also one of the hardest to bear. One monk fasted all day then ate only two hard biscuits. Another lived from the age of twenty-seven to thirty on just roots and wild herbs, then for the next four years on half a pound of barley bread a day and some herbs. Eventually he felt his eyes going dim while his skin became "as rough as a pumice stone." He added a little oil to his diet, then went on as before until he was sixty, to the awe and admiration of his fellow monks.[15] There had been asceticism before—but this went further. Others, like ruminants, lived on all fours, browsing for their food like animals. In some ways hunger helped: a famished monk would be less beset by the demons of fornication or anger than one with a full belly. "A needy body," as one put it, "is a tame horse."[16] But thoughts of food became an obsession with these men. In their reading of the Fall, the apple that Eve gives to Adam is not seen as a symbolic representation of sex; it is seen as nothing more, nor less, than an apple. Maslow's hierarchy of needs made monkish flesh.[17]

The monks tormented themselves by what they put on their bodies as much as what they put in them. Some chose to dress in woven palm fronds instead of any softer fabric. To wear the usual coarse monkish habit was regarded, in this extreme world, as being "foppishly dressed."[18] Others, under the desert sun, tortured their skin with abrasive hair shirts. Another dressed in an extraordinary leather costume (that would in a later era have different connotations) that left only his mouth and nose exposed. To be pleasing to the Lord, a monk's clothes must, it was said, be an offense against aestheticism: a habit should be tatty rather than smart, old rather than new, mended and re-mended and mended again. Anything less was vanity. A monk's clothes should be such that, if he threw his habit out of his cell for three days, no one would steal it. The monks' self-sacrifice was unquestionable; their smell must have been unspeakable.

If this sounds like a life lived on the edge of sanity, it was. In the searing heat of the desert day, reality shimmered, flickered and thinned.* One monk saw a dragon in a lake; another slew a basilisk. Another saw the Devil himself sitting at his window. Demons appeared then vanished like smoke; meditating monks turned into flames. Watch one monk as he prayed and you would see his fingers turn into lamps of fire. Pray well and you might yourself become all flame. Demons teemed around monks like flies around food. One monk was beset by visions of rotting corpses, bursting open as they decayed. Alone for weeks, months on end in their cells, with nothing more than aging hard bread to eat and an oil lamp to look at, monks were plagued by more tempting visions of sex, and food, and youth. Some monks lost their minds—if they had ever been in full possession of them. When Apollo of Scetis, a shepherd who later became a monk, spotted a pregnant woman in a field, he said to himself: "I should like to see how the child lies in her womb." He ripped the woman open and saw the fetus. The child and the mother died.[19]

The reasons for these peculiar practices are hard to fathom.

---

* The existence of monks in the Egyptian desert remains otherworldly. When the writer William Dalrymple traveled to St. Antony's monastery (a visit recounted in his wonderful book *From the Holy Mountain*) he found himself sitting at breakfast next to a brother who pointed to a space between two abbey towers. "In June 1987 in the middle of the night," the monk explained, "our father St Antony appeared there hovering on a cloud of shining light." You saw this? Dalrymple asked. "No," the monk replied. "I'm short-sighted . . . I can barely see the Abbot when I sit beside him at supper."

One theory is that Christian domination of the empire had brought many gains; but one of its great losses was that it had become considerably harder to be made a martyr by unsympathetic Roman governors. Deprived of the chance to die in one terrible, glorious, sin-erasing show, these men instead martyred themselves slowly, agonizingly, tormenting their flesh a little more every hour, thwarting their desires a little more every year. These practices would become known as "white martyrdom." The monks died daily in the hope that, one day, after they died, they might live. "Remember the day of your death," advised one monk. "Remember also what happens in hell and think about the state of the souls down there, their painful silence, their most bitter groanings, their fear, their strife, their waiting. . . ." A terrible enough plight, but the monk had not finished yet; he concluded his cheering list with "the punishments, the eternal fire, worms that rest not, the darkness, gnashing of teeth, fear and supplications."[20]

Grim tales taught monks the value of not giving in to their urges. One particularly vivid parable noted what happened to a disobedient monk named Heron. As the story opens, Heron, rather than spending his time weeping in his cell, is having a lovely time going about the fleshpots of his local city, frequenting the theater, the races and the taverns. At one of these, his resolve weakened by eating and drinking too much, he meets an actress, falls "into the mud of womanly desire" and has sex with her. This act was performed, as the story records with satisfaction, "to his own wounding . . . he developed a pustule on the penis itself and he was sick from this for six months until his genitals putrefied and fell off."[21] A lesson to us all.

Carpe diem, Horace had said. Eat, drink and be merry, for tomorrow you will be dead for eternity. The monks offered an alternative to this view: die today and you might live for eternity. This was a life lived in terror of its end. "Always keep your death in mind," was a common piece of advice: do not forget the eternal judgment.[22] When one brother started to laugh during a meal, he was immediately reproached by a fellow monk: "What does this brother have in his heart, that he should laugh, when he ought to weep?"[23] How should one live well in this new and austere world? By constantly accusing yourself, said another monk, by "constantly reproaching myself to myself."[24] Sit in your cell all day, advised another, weeping for your sins.[25]

A hint of desert isolationism started to find its way into pious city life, too. In John Chrysostom's writings, contact with women of all kinds was something to be feared and, if possible, avoided altogether. "If we meet a woman in the market-place," Chrysostom told his congregation, herding his listeners into complicity with that first-person plural, then we are "disturbed."[26] Desire was dangerously easy to inflame. Women who inflamed it were not to be relished as Ovid had relished them, but eschewed, scorned and denigrated in writings that made it abundantly clear that the fault of the man's desire lay with them. In this atmosphere a group of fashionable women with their low-cut necklines were not praised as beauties but excoriated as a "parade of whores."[27]

Eventually, clerical disapproval was reinforced by law. Pagan festivals, with their exuberant merriment and dancing, were banned. Dislike of them had been rumbling for decades: Constantine himself had poured scorn on the so-called religious festivals of the impious pagans and their drunken riotous feasts at which, "under the semblance of religion, your hearts are devoted to profligate enjoyment."[28] In AD 356, less than fifty years after Constantine had announced that "no man whatever should be refused complete toleration," the death penalty was instituted for those who made sacrifices.[29] In 407, the old merry ceremonies were forbidden. "It shall not be permitted at all to hold convivial banquets in honour of sacrilegious rites in such funereal places or to celebrate any solemn ceremony." If anyone declared themselves an official in charge of pagan festivals then, the law said, they would be executed.[30] John Chrysostom jubilantly observed their decline. "The tradition of the fore-fathers has been destroyed, the deep rooted custom has been torn out, the tyranny of joy [and] the accursed festivals . . . have been obliterated just like smoke."[31]

Such laws were easier to make than to police. How could Christians know what went on behind closed doors? In one infamous sermon, Chrysostom came up with a solution: Christian congregations were to spy on each other. They would watch their fellow congregation for sinners—and by "sinners" he meant people who dared go to the theater—and, when they found them, they would hound them, shun them, report them. Nowhere was to be beyond the gaze of the good Christian informer, even private homes. "Let us be meddle-some and search out those who had fallen," he advised in a ser-mon that encouraged Christians to hunt out those who were lapsing from true Christian ritual. "Even if we must enter into the fallen one's home, let us not shrink back from it."[32]

Lest any of his flock felt awkward about such an intrusion, they were reassured, once again, that what they were doing was not done to harm others but to help them.[33] Those who declined to act as informers would themselves be considered culpable, both in this world and in the next. Another vivid Chrysostom analogy sealed the point. In a household, "if one of the servants is caught stealing silver or gold, the thief him-self is not the only one punished, but also his conspirators and anyone who did not report him." In the same way, if a Chris-tian saw another going to the theater (or as he put it "departing into the place of the Devil") and kept silent, he would be pun-ished by God—and by him. It would cause Chrysostom pain, he said, but he would "spare nobody from the most grievous penalties."[34]

To turn on, hound and hunt your fellows in this way was not to harm them. No, Chrysostom reiterated, it was to *save* them. To turn another soul back from sin was the greatest thing that a Christian could do, better than fasting or even feeding the poor. In fiery prose, Chrysostom urged his congregation on: "Let us," he declared—you can imagine those famous flashing eyes glinting as he spoke—"take our wives, children, and households and go out after this game and quarry. Let us drag from the snares of the Devil those whom he has made captive to his will."[35]

Saint Apollonia Destroys a Pagan Idol, c. 1442–45 The saint calmly ascends to the idol, hammer in hand. Hagiographies frequently praised the flair with which saints smashed ancient temples and centuries-old statues.

CULT STATUE OF THE DEIFIED AUGUSTUS, EPHESUS Augustus, who was considered divine by polytheistic Romans, would have been considered demonic by Christians. He too has been disfigured by a crude carved cross.

THEOPHILUS STANDING ON THE SERAPEION In this manuscript, the bishop Theophilus stands triumphant over what had been widely considered to be the most beautiful temple in the world. Theophilus razed the temple in AD 392.

BYZANTINE CHAPEL IN A ROMAN AMPHI-
THEATER, DURESI, ALBANIA Laws encouraged Christians to use the remnants of
old temples to build and repair roads and
bridges. The well-cut stone suited those
purposes well, and was an added insult to
the old gods. Everywhere, Christians used
the remnants of Roman infrastructure to
construct churches.

HYPATIA, 1885 The great mathematician
and philosopher Hypatia, improbably un-
derdressed. Hypatia was renowned for her
chastity and wore an austere philosopher's
cloak. When one of her pupils fell in love
with her, she showed him her sanitary towel
to discourage him.

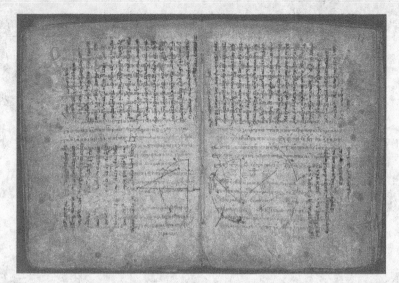

ARCHIMEDES PALIMPSEST, C. 10TH–13TH CENTURY A tenth-century copy of Archimedes's *Method of Mechanical Theorems*. In it, Archimedes had ingeniously applied mechanical laws, such as the law of the lever, to find the volume and area of geometric shapes. Two thousand years before Newton, he had come tantalizingly close to deriving calculus. However, in the thirteenth century this work was scraped off and overwritten with a prayer book.

THEOLOGICAL DEBATE BETWEEN CATHOLIC AND NESTORIAN CHRISTIANS AT ACRE, 1290 In 388, it was ruled that arguing about or even discussing religious matters in public was a "damnable audacity." Nestorius and his teachings were declared heretical.

SATYR AND MAENAD, FRESCO, POMPEII, 1ST CENTURY BC Later observers were shocked by the liberty with which pre-Christian Roman artists had depicted sex. "Lascivious frescoes and lewd sculptures," wrote one nineteenth-century American, "such as would be seized in any modern country by the police, filled the halls of the most virtuous Roman citizens and nobles."

PRIAPUS, C. 50–79 The modern world was shocked—or professed itself to be—by the bawdiness of many of the works of art that were uncovered from Pompeii. The city's eventual burial in ash was widely said to be the just deserts of an impious people.

HELL, 16TH CENTURY Early Christian texts described in precise detail the punishments meted out to sinners in hell. According to the Apocalypse of Peter, blasphemers would be hung up by their tongues, adulterers by their testicles, and women "who adorned themselves for adultery" would be strung up by their hair above the boiling mire.

ROMAN WOMEN PLAYING SPORTS, 4TH CENTURY AD The habit of bathing continued well into the Christian era, but more hard-line Christians looked with suspicion on bathhouses as immoral and the haunts of demons. Statues of Aphrodite and other gods, which often stood in the baths, were frequently mutilated and defaced by believers.

ST. JOHN CHRYSOSTOM, the charismatic and fiery-tongued preacher.

ST. SIMEON STYLITES SITTING ON HIS COLUMN, 5TH OR 6TH CENTURY Believers endured great trials for the love of God. St. Simeon spent over three decades on a column, until his feet and belly burst open from the pressure of continued standing.

ST. SHENOUTE, RED MONASTERY CHURCH, EGYPT, C. 7TH CENTURY St. Shenoute's face was said to be gaunt and hollow-eyed from continued fasting. Shenoute beat those in his care, hounded those suspected of paganism and declared that "there is no crime from those who have Christ."

EMPEROR JUSTINIAN I, C. 547 Justinian was determined to "close all the roads which lead to error." As part of this goal, he forbade anyone pagan from teaching, ordered the execution of anyone who was caught sacrificing to statues and forced the Academy in Athens to close.

CHAPTER FIFTEEN

"Merciful Savagery"

There is no cruelty in regard for God's honour.

—St. Jerome, Letter 109.32

IT HAD ALL SEEMED so simple: render unto Caesar what is Caesar's. Render unto God what is God's. As the fourth century drew to its close and the fifth century opened, caveats were added, complications brought to bear. What, asked some of the most powerful preachers, if God and Caesar both laid claim to the same thing? Well, said the great thinkers of the first Christian century, in that case God took precedence. As Augustine put it, if God's law diverged from Roman law then the Heavenly City and its inhabitants were compelled "to dissent, and to become obnoxious to those who think differently."[1] Everything—man, law and even bureaucracy—was now to give way to God. Or rather, to His Church. And if this meant some sticky moments on earth then so be it, for, argued another aggressive Christian cleric, the greatest wrong that one could do was not to disobey the law but to disobey God. "It is better to be deprived of empire, than to become guilty of impiety."[2]

One of those who policed the law of God most fiercely of all was the infamous Egyptian monk—now saint—Shenoute.

One night, at the turn of the fifth century, some hours after the blazing desert sun had set, there was a small bustle of activity outside Shenoute's monastery in Egypt. Usually at this time all would be quiet and the hundreds of monks behind the walls of the White Monastery would be asleep, enjoying the brief liturgical respite between final prayers and the knocking of the wooden bell that roused them from their beds just before dawn.

But if you had been standing outside the White Monastery on this particular night, you might have seen something unusual. Suddenly, in the stillness, there was movement. The door of the monastic gatehouse opened and a group of monks appeared. As they moved briskly away, the gate closed again behind them, shutting in the remaining monks, shutting out the demonic world. The small group moved away from the monastery, on down towards the river. Look closely, and you would have seen that there were eight of them. Look closer still, and your eye would almost certainly have been caught by one of them. Gaunt from constant fasting, his skin seemed to cling too closely to his bones. His deep-socketed eyes were as dark and sunken as holes in a stone wall—it was said that he did not sleep all night until daybreak, and only then for a moment. When he was awake, people said he wept constantly, tears as sweet as honey falling from his eyes, turning them black with his holy sorrow. This was Shenoute.

One should not, however, mistake weeping for weakness. Shenoute might weep for the sins of the earth but he walked with the angels—and smote demons. This was a man who, it was said, conferred with John the Baptist, spoke with Jesus Christ and had personally wrestled demons to the ground. Shenoute was a man to respect—and a man to fear. Under his charismatic leadership, male and female monks flocked in vast numbers to join the monastery's three communities, swelling its numbers into hundreds, perhaps even thousands. Once in his care, these men and women faced stringent discipline. Beatings were administered to those who strayed from the monastery's numerous rules. A nun who "stealthily took things" received twenty blows of the rod. Another who ran after a sister "in friendship and with fleshly desire" received fifteen.[3] More pain was added by the humiliating method in which such beatings were delivered: elder nuns held their errant sister down while a monk beat the soles of her feet.

On this particular night, the gaze of Shenoute's black, tear-washed eyes was not directed at those within his monastery, but at a man outside it. In the stillness of the desert dark, Shenoute and his seven fellow monks hurried towards the Nile and crossed it. Later it was said that they had not needed any boat or sailor for this crossing: divine providence alone had carried them, miraculously, to the other bank. Whatever the conveyance, once they reached the other side, they moved on once again towards the city of Panopolis.

If any locals had seen the dark-robed group as they moved through the darkness they might well have felt the stirrings of fear. Monks—anonymous, rootless, untraceable—were able to commit atrocities with near impunity. "Our angels" some Christians called them. Rubbish, said non-Christians. They were not angels but ignorant, boorish thugs, men in appearance only who "led the lives of swine, and openly did and allowed countless unspeakable crimes." As the author Eunapius wrote with sardonic distaste: "in those days every man who wore a black robe and consented to behave in unseemly fashion in public, possessed the power of a tyrant, to such a pitch of virtue had the human race advanced!"[4] Even a wholeheartedly Christian emperor mutedly observed that "the monks commit many crimes."[5]

And on that night, these monks were about to commit another. Shenoute's target was not, this time, one of his monks but one of the wicked, godless pagans. In sermon after furious sermon Shenoute had turned his famously fiery prose on these people. Their hearts were "the nests of the spirits of wickedness."[6] If disturbed then these evil people would spit out poison.[7] The Bible, Shenoute told his congregants, said that those who set up pagan images should be killed.[8] As he put it in one particularly vigorous sermon, God wished His people to "remove the abominations from His presence." The emperors, Shenoute thundered, had declared that the entire earth must be cleansed of perversions. No stone was to be left on top of any other stone of any pagan temple.[9] Not one. In the entire earth.

But on that particular night Shenoute and his seven companions would start small. They would start with the house of one single man: a local named Gessius.

It was still pitch dark when the monks arrived outside the entrance to Gessius's house. Gessius—to give him his full, grandly Roman name, Flavius Aelius Gessius—was a Roman citizen, a prominent landowner and a former governor, as Pliny had been. Gessius was an enviable member of the empire's tiny elite ruling class. He was also, on that night, a marked man. For this Gessius, uncowed by Shenoute's blustering, had committed several unpardonable crimes. On one occasion he had been overheard bluntly declaring that "Jesus was not divine."[10] On another, he had gone into a recently ruined pagan temple and, despite the laws forbidding it, had made a sacrificial offering by scattering roses. This was not only a crime, it was, perhaps more importantly, an insupportable snub to the area's most powerful Christian, Shenoute.

And so, on that dark night, Shenoute was going to make Gessius pay. The monks gathered round Gessius's heavy, locked front door—and opened it. If that seems a rather simple gloss on what must have been a complicated or at the very least physically demanding procedure, then that is because Shenoute said afterwards that it was simple. The monks, he said, did not open the front door: God did.

Shenoute and his monks then entered the dark house—which, Shenoute later explained, was not merely dim with the darkness of night but black with the darkness of evil. Despite such logistical difficulties, the monks' progress never wavered and they moved on, through the atrium and up the stairs into the heart of Gessius's home. Again, if the claim that a band of eight monks managed not only to break into and enter a locked house, but also to move through its Stygian gloom without rousing anyone or taking a wrong turn seems improbable, then Shenoute had an explanation for that too: God was guiding them.[11]

Their divine fixer helped them once again when they finally came to Gessius's locked private chamber. There was no need for them to put their shoulders to the door or bash it open: it merely "popped out" when Shenoute grasped it, and fell off its hinges of its own accord, allowing the monks to carry it away easily. Later it would become clear that not everyone in the town was wholly convinced by this account. Indeed, impious tongues seem to have wagged, disparaging the idea that "the doors opened by themselves" as "big claims." Shenoute defended himself hotly: "We did not say that they opened [for us] by themselves," he blustered, "but rather we opened them as the Lord ordained." A somewhat Jesuitical distinction that may not have gone a long way to reassuring his doubters.[12]

Afterwards, Shenoute would speak of what happened in the next moments inside Gessius's house with revulsion. Being in that room, he said, was like being in a pagan temple once again, back in those dark days before the righteous emperors had ordered them to be laid waste. For as they went through the door, the monks found themselves in a room whose air was heavy with incense and where the light of numerous lamps glimmered on countless carved surfaces: they were in a chamber full of heathen idols. Here was a statue of the lecherous parricide Zeus; there was one of Zeus's father, Kronos; there was the deceitful Hecate . . .

The entire room — or so he later claimed — was crowded by "lewd and licentious" deities. Incense smoldered on small altars; lamps, lit by a reverential hand, cast flickering light over the faces of the pagan gods. A terrible sight for a devoted Christian monk to behold. But it is hard to imagine that, as the light caught Shenoute's own hollow-eyed face, there was not at least a small flicker of victory on it. For Shenoute — an arch-self-publicist — would have known well that if this was an awful moment then it was also a magnificent one. He had caught his enemy in the act of pagan worship. In the dim light, the dark figures of the monks moved about the room, gathering up the accursed statues, before hurrying out of the house, helped once again, of course, by God.[13]

In the street outside the house, the deep blue of the Egyptian night must have seemed almost light by comparison. The monks set off, back to the river, and standing on the banks of the Nile, they smashed the statues and threw the broken fragments in. The waters swirled, then swallowed the remnants of Gessius's paganism without a trace. A nest of Satan had been emptied.

Later, when Shenoute was criticized for breaking and entering into another man's house, he was utterly intransigent. "There is no crime," he declared, "for those who have Christ."[14]

The laws of the land may not have mattered to Shenoute. The laws of his monastery were, on the other hand, to be obeyed at all times. And there were a lot of them. More than five hundred rules circumscribed every aspect of Shenoute's monks' lives from the moment they got up, just before dawn, to the moment that they went to sleep, and everything they did in between. There were rules on what the monks wore; what they ate (precious little, mainly bread); when they ate (infrequently); when they prayed (relentlessly); how they prayed (audibly); where they had their hands when they prayed (emphatically, for some reason, not near their ribs); how they slept (alone and without erotic desire); how they washed (infrequently, without looking at one another's bodies or their own); whether or not they shaved (absolutely not, except with permission, for: "Cursed shall be any who shaves himself . . ."); and even where they defecated. As one rule (that perhaps raises more questions than it answers) explained: if anyone needs to "defecate into a pot or a jar or any other vessel . . . they shall ask the Male Eldest."[15]

Once inside a monastery, the monk's life was no longer his own. Certainly his property was not. Even clothes had to be given up and left outside so that the monks might obtain equality "in all things and desire might not find a place among foolish people." The monastery itself, however, not only desired possessions but categorically demanded them: a condition of entering was that each monk and nun must sign all their earthly possessions over to the monastery, in writing, within three months of joining. If they did not, then for this too they would find themselves, in the words of the rules, "cursed."[16]

The lands of these simple monks, naturally, began to spread. Soon the monastery grounds took in not just the monks' buildings but also palm groves, orchards, vegetable gardens, farm animals, fields . . . The monastery even controlled minds—or attempted to. From the moment of waking, monks in Shenoute's monastery were rarely at rest, their days filled with a punishing regime of physical work and prayer. They were even more rarely silent. Lest their minds wander onto ungodly paths as they performed the tedious basket-weaving that was a monk's lot, they were encouraged to chant constantly— prayers, or passages of scripture—anything at all. Just as the weaving chained hands, keeping them from sin, so the chanting chained wandering minds. It has been said that the monastery at work would have sounded like nothing so much as a swarm of bees in flight.[17]

Why did people sign up for such an unappealing life? It is possible that they didn't know the full extent of its austerity when they joined. Monks who entered Shenoute's monastery were not presented with a comprehensive contract at the door, or read their rights upon arrival. Instead, monastic discipline was more of a revealed religion, the full extent of the White Monastery laws being only slowly explained to each new entrant, little by little, once they were already inside. This may have been less Machiavellian than it sounds: to hear all the laws in one go would have made for a long evening. Nevertheless, by the time monks fully realized the form of their new life they would—now bereft of their money, their land and even their own clothes—have been almost powerless to leave it.

Once a monk had given himself to his new monastic master he had to obey him—or face the consequences. Numerous rules begin with the formulation "Cursed be . . . " Cursed were those who didn't give all their wealth to the monastery; cursed were those who shaved without having been ordered to; cursed were those who looked at another monk with desire. If a monk ate, say, the forbidden fruit of cucumber at the wrong time then, the law informed him, "he sins." At least sixty of the rules were devoted to sexual transgressions. Looking desirously at the nakedness of your neighbor while he washed was wrong; as was staring "with desirous feeling" at your own nakedness; those who sat "close to one's neighbour with a filthy desire in their heart" were also "cursed."[18]

Note that last one: "with a filthy desire *in their heart*." No sin had been committed. The mere intention of sin was now a sin in itself. In Shenoute's monastery even thoughts were policed. "Can any hide himself in secret places that I shall not see him?" the Lord had asked.[19] The answer from the White Monastery at least was a resounding no. As this new generation of hardline Christian preachers constantly reminded their congregations in fierce, hectoring speeches, there was nowhere to hide from the all-seeing eyes of the Lord.

Shenoute conducted frequent verbal inquiries and physical searches of those in his care. A period of four weeks every year was given over to a public examination of the monks. During this time, all the monks would gather together and publicly "scrutinize our words and deeds." This was supplemented by frequent physical inspections during which an official would search the cell of each monk. As the monastic rules declared with precision: "Twelve times per year—once a month—the Male Eldest shall enter all the Houses of the congregation and inspect all the cells within them." Man looks upon your face; God sees into your soul. Shenoute looks into your room.[20]

It is clear that Shenoute's monks were terrified of him. He was determined that the monks behind his walls—hundreds, possibly thousands of them—were to be as one: they were to work at the same time, pray at the same time, pause at the same time. There was a time to rise, a time to pray, a time to eat, a time to sleep . . . A time to be obedient. The monks were to move with one mind, as one body; a single swarm rather than a collection of individuals. The possessive pronoun was forbidden: one could not say "my bread" as all things belonged to everyone—and to no one. All must obey the clacking of the wooden monastic bell instantly—and woe betide anyone who did not. The bell was sounded twice: the first sounding indicated that the monks should stop what they were doing and pause; the second that they should move on to the next activity. Once, one of Shenoute's monks happened to be putting wood into the oven in the monastery's bakery when the first bell went. Obediently, the monk waited, hand in the heat, until the bell sounded again—whereupon he finally removed his ruined hand.[21]

It wasn't only monks who felt Shenoute's anger. He could vent the righteous wrath of God on anyone who he felt deserved it, including demons. One evening, a bureaucrat was due to inspect the White Monastery—possibly to investigate the terrible disciplinary violence that was rumored to be inflicted against erring monks. Shenoute saw the figure entering the monastery without knocking. According to legend, the official then grabbed Shenoute, whereupon Shenoute wrestled back, finally overcoming the man by putting him in a scissor hold between his thighs. This, Shenoute realized, was not some local official or an angel: it was a demon. In another retelling, the figure is the Devil himself, while Shenoute's wrestling becomes even more athletic: the anecdote concludes with Shenoute hurling the demon to the ground and putting his foot on his head.[22]

Religious intensity was not new. Greece and Rome had known those who took religion to extremes and who had gone about their lives feeling humbled and crushed by fear of the gods. Generally, though, religious fervor had been a private passion—and it had kept within the confines of the law. But as Christianity gained control, religiosity started to become a public duty and would, with self-righteous pride, overstep the boundaries of the law. Some of the most important thinkers of the era supported such behavior. If necessary, one must make oneself obnoxious. One must stop at nothing—even harming other people—in the service of the Lord. There is, after all, no crime for those who have Christ.

To punish a sinner violently, to flog them, beat them, make them bleed—this was not to harm them but to help them, by saving them from worse punishments to come. Shenoute worried that if he didn't beat the monks in his care then he was offending God. Punishments used against erring Christians even in Augustine's time ranged from the confiscation of property to being barred from church, beatings and floggings with rods. It is better, said Augustine, "with severity to love, than with gentleness to deceive."[23] This was not cruelty. Did not the shepherd bring wandering sheep back to the flock with his rod?[24] The Church, he wrote, "persecutes in the spirit of love."[25]

This was holy violence. Jesus may have told his followers that they should, when struck by an aggressor on their right cheek, offer him the other, but his fourth- and fifth-century followers were less forgiving. As John Chrysostom explained, if a Christian happens to hear someone blaspheme, then, far from turning their own cheek, they should "go up to him and rebuke him; and should it be necessary to inflict blows, spare not to do so. Smite him on the face; strike his mouth; sanctify thy hand with the blow." Murder committed for the sake of God, argued one writer, was not a crime but actually "a prayer."[26]

Some of Chrysostom's and Shenoute's methods of control would be mirrored, a hundred or so years later, for very similar reasons, in imperial law. When the emperor Justinian came to power in AD 527, he set about reforming the morals of his subjects with a zeal and a legal thoroughness as yet unseen. He had a good incentive: if he did not punish them then, he firmly believed, God would punish him.

Civil officials now found themselves required to enforce laws about what went on in private homes. Church officials found themselves pressed into service as de facto spies. Roman emperors had always used informers—"delatores." Now, they were put to the service of the Church. Men of all ranks were required to become informers. Any breach of the laws was to be reported. Bishops were required to become the emperor's spies and report back on their fellow officials. If they refused or failed in their duties, then they themselves would be held accountable. Among those whom the clergy were tasked with reporting on were actors, actresses and, as one revealing little law added, prostitutes "who wore monastic habits."[27] The punishments could be terrible. If a nurse aided and abetted an affair of a young woman in her charge, she would be punished by having molten lead poured down her throat. Correction was paramount. Justinian, as the chronicler Procopius put it, was determined to "close all the roads which lead to error."[28]

Some of the "holy" violence alarmed even the Church. In North Africa at the turn of the fifth century, the circumcellions became notorious not only for their suicides but for their vicious attacks on those who didn't share their particular Christian beliefs. One bishop was standing next to his altar when suddenly he found himself surrounded and beaten by men with clubs. Then his attackers tore his altar apart, beat him with its remnants, before finally stabbing him in the groin. Another priest found himself dragged from his house and, once the circumcellions had him outside, they gouged out his eye. Like the tailor-made tortures that awaited sinners in hell, where blasphemers were strung up by their tongues, there was a ghoulish appositeness to these assaults. Eyes of the erring were gouged out because those who couldn't see the true religion were "blind" anyway. Another bishop was seized, his hands chopped off and his tongue, which had preached falsehoods, cut out.[29]

The circumcellions roamed widely, vandalizing property, setting light to churches and torching houses. Just when people thought that these "warriors," as they called themselves, could not have gotten any worse, they invented what Augustine called a "new and unspeakable kind of violence, a piece of cruelty deserving of the Devil Himself."[30] By mixing together caustic lime powder and vinegar they created a solution strong enough to burn human skin. This they took to throwing into the eyes of priests, blinding them. Nowhere was safe: if a "traitor"—as they called those who didn't share their beliefs—was known to be at home, the circumcellions would go into their house, drag them out and then attack them. The more unexpected the attack, the more glorious the effect.

Festivals of the old gods were a favorite target: circumcellions raided these, smashing statues and shouting their rallying cry of "Laudes Deo"—"Praise the Lord"—as they went. In a moment, a joyful, drunken celebration could be reduced to sheer chaos. Like so many before and since, these men wanted religious conformity and they would stop at little to get it. Because Matthew 26:52 advised Christians to "sheathe your sword," with almost Jesuitical precision they adopted the club as their weapon of choice. Appalling violence could thus be done while sin was avoided. Besides, a club was efficient enough: they would beat to death as many as they could before melting back into the landscape.[31] The sticks with which these men carried out this work became their proud trademark; they called them their "Israels."

Augustine and others might have been shocked by such acts —but to an extent the Church was reaping what had been sown. A few decades earlier, as the academic Brent D. Shaw has pointed out, Christian preachers had been glad of the circumcellions' violence and cultivated it: in the attacks against the temples such freelance destroyers had been eminently useful and were drafted in to do the strong-arm work of pulling these buildings down. Schooled and encouraged in violence and thuggery, the group suddenly became, to the dismay of those who had once encouraged them, much less biddable.[32]

If circumcellions ignored the law, then they were in good company. At the highest level the Church was starting to challenge the power of the state. Roman observers had long noticed the Christian tendency to consider themselves above the law—and been irritated by it. When Pliny the Younger had put his slaves on trial he had executed them almost as much for their obstinacy as for their Christianity. Romans had frequently found the insolent conduct of Christians in court enraging. The Christian who had refused to answer any question in court—even the question of his name—with any words other than the phrase "I am a Christian"[33] was admired by other Christians for his fortitude. To the Romans his behavior would have seemed stubborn to the point of infantile.

As Christianity gained in power their acts of defiance gained in boldness. Courtrooms in the east of the empire were disrupted by sinister groups of dark-clad, psalm-chanting monks. Christians demanded the right to sanctuary in churches: the request became law.[34] In Antioch, fear of the monks grew so great that one judge didn't even wait for them to arrive in his court: hearing the sound of the monks approaching, chanting hymns, he simply jumped up from his seat, adjourned the court and fled from the city. "Justice cannot be exercised once they have appeared," he said as he escaped.[35]

In Caesarea, a judge dared to rule against a Christian bishop. He compounded his crime in the eyes of the Church by then declaring that everyone, whether they were Christian or not, should yield to the rule of law. He came to regret it. A mob of Christians, "like a hive roused by smoke," surged around, "torch in hand, amid showers of stones, with cudgels ready, all ran and shouted together in their united zeal." It was an effective technique. As one gloating Christian recorded: "What then was the conduct of this haughty and daring judge? He begged for mercy in a pitiable state of distress, cringing before them to an unparalleled extent." This, the chronicler concluded with satisfaction, "was the doing of the God of Saints, Who works and changes all things for the best."[36]

It did not seem to be "for the best" to many non-Christians. Elite writers expressed their disgust at the disorder. As the philosopher Celsus had observed so many years before, one should not defile the laws because if everyone did so it would be impossible for the law to function at all. The sort of intimidation that zealous Christians indulged in was not, another writer protested, the way that crime and punishment should work in the Roman Empire. "Nobody draws his sword against the murderer and puts it to his throat, employing force in place of the forms of law," said the orator Libanius. Instead, in a civilized society, "the place of swords is taken by impeachments and processes, civil and criminal." The Christians, he wrote with disdain, seemed to have no time for that: "these people here were the only ones ever to judge the cases of those whom they accuse and, having passed judgement, themselves to play the hangman's part."[37]

Christian preachers, however, were intransigent. They, they said, were answerable to a higher power than the mere law of the land. Their eye was upon heaven. As they reminded their flocks, it was not the law of some imperial bureaucrat that mattered. It was the law of God. Anything that saved a soul — even if it did so at the expense of law, order or even the body that that soul inhabited—was an acceptable act. To attack the houses, bodies and temples of those afflicted by the "pagan error" was not to harm these sinners but to help them. This was not brutality. This was kindness, education, reformation.

A rich tapestry of metaphor was brought out, cloaking what otherwise would have looked like naked aggression. Chrysostom wrote of hunting with nets to describe how one ought to herd the erring back to the true path. Augustine used the argument of the banquet described in Luke. Had not the lord of the house, when holding a feast, said to his servant: "Go out into the highways and hedges, and compel them to come in, that my house may be filled"?[38] Well then. Even the unwilling must be compelled to come into the house of the Lord. The arguments went further: those punishing errant Christians were not brutes; on the contrary, Augustine said that they were like a doctor tending to a sick patient. "When surgeons see that a gangrene must be cut away or cauterized, they often, out of compassion, turn a deaf ear to many cries." In the same letter, Augustine likened the concerned Christian to someone who pulls a boy's hair to stop him provoking serpents and a parent who removes a sword from a child's hand. "Such punishments are administered by wise care, not by wanton cruelty."[39]

In a now-familiar paradox of punishment it was explained again and again that all these physical attacks were a kindness. The Church persecutes, Augustine said, in the spirit of love. Jerome, the biblical scholar and saint, concurred: it was not cruel to defend God's honor—in the Bible sinners suffer punishments up to and including death.[40] Chrysostom agreed: if he were to punish your earthly body, he reassured his listeners, it was only to protect your eternal one so that "you may be saved, and we may rejoice, and God may be glorified now and always, for ever and ever without end. Amen."[41] Those receiving such salvation might, not unreasonably, have felt otherwise. One monk in Shenoute's care was saved with beatings so savage that he died of his injuries.

And what if people, disinclined to rejoice, became frightened by the fact that their neighbors were spying on them, reporting on them, hounding them in their homes? Well, fear too had its benefits. Better to be scared than to sin. "Where there is terror," said Augustine, "there is salvation . . . Oh, merciful savagery!"[42]

The intellectual foundations for a thousand years of theocratic oppression were being laid.[43]

CHAPTER SIXTEEN

"A Time of Tyranny and Crisis"

Moreover, we forbid the teaching of any doctrine by those who labour under the insanity of paganism.

—Justinian Code, 1.11.10.2

THE PHILOSOPHER DAMASCIUS was a brave man: you had to be to see what he had seen and still be a philosopher. But as he walked through the streets of Athens in AD 529 and heard the new laws bellowed out in the town's crowded squares, even he must have felt the stirrings of unease.[1] He was a man who had known persecution at the hands of the Christians before. He would have been a fool not to recognize the signs that it was beginning again.

As a young man, Damascius had studied philosophy in Alexandria, the city of the murdered Hypatia.[2] He had not been there for long when the city had turned, once again, on its philosophers. The persecution had begun dramatically. A violent attack on a Christian by some non-Christian students had started a chain of reprisals in which philosophers and pagans were targeted. Christian monks, armed with an axe, had raided, searched, then demolished a house accused of being a shrine to "demonic" idols.[3] The violence had spread and Christians had found and collected all images of the old gods from across Alexandria, from the bathhouses and from people's homes. They had placed them on a pyre in the center of the city and burned them. As the Christian chronicler Zachariah of Mytilene comfortably observed, Christ had declared that he had "given you the authority to tread on snakes and scorpions, and over all enemy power."[4]

For Damascius and his fellow philosophers, however, all that had been a mere prelude to what came next. Soon afterwards, an imperial officer had been sent to Alexandria to investigate paganism. The investigation had rapidly turned to persecution. This was when philosophers had been tortured by being hung up by cords and when Damascius's own brother had been beaten with cudgels—and, to Damascius's great pride, had remained silent.[5]

Philosophers weren't only attacked in Alexandria—and they didn't always bear the attacks with such mute suffering. When one philosopher was being beaten in a courtroom in Constantinople, the blood started flowing down his back. The man allowed some of it to pool in his hand. You savage, he said to the judge. "You want to devour the flesh of men? Then have something to wash it down with." He threw a palmful of blood over the official: "Drink this wine!"[6]

Damascius would come out of the Alexandrian persecutions a changed man. He had never originally intended to study philosophy at all; the privileged son of wealthy parents from Damascus, he had hoped to pursue the more glamorous life of a public orator. Mere chance had brought him into the philosophical fold, but once he had converted to the cause he not only devoted his life to philosophy, he also risked his life for it, repeatedly. He would develop a deep contempt for anyone who did anything less, and in his writings poured scorn on those who were adept at talking about what should be done but inept at actually doing anything.[7] Words without deeds were useless. Action, then. When the persecutions in Alexandria became intolerable, Damascius decided to flee. In secret, he hurried with his teacher, Isidore, to the harbor and boarded a boat. Their final destination was Greece, and Athens, the most famous city in the history of Western philosophy.

It was now almost four decades since Damascius had escaped to Athens as an intellectual exile. In that time, a lot had changed. When he had arrived in the city he had been a young man; now he was almost seventy. But he was still as energetic as ever, and as he walked about Athens in his distinctive philosopher's cloak — the same austere cloak that Hypatia had worn — many of the citizens would have recognized him. For this émigré was now not only an established fixture of Athenian philosophy and a prolific author, but also the successful head of one of the city's philosophical schools: the Academy. To say "one of" is to diminish this institution's importance: it was perhaps the most famous school in Athens, indeed in the entire Roman Empire. It traced its history back almost a thousand years and it would leave its linguistic traces on Europe and America for two thousand years to come. Every modern academy, *académie* and *akademie* owes its name to it.[8]

Since he had crossed the wine-dark sea, life had gone well for Damascius — astonishingly well, given the turbulence he had left behind. In Alexandria, Christian torture, murder and destruction had had its effect on the intellectual life of the city. After Hypatia's murder the numbers of philosophers in Alexandria and the quality of what was being taught there had, unsurprisingly, declined rapidly. In the writings of Alexandrian authors there is a clear mood of depression, verging on despair. Many, like Damascius, had left.

In fifth-century Athens, the Church was far less powerful and considerably less aggressive. Its intellectuals had felt pressure nonetheless. Pagan philosophers who flagrantly opposed Christianity paid for their dissent. The city was rife with informers and city officials listened to them. One of Damascius's predecessors had exasperated the authorities so much that he had fled, escaping — narrowly — with his life and his property. Another philosopher so vexed the city's Christians by his unrepentant "pagan" ways that he had had to go into exile for a year to get away from the "vulture-like men" who now watched over Athens. In an act that could hardly have been more symbolic of their intellectual intentions, the Christians had built a basilica in the middle of what had once been a library. The Athens that had been so quarrelsome, so gloriously and unrepentantly argumentative, was being silenced. This was an increasingly tense, strained world. It was, as another author and friend of Damascius put it, "a time of tyranny and crisis."[9]

The very fabric of the city had changed. Its pagan festivals had been stopped, its temples closed and, as in Alexandria, the skyline of the city had been desecrated—here, by the removal of Phidias's great figure of Athena. Even Athens's fine philosophical traditions had been debased—though as much by incompetent philosophers as by anything the Christians did. When Damascius and his teacher arrived in the city at the end of the fifth century, they had been utterly underwhelmed by it. "Nowadays," Isidore observed, "philosophy stands not on a razor's edge but truly on the brink of extreme old age."[10] Damascius had "never heard of philosophy being so despised in Athens" as it was then.[11] It is a mark of quite how uncongenial the empire had become to non-Christians that despite this, Athens had seemed the most congenial place for them to flee to.

Yet Damascius had turned Athenian philosophy around. In the decades since his arrival in the city, he had taken its philosophical schools from decrepitude to international success. Once again, the Academy was attracting what one ancient writer called the "quintessential flower of the philosophers of our age" to come there to study.[12] Its philosophers were hugely prolific—and knowledgeable: Damascius and his fellow scholars were producing works that have been called the most learned documents ever to have been produced by the ancient world.[13] As well as all of this, the inexhaustible Damascius would also find time to deliver densely academic lectures on Aristotle and Plato and produce a series of subtle works on metaphysical philosophy, Plato and mathematics.[14]

Despite his success, Damascius had not forgotten what he had seen in Alexandria—and had not forgiven it, either. His writings show a never-failing contempt for the Christians. He had seen the power of Christian zeal in action. His brother had been tortured by it. His teacher had been exiled by it. And, in the year 529, zealotry was once again in evidence. Christianity had long ago announced that all pagans had been wiped out.[15] Now, finally, reality was to be forced to fall in with the triumphant rhetoric.

The determination that lay behind this threat was not only felt in Athens in this period. It was in AD 529, the very same year in which the atmosphere in Athens began to worsen, that St. Benedict destroyed that shrine to Apollo in Monte Cassino.[16] A few years later, the emperor Justinian decided to destroy the frieze in the beautiful temple of Isis at Philae in Egypt: a Christian general and his troops duly methodically smashed the faces and hands off the demonic images. Go to Philae today, and you can see the frieze—much of it still intact, except that many of the carved figures are missing faces and hands.

In Athens, it wouldn't be temples but something far more intangible—and potentially far more dangerous—that was targeted: philosophy. Previous attacks on Damascius and his scholars had largely been driven by local enthusiasms: a violently aggressive band of Alexandrian monks here, an officious local official there. But this attack was something new. It came not from the enthusiasm of a hostile local power; it came in the form of a law—from the emperor himself. Actually, what befell the philosophers in AD 529 was not just one single law but a staccato burst of legal aggression issued by Justinian. "Your Clemency . . . the Glorious and Indulgent" Justinian is how laws of this period referred to him. Justinian's reverence, the legal code of the time announced, shone out "as a specially pure light, like that of a star," while Justinian himself was referred to as "Your Holiness," the "glorious emperor."[17]

There was little glorious or indulgent about what was coming. And there was certainly nothing that was clement. This was the end. The "impious and wicked pagans" were to be allowed to continue in their "insane error" no longer.[18] Anyone who refused salvation in the next life would, from now on, be all but damned in this one. A series of legal hammer blows fell: Anyone who offered sacrifice would be executed. Anyone who worshipped statues would be executed. Anyone who was baptized—but who then continued to sacrifice—they, too, would be executed.[19]

The laws went further. This was no longer mere prohibition of other religious practices. It was the active enforcement of Christianity on every single, sinful pagan in the empire. The roads to error were being closed, forcefully. Everyone now had to become Christian. Every single person in the empire who had not yet been baptized now had to come forward immediately, go to the holy churches and "entirely abandon the former error [and] receive saving baptism." Those who refused would be stripped of all their property, movable and immovable, lose their civil rights, be left in penury and, "in addition"—as if what had gone before was not punishment but mere preamble—they would be "subject to the proper punishment." If any man did not immediately hurry to the "holy churches" with his family and force them also to be baptized, then he would suffer all of the above—and then he would be exiled. The "insane error" of paganism was to be wiped from the face of the earth.[20]

In such an atmosphere, it took something for a law to stand out as particularly repressive. Yet one law did. Out of all the froth and fury that was being issued from the government at the time, one law would become infamous for the next 1,500 years. Read this law and, in comparison to some of Justinian's other edicts, it sounds almost underwhelming. Filed under the usual dull bureaucratic subheading, it is now known as "Law 1.11.10.2." "Moreover," it reads, "we forbid the teaching of any doctrine by those who labour under the insanity of paganism" so that they might not "corrupt the souls of their disciples."[21] The law goes on, adding a finicky detail or two about pay, but largely that is it.

Its consequences were formidable. This was the law that

forced Damascius and his followers to leave Athens. It was this law that caused the Academy to close. It was this law that led the English scholar Edward Gibbon to declare that the entirety of the barbarian invasions had been less damaging to Athenian philosophy than Christianity was.[22] This law's consequences were described more simply by later historians. It was from this moment, they said, that a Dark Age began to descend upon Europe.

It didn't descend immediately. Like most "turning points" in history this one was in reality more of a tilting. Night didn't suddenly fall; the world did not suddenly go black. At the very most it merely dimmed, in one place, a little. The immediate consequences of the law were less dramatic than the language in which it was written. For a while, Damascius and his fellow philosophers continued to teach and their school continued to function. They almost certainly kept giving lectures; they definitely continued writing books. And it is impossible to imagine that the philosophers would have stopped bickering among themselves about the minutiae of Neoplatonic interpretation.

Little else is known from this period apart from one tantalizing possibility. It seems that we might know precisely which building these men, the last philosophers of the Academy, the last true philosophers of Athens, occupied during their final months and days in the city.[23] In the 1970s, excavations on the Athenian Agora uncovered an enviably elegant house. Today, this Roman-style villa is known by the unprepossessing name of "House C." This does little justice to its beauty. From the outside, admittedly, the house was unassuming enough. Set in a narrow street, just off the main square of the Agora, it presented no more than a featureless and rather dull wall to the outside world. Only this wall's length, an impressive 40-odd meters, and its location, in the shadow of the Acropolis, might have hinted discreetly at something more.

Step through the door in that wall, out of the sunshine of an

Athenian afternoon, into a dim entrance hall, and you would have entered another world. After the noise and the filth of an Athenian street, you would have found yourself in a cool, shaded courtyard with a colonnade running round all sides. The walls and floor were stone, cool to the touch even on the hottest day, and from somewhere just beyond the courtyard came the sound, tantalizing in the heat, of water. More remarkable than all of this, however, was the art.

You can tell a lot from the art that people choose for their house. The twelve statues that have been recovered from House C were not the collection of an ignorant nouveau. It isn't just the quality of their craftsmanship that impresses — though that is extraordinary: the delicate lines on this woman's mouth, the plump pout on that statue of the goddess Nemesis, the realism that was able to show individual hairs on the eyebrows of that emperor . . . What also impresses about these statues is their age. These pieces were antique — ancient — even when the philosophers lived here: in Damascius's day one of them was already over eight hundred years old.[24] One of the most interesting works was a large but delicately carved relief that depicted the gods Hermes, Apollo and Pan, and a cluster of nymphs, all overlooked by a bearded Zeus. This art collection was an eclectic, antiquarian delight that would have impressed visitors in any century. In the early sixth century, when religious artworks in the city outside the walls of House C had been relentlessly smashed, attacked and defaced, it must have been astonishing.

Walk on, past the statues, over the light-dark stripes of the shadows cast by the stone columns, and the sound of water would have grown louder still. In a world in which piped water was an expensive rarity, this was a house that dripped, quite literally, with wealth. Go down some steps and here, beneath generous arches, bright in the Athenian sun, was a large semicircular pool and shrine. It must have been a delightful place to stop on a punishingly hot Athenian afternoon. Like Pliny

the Younger, reveling at the sight of the glass-clear waters at
a shrine to the river god, one could have worshipped not only
divinity but beauty here.

It is entirely plausible that House C was the place where
Damascius and his fellow scholars spent their last years in
Athens. It would have been perfect for them. Everything they
might have needed was here, from lecture rooms to teach
in, to shrines to the old gods to worship at, and a large dining room—decorated with scenes featuring those gods—at
which Damascius could have given the dinners that tradition
required him to hold.

At such meals Damascius must have made for an entertaining, albeit sharp-tongued, companion. It's quite clear from his
writings that he had an excellent eye for anecdote: it is to his
pen that history owes the story of Hypatia and her sanitary
towel.[25] It is also clear that he would not have been willing to
sugar his speech to suit his listener. His accounts of his fellow
philosophers have a warts-and-all feel to them. One scholar,
whose mind most think is perfect, is dismissed by him as being
only of "uneven intelligence."[26] Others receive similar slights.
Still, barbed or not, the company would have been fun and, in
its way, exhilarating. An illicit glamour must have clung to this
cool, otherworldly courtyard and to its philosophers as they
walked about in their defiant philosophers' cloaks, criticizing
each other's theories and arguing about forbidden things.

Without a doubt they would have talked, too, about what
was fast becoming the most important force in their lives:
Christianity. As the modern scholar Alan Cameron has put
it: "In 529 the philosophers of Athens were threatened with
the destruction of their entire way of life."[27] The Christians
were behind this—yet you will search almost in vain for the
word "Christian" in most of the writings of the philosophers.
That is not to say that evidence of them is not there. It is. The
miasmatic presence of the religion is keenly felt on countless
pages: it is Christians who are driving persecutions, torturing

their colleagues, pushing philosophers into exile. Damascius and his fellow scholars loathed the religion and its uncompromising leaders. Even Damascius's famously mild and gentle teacher, Isidore, "found them absolutely repulsive"; he considered them "irreparably polluted, and nothing whatever could constrain him to accept their company."[28]

But the actual word Christian is missing. As if the very syllables were too distasteful for them to pronounce, the philosophers resorted to elaborate circumlocutions. At times, the names they gave them were muted. With a masterful understatement, the present system of Christian rule, with its torture, murder and persecution, was referred to as "the present situation" or "the prevailing circumstances."[29] At another time the Christians became—perhaps a reference to those stolen and desecrated statues—"the people who move the immovable."[30] At other times the names were blunter: the Christians were "the vultures" or, more simply still, "the tyrant."[31]

Other phrases carried a contemptuous intellectual sneer. Greek literature is awash with hideously rebarbative creatures, and the philosophers turned to these to convey the horror of their situation: the Christians started to be referred to as "the Giants" and the "Cyclops." These particular names seem, at first sight, an odd choice. These are not the most repellent monsters in the Greek canon; Homer alone could have offered the maneating monster Scylla as a more obvious insult. That would have missed the point. The Giants and the Cyclops of Greek myth aren't terrible because they are not like men— they are terrible because they are. They belong to the uncanny valley of Greek monsters: they look, at first glance, like civilized humans yet they lack all the attributes of civilization. They are boorish, base, ill-educated, thuggish. They are almost men, but not quite—and all the more hideous for that. It was, for these philosophers, the perfect analogy. When that philosopher had been beaten till the blood ran down his back, the precise insult that he hurled at the judge had been: "There,

Cyclops. Drink the wine, now that you have devoured the human flesh."[32]

If the philosophers loathed the Christians then the Christian authorities, for their part, found themselves profoundly irritated by the philosophers. Some of what they taught expressly and intolerably contradicted Christian doctrine. Any suggestion from philosophers that the world was eternal, for example, could not be countenanced if the doctrine of the Creation was to be believed. Moreover, this was an age in which philosophy and theology frequently blended into one (to Christian eyes) ominous whole.[33] Worse still, what was being studied in the Academy was not pure Plato but the dubious Neoplatonism—much to the horror of later scribes. A tenth-century text that preserves some of Damascius's writings intersperses quotations from them with bursts of Christian revulsion towards this "impious" man,[34] and the "impossible, unbelievable, ill-conceived marvels and folly" that he, in his "godlessness and impiety," believed.[35]

The Christians would not need to put up with such irritations for much longer. In AD 529 the law forbade the philosophers—suffering, as they did, from the "insanity of paganism" —from teaching.[36]

What did the philosophers say to each other as they walked along the cool marble hallways of House C? What would have gone through their minds when they learned that, if they didn't immediately present themselves for baptism then, according to the law, they would be stripped of all their rights and their possessions—including that wonderful villa? What would they have thought when they heard that, if they did accept baptism and later lapsed, and put an offering at the shrine next to their beautiful pool, then, according to the law, their fate should be execution?

What conversations must they have had in the months that followed as the new laws began to take effect and as that flow of brilliant pupils to those marble classrooms had slowly petered out; as the fees had stopped coming in and dented their wealth; and as the bequests they had once relied on had finally dried up?

Like so much else from this period, it is impossible to know. It is thought that one of the philosophers wrote an account of what happened next but if so it has been lost. Some facts, through the thin web of surviving texts, are clear.[37] It is clear that the philosophers didn't leave immediately after the infamous law was announced. They seem, instead, to have lain low—not a mark of the cowardly man, in their philosophy, but the sensible one. Almost two hundred years of aggressive Christianity had taught them the value of this. Philosophers, as one of their number put it, should let "sleeping beasts lie" and "at such times of crisis, be careful to avoid clashes with the authorities and untimely displays of outspokenness."[38]

But the sleeping beasts didn't lie. On the contrary, the Christian "beasts" started to roar with ever-increasing ferocity. Then the confiscations began. The philosophers couldn't earn money; they couldn't work; they couldn't practice their religion, and now they couldn't even hold on to what property they did have. By about 532, it seems that life had become intolerable for them. They decided to leave. Athens, the mother of Western philosophy, was no longer a place for philosophers —or at any rate for philosophers who refused to turn their philosophical tools to suit their Christian masters.

Damascius was now in his late sixties; yet he was not going to give up. He had traveled thousands of miles to get this far. He would now simply have to travel a few thousand more. His sense of duty demanded it. "A desire to do good is not enough," he wrote. "One also needs strength of character and single-mindedness."[39] Still, even by Damascius's standards the journey that he decided on was a bold one. The philosophers had heard that there was a new king in Persia, King Khosrow. He was renowned as a lover of literature and said to be a great student of philosophy. The rumors were beguiling: he had had whole works translated from Greek into Persian for him to read. His mind was filled with the doctrines of Plato—he even, it was whispered, understood the fiendishly difficult *Timaeus*. Persia itself received a similarly excitable billing. This was a land so justly ruled that it suffered from no theft, brigandage or crime. It was, in short, the land of Plato's philosopher king.

The journey would not be easy. Its length alone was daunting. Damascius, however, was not a man to be put off by fear. "Nothing human is worth as much as a clear conscience," he had once written. "A man should [never] give greater importance to anything other than truth—not the danger of an impending struggle, nor a difficult task from which one turns away in fear."[40]

And so it was that one day, probably about three years after Law 1.11.10.2 was issued, these seven men, the last philosophers of the great Academy, set out from Athens. For the second time in his life, Damascius had been made an exile by the Christians. For the second time in his life, he would have had to pack his bags, bundling up his possessions and his books as he had done in Alexandria.[41] He had arrived in Athens as a young man and an exile. Since then, he had achieved so much. He had saved Athenian philosophy and made the Academy the greatest philosophical school in the empire. And he had done all this while tiptoeing round the "sleeping beasts" of the Christians.

It hadn't been enough. Damascius was, once again, creeping out of a city like a criminal. More than that. Not like a criminal: as a criminal. And one who, as the hysterical language of the laws put it, was insane, wicked and iniquitous. Their beautiful house was prepared for desertion. In 532, the philosophers finally left Athens. The Academy closed. True—free—Athenian philosophy was over.

The trip was not a success. Far from being a society of such perfect justice that there was no crime, they discovered a land where the poor were treated with even more brutality and inhumanity than at home. They were dismayed to discover that Persian men took multiple wives—and even more dismayed to learn that they still committed adultery, a state of affairs that seemed to bother them less for the infidelity than for the incompetence. Almost more upsetting than the treatment of the living was the Persians' treatment of the dead: according to ancient Zoroastrian custom, corpses were not immediately buried but left above the ground to be eaten by dogs. In Greek culture this was profoundly shameful: *The Iliad* opens by describing how the war had "hurled down to Hades many mighty souls of heroes, making their bodies the prey to dogs and the birds' feasting."[42] In Homer, it is the epitome of humiliation. In Persia, it was normal practice.

The philosophers were also disappointed in their host, King Khosrow. They had hoped for a philosopher king, but found instead "a fool." Far from being well read, Khosrow's famed "great learning" amounted to no more than an interest in "a smattering of literature."[43] Far from being an acute Platonic intellect this man, it was said, was the sort of intellectual lightweight who could be taken in by charlatans. A favorite at Khosrow's court was a drunken Greek who mainly spent his days eating, drinking and then impressing people by saying the odd clever thing. An intelligence of sorts, but not the kind to impress the austere philosophers of Athens.

Damascius and his philosophers were bitterly downcast. Khosrow, who along with his lack of perspicacity in philosophical matters seems to have had a certain blithe unawareness in social ones, doesn't seem to have noticed their disgust and, regarding them with affection, even invited them to stay on longer. They declined. Reproaching themselves for ever having come, they decided to return home as soon as they possibly could. According to one historian, their somewhat melodramatic feeling was that "merely to set foot on Roman territory, even if it meant instant death, was preferable to a life of distinction in Persia."[44]

It seems that the philosophers underestimated their host, however. For while they might prefer instant death to remaining in Persia, Khosrow had gone out of his way to protect them. At the time when they were leaving court, the king had fortuitously been concluding a peace treaty with Emperor Justinian. Khosrow now used his military sway with Justinian to extort safe passage home for the philosophers. The precise wording of this clause has been lost but its essence has been preserved: the treaty demanded that "the philosophers should be allowed to return to their homes and to live out their lives in peace without being compelled to alter their traditional religious beliefs or to accept any view which did not coincide with them."[45] This clause was the only declaration of ideological toleration that Justinian would ever sign. It was, in some ways, a liberal landmark — and a sign of how illiberal the empire had become that it was needed at all.

The philosophers, homeless yet again, set out for a final time together. Their journey must have been a miserable one. What happened to them next is not certain. Some scattered facts remain. The philosophers do indeed seem to have returned to the Roman Empire, but not to Athens. It is certain that they didn't give up philosophy. Scraps of their writings drift back to us: an epigram that is almost certainly by Damascius; a treatise from another philosopher, entitled "Solutions to those points that Khosrow, King of the Persians, was considering."[46] They had been exiled, outlawed and impoverished but they had still not relinquished philosophy.

And then, slowly, with a whisper rather than a shout, the philosophers are gone. Their writings peter out. The men, scattered across the empire, die.

The philosophy they had lived for starts to die itself. Some strands of ancient philosophy live on, preserved by the hands of some Christian philosophers — but it is not the same. Works that have to agree with the pre-ordained doctrines of a church are theology, not philosophy. Free philosophy has gone. The great destruction of classical texts gathers pace. The writings of the Greeks "have all perished and are obliterated": that was what John Chrysostom had said. He hadn't been quite right, then; but time would bring greater truth to his boast. Undefended by pagan philosophers or institutions, and disliked by many of the monks who were copying them out, these texts start to disappear. Monasteries start to erase the works of Aristotle, Cicero, Seneca and Archimedes. "Heretical"—and brilliant—ideas crumble into dust. Pliny is scraped from the page. Cicero and Seneca are overwritten. Archimedes is covered over. Every single work of Democritus and his heretical "atomism" vanishes. Ninety percent of all classical literature fades away.

Centuries later, an Arab traveler would visit a town on the edge of Europe and reflect on what had happened in the Roman Empire. "During the early days of the empire of the Rum," he wrote—meaning the Roman and Byzantine Empire—"the sciences were honoured and enjoyed universal respect. From an already solid and grandiose foundation, they were raised to greater heights every day, until the Christian religion made its appearance among the Rum; this was a fatal blow to the edifice of learning; its traces disappeared and its pathways were effaced."[47]

There was one final loss, too. This loss is even more rarely remembered than all the others, but in its way it is almost as important. The very memory that there was any opposition at all to Christianity faded. The idea that philosophers might have fought fiercely, with all they had, against Christianity was—is—passed over. The memory that many were alarmed at the spread of this violently intolerant religion fades from view. The idea that many were not delighted but instead disgusted by the sight of burning and demolished temples was—is—brushed aside. The idea that intellectuals were appalled—and scared—by the sight of books burning on pyres is forgotten.

Christianity told the generations that followed that their victory over the old world was celebrated by all, and the generations that followed believed it.

The pages of history go silent. But the stones of Athens provide a small coda to the story of the seven philosophers. It is clear, from the archaeological evidence, that the grand villa on the slopes of the Acropolis was confiscated not long after the philosophers left. It is also clear that it was given to a new Christian owner.

Whoever this Christian was, they had little time for the ancient art that filled the house. The beautiful pool was turned into a baptistery. The statues above it were evidently considered intolerable: the finely wrought images of Zeus, Apollo and Pan were hacked away. Mutilated stumps are now all that remain of the faces of the gods, ugly and incongruous above the still-delicate bodies. The statues were tossed into the well. The mosaic on the floor of the dining room fared little better. Its great central panel, which had contained another pagan scene, was roughly removed. A crude cross pattern, of vastly inferior workmanship, was laid in its place.

The lovely statue of Athena, the goddess of wisdom, suffered as badly as the statue of Athena in Palmyra had. Not only was she beheaded, she was then, a final humiliation, placed face-down in the corner of a courtyard to be used as a step. Over the coming years, her back would be worn away as the goddess of wisdom was ground down by generations of Christian feet.[48]

The "triumph" of Christianity was complete.

Acknowledgments

There are so many people to thank. My agent, Patrick, for being tremendous. My publisher, George Morley, for not only being a brilliant editor but also making me laugh.

I owe a deep debt of gratitude to all the academics who have answered my questions, broadened my horizons and gently pointed out mistakes. Particular thanks go to Tim Whitmarsh, a man for whom the phrase "boyish enthusiasm" might have been invented. Also to David Brakke, who is not only a world expert on demons and their devious ways, but a very close reader. Dirk Rohmann was infinitely helpful and kind: he not only wrote the book on the Christian destruction of books, he also read sections of my own book with care and patience. Huge thanks too to John Pollini, who has written so lucidly on the Christian destruction of the ancient world — and the academic reluctance to address it.

So many others have helped. I am grateful for James Corke-Webster for his compendious knowledge of martyrs (and excellent writings on them); to Matthew Nicholls, who knows the streets of ancient Rome like the back of his hand, and has created a virtual model of it to prove it. Many thanks to Glen Bowersock for his comments on Hypatia — and for telling me one of the most amusing anecdotes about mathematicians that I have ever heard. Eberhard Sauer was enormously helpful on the destruction of statues. Very great thanks go to Stephen Emmel not just for his brilliant writings on Shenoute but for proofreading my own writing on him with an eagle eye. Many

thanks too to Gill Evans at Cambridge, who was very illuminating on the history of Oxford and Cambridge. Thanks are
also due to Edward Watts not only for being a lucidly readable
academic but also a close and helpful reader. There are many
more to thank, particularly Rebecca Flemming, Elise Friedland,
Hal Drake, Troels Myrup Kristensen and Phil Booth. Your help
has been more generous and more helpful than I can say. Any
mistakes are my own.

Beyond academia I am grateful to the Jerwood Foundation
and the Royal Society of Literature, whose generous Jerwood
Award enabled me to find the time to actually write this book.
I am more grateful than I can say to my family, and to my
friends. To Erica and to Tom Gatti, for inspiring me to get on
with it; to Zarah, for enabling me to actually get on with it.
To Mima and Anne, for being unfailingly excellent. To Anne
and Dave, for helping me more than I can say. To Dana, for the
same. To my parents who, despite their past, were never dogmatic. To my mother in particular, who always answered my
questions. To my father, who is always optimistic and never
doubts. To Peter, who is endlessly enthusiastic. To F. and to W.

And finally, thank you to Tom. For deciphering my handwriting, as they say, and everything else besides.

Notes

LIST OF ABBREVIATIONS

ACM The Acts of the Christian Martyrs

AGT John Chrysostom, *Against the Games and Theatres*

Anth. Pal. Palladas, *Anthologia Palatina*

AP Apophthegmata Patrum, *The Sayings of the Desert Fathers: The Alphabetical Collection*

C. Just. Codex Justinianus

C. Th. Codex Theodosianus

CC Origen, *Contra Celsum*

EH Sozomen, *The Ecclesiastical History*

HC Eusebius, *The History of the Church from Christ to Constantine*

LC Eusebius, *Life of Constantine*

OAP Galen, *On Anatomical Procedures*

ONT Lucretius, *On the Nature of Things*

PH Damascius, *Philosophical History*

PROLOGUE: A BEGINNING

1. Coptic pilgrims' chant, quoted in Kristensen (2013), 85.

INTRODUCTION: AN ENDING

1. Athanassiadi (1993), 4; Marinus, *Life of Proclus*, 26.
2. *PH*, 124.
3. *PH*, 117C; Olympiodorus, *Commentary on the First Alcibiades*, quoted in Cameron (1969), 15.
4. *C. Th.*, 16.4.4.2, dated 16 June 388.
5. *AGT*.
6. *PH*, 119.
7. *PH*, 42.

8. Palladas, 10.90 and 10.82.

9. The precise criteria for a triumph varied; the stipulation of thousands dead was, for a time, one of them. Deciding when a triumph had been won was usually more an art than a science. See Beard (2007).

10. Greenblatt (2012), 43–44.

11. For paganism as insanity, sickness, etc., see C. Th., 16.10.1–21 and C. Just., 1.11.10.

12. Augustine, Sermon 24.6, quoted in MacMullen (1984), 95.

13. *AGT.*

14. Augustine, Sermon 279.4, quoted in Shaw (2011), 682.

15. Eusebius, *The History of the Church from Christ to Constantine*, 10.9.7.

16. Johnson, 15 April 1778, quoted in MacMullen (1997), 169 n. 37, to whom this paragraph is indebted.

I. THE INVISIBLE ARMY

1. Chitty (1966) calls it a pigsty, though this may not be strictly accurate: the Greek refers to him moving "just outside his house"—presumably to some sort of simple structure there. Nonetheless, the idea of a pigsty confers well the idea of simplicity—even squalor—that would no doubt have been appropriate.

2. Clement, *The Instructor*, 3.5.

3. Matthew 19:21.

4. Augustine, *Confessions*, 8.7–8.

5. *Life of Antony*, 5.

6. *Life of Antony*, 5–6.

7. *Life of Antony*, 24.

8. Cyprian, Bishop of Carthage, *On the Mortality*, 14.

9. Dodds (1965), 133–34.

10. Palladas, *Palatine Anthology*, 10.72, quoted in Dodds (1965), 11.

2. THE BATTLEGROUND OF DEMONS

1. Augustine, *Confessions*, 8.7.

2. Mark 5:9.

3. Augustine, *City of God*, 4.27.

4. Origen, *Homilies on Joshua*, 15.5.

5. Tertullian, *Apology*, 22.8.

6. Tertullian, *Apology*, 22.4.

7. Evagrius, *Praktikos*, 12; Evagrius, *Eight Spirits*, 13–14, quoted in Brakke (2006), 65–66.

8. Evagrius, *Talking Back*, 1.22.

9. Evagrius, *Talking Back*: naked women, 2.15; monks, 2.24; fire, 2.63, 2.23; walk, 2.25.

10. John Moschos, *The Spiritual Meadow*, 160.

11. Evagrius, *Talking Back*, 4.25.

12. Tertullian, *Apology*, 22.4.

13. Augustine, *Exposition on Psalm 94*.

14. Tertullian, *Apology*, 22.6.

15. Tertullian, *Apology*, 22.10.

16. Augustine, Letter 46 from Publicola.

17. Augustine, Letter 47.

18. Tertullian, *Apology*, 27.3.

19. Minucius Felix, *The "Octavius,"* XXVII.

20. For a discussion of the difficulty of assessing the Christianization of individuals as opposed to that of their clergy, see Rebillard (2012), especially Chapter 3, "Being Christian in the Age of Augustine."

21. Augustine, Homily 34 on John 8:12, quoted in MacMullen (1997), 121, to whom this paragraph is indebted.

22. For a discussion of the coin and the vision, see Drake (2014), 71.

23. Encyclical of Pope Leo XIII, *On the Nature of Human Liberty*, 6.

24. Augustine, ed. Dolbeau (1996), 266.

25. Deuteronomy 12:3.

3. WISDOM IS FOOLISHNESS

1. *OAP*, VIII.8.

2. Galen, *On Diagnosing and Curing the Affections and Errors of the Soul*, 3.5.70K, quoted in Mattern (2013), 64.

3. These observations and indeed this paragraph are indebted to Gross (1998), passim.

4. *OAP*, VIII.4; *OAP*, VIII.5; and *OAP*, VIII.4.

5. *OAP*, VII.16.

6. Galen, *De Pulsuum Differentiis*, iii, 3, quoted in Walzer (1949), 14.

7. Galen, *De Pulsuum Differentiis*, ii, 4, quoted in Walzer (1949), 14.

8. Galen, *On Hippocrates' Anatomy*, quoted in Walzer (1949), 11.

9. *CC*, I.32.

10. *CC*, VI.60; *CC*, V.14.

11. Gibbon, *Decline and Fall*, Vol. IV, Chapter 38, 163.

12. Gibbon, *Decline and Fall*, Vol. II, Chapter 15, 38.

13. Gibbon (1796), 97.

14. C. Th., 16.4.1, 386.

15. Gibbon, *Decline and Fall*, Vol. II, Chapter 15, 39.

16. *CC*, I.39.

17. *CC*, VI.32.

18. CC, VI.49.
19. CC, V.14.
20. CC, VI.37.
21. CC, VII.18.
22. CC, IV.7.
23. CC, VI.78.
24. CC, IV.3.
25. CC, II.70.
26. CC, II.55.
27. CC, II.60.
28. CC, II.16.
29. CC, III.62–64.
30. CC, VI.60–61.
31. ONT, 1.419–21.
32. Minucius Felix, The "Octavius," V.
33. ONT, 5.855–77.
34. Minucius Felix, The "Octavius," V.
35. ONT, 1.150.
36. Plutarch, On Superstition, 2.
37. ONT, 1.151–54.
38. ONT, 1.146.
39. John Chrysostom, Homily 7 on First Corinthians, 9. For this and other points, see the excellent and original book by Dirk Rohmann, Christianity, Book-Burning and Censorship in Late Antiquity, to which this paragraph and the following are much indebted. It is striking—and an indication of where academic sympathies have lain in recent decades—that Rohmann's book is the first to deal in depth with this topic.
40. Rovelli (2016), 19.
41. This paragraph is indebted to Greenblatt (2012), 11–14. His wonderful book The Swerve: How the Renaissance Began tells this story beautifully.
42. CC, III.44.
43. CC, III.55.
44. CC, I.9.
45. Origen, Homilies on Genesis, 9.2.
46. Augustine, Sermon 198, quoted in Brown (1967), 458.
47. Ovid, Metamorphoses, 1.1–362.
48. Genesis 1:1–6:7.
49. CC, IV.41.
50. Buckland (1820), 24.
51. CC, I.50.
52. CC, II.58.
53. Lucian, Passing of Peregrinus, 33.
54. Lucian, Passing of Peregrinus, 37.

55. Lucian, *Passing of Peregrinus*, 33.

56. Lucian, *Passing of Peregrinus*, 34.

57. Lucian, *Passing of Peregrinus*, 1.

58. Lucian, *Passing of Peregrinus*, 41.

59. Lucian, *Passing of Peregrinus*, 40.

60. Suda, under Loukianos, quoted in Whitmarsh (2015), 221.

61. Quoted in Whitmarsh (2015), 221, to whom this paragraph is indebted.

62. *CC*, II.32.

63. *CC*, I.68.

64. Observation indebted to Wilken (1984), 98–99.

65. Justin Martyr, *Apology*, 1.26.

66. Justin Martyr, *Apology*, 1.26.

67. Lucian, *Demonax*, 27.

68. Cicero, *On the Nature of the Gods*, 2.7.

69. Pliny, *Natural History*, 2.14.

70. Pliny, *Natural History*, 2.18, *"deus est mortali iuvare mortalem"*; lovely translation from Whitmarsh (2015), 220. For an excellent discussion of ancient atheism, see Whitmarsh's *Battling the Gods*.

71. Suetonius, *The Twelve Caesars, Vespasian*, 23.

72. *ACM*, 3; see Wilken (1984), 62ff., for a discussion.

73. Livy, *The Early History of Rome*, 5.16.11, quoted in Frend (1965), 105.

74. Cicero, *On the Nature of the Gods*, 2.7.

75. Minucius Felix, *The "Octavius,"* VIII.

76. *CC*, V.34.

77. *CC*, IV.70.

78. *CC*, V.34.

79. *CC*, V.34.

80. Garnsey (1984), 17.

81. Augustine, Letter 104.2.7.

82. Porphyry quoted in Augustine, Letter 102.30.

83. Eusebius, *Preparation for the Gospel*, 1.3.1, quoted in Wilken (1984), 161.

84. Porphyry in Augustine, Letter 102.8.

85. *Another Epistle of Constantine*, in Socrates, *Ecclesiastical History*, 1.9.

86. Celsus, *On the True Doctrine*, tr. Hoffmann, 29.

87. Augustine, Letter 93.1.2.

88. Augustine, Letter 93.II.4.

89. *CC*, V.34.

4. "ON THE SMALL NUMBER OF MARTYRS"

1. *HC*, 2.25.

2. Suetonius, *The Twelve Caesars, Nero*, 6.1.

3. Suetonius, *The Twelve Caesars, Nero*, 28.2.

4. Suetonius, *The Twelve Caesars, Nero*, 29.

5. Pliny, *Natural History*, 36.108 (possibly exaggerating).

6. Juvenal, Satire 3, 193–96.

7. Juvenal, Satire 3, 200–202.

8. Suetonius, *The Twelve Caesars, Nero*, 38.

9. Suetonius, *The Twelve Caesars, Nero*, 31.2.

10. Tacitus, *Annals*, 15.44.

11. Suetonius, *The Twelve Caesars, Claudius*, 25.4. See Frend (1965) for the possibility that this "Chrestus" wasn't Christ but someone else with a similar name.

12. Tacitus, *Annals*, 15.44.

13. Tacitus, *Annals*, 15.44.

14. Tacitus, *Annals*, 15.44.

15. *The Golden Legend*, Vol. III, *The Life of St. Alban and Amphiabel*.

16. *HC*, 8.9.

17. Tertullian, *Apology*, 50.

18. Basil, Letter 164.1.

19. This observation is indebted to Lane Fox (1988), 419.

20. From "First of Martyrs, Thou Whose Name" and "The Son of God Goes Forth to War." Often these hymns were, directly or indirectly, translating Latin versions that went back centuries.

21. Sienkiewicz (1895), Epilogue.

22. *Quo Vadis*, MGM (1951).

23. Hopkins, "Christian Number and Its Implications," no. 4.

24. Origen, *Exhortation* 16, in Corke-Webster (2013). I am indebted to James Corke-Webster for drawing my attention to this.

25. Gregory Nazianzen, *First Invective Against Julian*, Oration 4.58.

26. "The Martyrdom of Saints Marian and James," in *ACM*, 14.8.

27. Prudentius, *Crowns of Martyrdom*, V.111–16; see the very interesting discussion in Corke-Webster (2012).

28. Acts of Paul, II.18, in Anon., *The Apocryphal New Testament*, 24.

29. Prudentius, *Crowns of Martyrdom*, X.710ff.

30. *CC*, III.8.

31. Dodwell (1684).

32. Gibbon, *Decline and Fall*, Vol. II, Chapter 16, 138.

33. De Ste. Croix (2006), 42.

5. THESE DERANGED MEN

1. This paragraph is indebted to Wilken (1984), who spotted the drama of this moment.

2. Pliny the Younger, Letter 10.17a and b.

3. "My dear": Pliny the Younger, Letter 10.20; illness: Letter 10.18; special mission: Letter 10.18.

4. Pliny the Younger, Letter 10.42.

5. Pliny the Younger, Letter 10.32.

6. Prudentius, *Crowns of Martyrdom*, 3.90; Justin Martyr, *Apology* 1.5.

7. See "The Martyrdom of Polycarp," in *ACM*, 1.17; *HC*, 5.1; "Letter of the Churches of Lyons and Vienne," in *ACM*, 5.7; "Acts of Carpus, Papylus and Agathonice," in *ACM*, 2.4; see also Martyrs of Lyons, in *HC*, 5.1.

8. Pliny the Younger, Letter 10.98.

9. Justinian, *Digest*, 1.18.13.

10. *HC*, 5.1.

11. Pliny the Younger, Letter 8.8.

12. Tertullian, *The Address of Q. Sept. Tertullian to Scapula Tertullus*.

13. Tertullian, *The Address of Q. Sept. Tertullian to Scapula Tertullus*.

14. *Life of Antony*, 46–47.

15. Pseudo Jerome, *Indiculus de Haeresibus*, 33, quoted in Drake (2011), 182.

16. Augustine, Letter 88.8.

17. Augustine, *Liber de Haeresibus*, 69.3, in Shaw (2014), 183–84.

18. Ambrose, *Letters to His Sister*, 60.

19. Augustine, Letter 185.12.

20. Filastrius, quoted in Shaw (2014), 181–83; "orgiastic" behavior: Augustine, *Letter to Catholics of the Donatist Sect*, 19.50; Augustine, *Against the Letter of Parmenianus*, 2.9.19, both mentioned in Shaw (2011), 660ff.

21. Cyprian, *On the Unity of the Church*, 1.20.

22. Prudentius, *Crowns of Martyrdom*, VI.36.

23. "The Martyrdom of Saint Irenaeus Bishop of Sirmium," in *ACM*, 23.2ff.

24. Prudentius, *Crowns of Martyrdom*, III.104ff.

25. "The Martyrdom of Saint Conon," in *ACM*, 13.4.

26. "The Martyrdom of Justin and Companions," Recension C, in *ACM*, 4.1–4.

27. S. Coluthus, 90–92, in Reymond and Barns, *Four Martyrdoms from the Pierpont Morgan Coptic Codices* (1973), 148–49.

28. "The Martyrdom of Julius the Veteran," in *ACM*, 19.2.

29. Prudentius, *Crowns of Martyrdom*, III.122–25.

30. "The Martyrdom of Saint Conon," in *ACM*, 13.4.

31. "The Martyrdom of Julius the Veteran," in *ACM*, 19.2.

32. Frend (1965), 413.

33. S. Coluthus, 90–92, in Reymond and Barns, *Four Martyrdoms from the Pierpont Morgan Coptic Codices* (1973), 148–49.

34. "The Martyrdom of Saint Conon," in *ACM*, 13.5.2.

35. "The Martyrdom of Julius the Veteran," in *ACM*, 19.2.

36. Pliny the Younger, Letter 10.96.

37. "The Martyrdom of Saint Conon," in *ACM*, 13.4.

38. "The Martyrdom of Julius the Veteran," in *ACM*, 19.2.

39. Marcus Aurelius, *Meditations*, 11.3.

40. Lucian, *The Passing of Peregrinus*, 13.

41. See Wilken (1984), 23, to whom these paragraphs are much indebted.

42. *HC*, 5.1.20.

43. Pliny the Younger, Letter 10.97.

44. De Ste. Croix (1963), 6–7; Lane Fox (1988), 423ff.

45. The status or even existence of these is contested. Watts (2015), 46ff., provides a very interesting discussion of them.

46. *LC*, 2.45.

47. C. Th., 16.10.6, dated to 20 February 356.

48. C. Th., 16.10.22, dated to 9 April 423; see also the discussion in Geffcken (1978), 224.

6. THE MOST MAGNIFICENT BUILDING IN THE WORLD

1. Ammianus Marcellinus, *The Later Roman Empire*, 22.16.12.

2. Anon., *Expositio Totius Mundi et Gentium*, ed. Rougé, 34, quoted in Hahn (2008), 335.

3. Ammianus Marcellinus, *The Later Roman Empire*, 16.12.

4. Russell (2007), 69.

5. Rufinus, *Church History*, 11.23.

6. Rufinus, *Church History*, 11.23.

7. Eunapius, *Lives of the Philosophers*, 472.

8. Eunapius, *Lives of the Philosophers*, 472.

9. Canfora (1990), 192.

10. Gibbon, *Decline and Fall*, Vol. IV, Chapter 28, 201.

11. Palladas, *The Greek Anthology*, 9.501.

7. TO DESPISE THE TEMPLES

1. This is the version from Eusebius's *Life of Constantine* that, he says, Constantine told him with his own mouth. It was, Eusebius noted, an account that "might have been hard to believe had it been related by any other person" (*LC*, 1.26ff.). Historians have later found it hard to believe anyway. The other account in Lactantius (*On the Deaths of the Persecutors*, 44.3ff.) is slightly different: in this, Constantine was told in a dream to mark the heavenly sign of God on the shields of his army, which he did, in the form of the chi-rho sign: as Lactantius put it, "he marked Christ on the shields."

2. Edict of Milan, AD 313, from Lactantius, *On the Deaths of the Persecutors*, 48.2–12, quoted in Stevenson (1987), 284–85.

3. *HC*, 10.9.7.

4. *HC*, 10.9.6.

5. Zosimus, *The History*, Book 2, 51.

6. Eusebius, *Oration in Praise of Constantine*, 5.6.

7. *HC*, 10.6.3.

8. Egeria, a Spanish pilgrim, quoted in the excellent Brown, *Authority and the Sacred* (1997), 38, to whom this paragraph is indebted.

9. *LC*, 2.56; *EH*, 2.5; *LC*, 3.53.2.

10. *EH*, II.5.

11. Deuteronomy 12:2–3, discussed in Watts (2015), 46–47.

12. *LC*, 3.54.6.

13. *EH*, II.5.

14. *LC*, 3.54–57.

15. *LC*, 3.54.

16. *EH*, II.5.

17. Julian quoted in Frend (1965), 160.

18. *EH*, II.5.

19. See the excellent "Lambs into Lions: Explaining Early Christian Intolerance," by H. A. Drake (1996), for a fascinating discussion on this point.

20. Firmicus Maternus, *The Error of the Pagan Religions*, 29.1–3.

21. Marinus, *Life of Proclus*, 30.

22. Palladas, *The Greek Anthology*, 9.528.

23. This version of the Seven Sleepers is taken from Jacobus de Voragine, *The Golden Legend*.

24. *Decline and Fall*, Vol. II, Chapter 15, 55.

25. Grindle (1892), 16.

26. Dodds (1965), 132–33; Geffcken (1978), 25–34.

27. Lacarrière (1963), 87.

28. Geffcken (1978), vii.

29. De Hamel (2016), 19.

30. Stevenson (1987); see Chapter 24, entitled "Constantine and the End of Persecution, 310–313," 282ff.

31. For the numbers, see Stark (1996), Kaegi (1968) and Hopkins (1998).

32. Evans (2010), 270–71.

33. Wilken (1984), xv.

34. Although shades of paganism survive even now. When the academic John Pollini was excavating in Turkey in the 1970s at the Greco-Roman site of Aphrodisias, he climbed Baba Dagh (Father Mountain), the highest mountain in that part of Turkey. Near the summit, his Turkish guide and he met some shepherds, who, Pollini recalled, "were bringing sheep to sacrifice not to Allah but to the local god of the mountain, the genius loci." In the ancient manner, they also tied fillets around sticks planted in a pile of rocks. Shadows survived; the religious system itself had gone.

8. HOW TO DESTROY A DEMON

1. Pollini (2007), 212ff.
2. Trombley (2008), 152; Kaltsas (2002), 510.
3. It is Troels Myrup Kristensen's brilliant *Making and Breaking the Gods: Christian Responses to Pagan Sculpture in Late Antiquity* (2013).
4. *HC*, 10.4.16.
5. Firmicus Maternus, *The Error of the Pagan Religions*, 28.1–29.1.
6. Exodus 20:4–5; see also Deuteronomy 12:2–3.
7. *HC*, 10.5.1–14; see discussion in Garnsey (1984).
8. *LC*, 2.44–45; see excellent discussion in Watts (2015), 46–47, about these laws.
9. On sacrifices: C. Th., 16.10.7 and 11; death penalty: C. Th., 16.10.6.
10. Madmen: C. Th., 10.6.7; completely eradicated: C. Th., 16.10.3; sin: C. Th., 16.10.4; avenging sword: C. Th., 16.10.4.
11. *EH*, V.15.
12. Libanius, *Oration* 30.8–9.
13. Libanius, *Oration* 30.44–45.
14. Libanius, *Oration* 30.43.
15. Libanius, *Oration* 30.8.
16. Libanius, *Oration* 30.8.
17. C. Th., 16.10.11–12.
18. C. Th., 16.10.16, dated to 399.
19. *Constitutiones Sirmondianae*, 12, tr. Pharr, quoted in Fowden (1978), 56; see Beard et al., eds. (1998), 375, for the difficulty of knowing why laws were repeated.
20. Theodoret, *Ecclesiastical History*, V.21.
21. Observation indebted to Hahn (2008), passim.
22. Sulpicius Severus, *Life of St. Martin*, 14.1–7.
23. *Life and Times of Saint Benedict of Nursia*, quoted in Kristensen (2013), 86–87, to whom this chapter is indebted.
24. Eyes: Brown (2008), 318; performance: *On the Priesthood*, quoted in Brown (2008), 307, to whom this observation is indebted.
25. Theodoret, *Ecclesiastical History*, V.29.
26. Augustine, Letter 47, ed. Schaff.
27. Augustine, Sermon 24.6, quoted in MacMullen (1984), 95, to whom this paragraph is indebted.
28. Augustine, Sermon 24.5, quoted in Shaw (2011), 230–1, to whom this paragraph also is indebted.
29. Zachariah of Mytilene, *The Life of Severus*, 33.
30. Jacob of Serugh and Eusebius, *Triennial Oration*, quoted in Stewart (1999), 177–79.
31. In Kristensen (2013), 85.

32. *Avodah Zarah* 4:5, tr. Elmslie, quoted in Trombley (2008), 156–57.

33. Theodoret, *Treatment of Greek Diseases*, 3.79, tr. Gazda (1981), quoted in Kristensen (2013), 224.

34. C. Th., XV.1.36, dated 1 November 397.

35. Chuvin (1990), 79.

36. Jacob of Serugh in Stewart (1999), 177, to whom these paragraphs are indebted.

37. Theodoret, *Ecclesiastical History*, V.21.

38. Augustine, *Expositions on the Psalms*, 98.2 and 98.14, quoted in Shaw (2011), 234.

39. Elvira Canon 60; see Stewart (1999), 173; Gaddis (2005), 176, for discussion.

40. Mark the Deacon, *The Life of Porphyry*, 61.

41. *Acts of John*, 37–43, in Anon., *The Apocryphal New Testament*.

42. Theodoret, *Ecclesiastical History*, V.21.

43. Theodoret, *Ecclesiastical History*, V.21.

44. Sulpicius Severus, *Life of St. Martin*, XIV.1–2.

45. Attwater (1965), 233–34.

46. Pollini (2007), 212–13.

47. Brown, *Authority and the Sacred* (1997), 49.

48. Mark the Deacon, *Life of Porphyry*, 61–62.

49. Theodoret, *Ecclesiastical History*, V.21.

50. Libanius, *Oration* 30.28–29.

51. On the vexed question of whether this was true religious tolerance, see Garnsey (1984).

52. Themistius, *Speech* 5.68b–c.

53. Augustine, *City of God*, 18.54.

54. Sulpicius Severus, *Life of St. Martin*, 14–15.

55. For a full discussion on the stone, the probable composition of the cross that is likely to have stood on this, and the question of whether or not there was a statue of Artemis there beforehand, see Kristensen (2013), 9–13.

56. Libanius, *Oration* 18.23.

57. Figures from Kaegi (1968), 249.

58. Isidore of Pelusium, Ep 1.270 PG LXXVIII.344A, quoted by Brown in Cameron and Garnsey, eds. (1997), 634.

59. Symmachus, *Memorandum* 3.8–10, in Lee (2000), 115ff.; see Cameron (2011), 37, on Symmachus's moderation as a "pagan."

60. Deuteronomy 12:2–3; see also Pollini (2008), 186, and Shaw (2011), 229, for the fact that to do so was thus not wrong but part of a "beneficent process."

61. MacMullen (1997), 14.

62. Cyril of Jerusalem, *Mystagogic Catecheses* 1.4–8, quoted in Tsafrir (2008), 122.

63. C. Th., 16.10.19.2.

64. Symmachus, *Memorandum* 3.10.

9. THE RECKLESS ONES

1. This translation assumes that the correct spelling was *"parabolani"* and that it subsequently became changed to *"parabalani"* as the years went on.
2. Procopius, *History of the Wars*, II.xxii.
3. On taking risks to do good deeds: Bowersock (2010), passim.
4. Bowersock (2010), passim; on lack of education: Dzielska (1995), 96.
5. Number: Dzielska (1995), 96.
6. See Brown (1992), 103, to which this paragraph and the next are indebted; Ignatius of Antioch, to Polycarp, 6, quoted in Hopkins (1998), 9; see Ammianus Marcellinus, *The Later Roman Empire*, 27.3.12 for the description of the "alarming" violence: "adherents of both did not stop short of wounds and death"; for the admission, see Ambrose, *Epistles*, 40.6.
7. Bowersock (2010), passim; C. Th., 16.2.42 (29 September 416).
8. In March, according to Socrates, *Ecclesiastical History*, VII.15.
9. Synesius, *Dion*, 9, quoted in Dzielska (1995), 48, to whom this section on Hypatia is indebted; painting is by Charles William Mitchell (1885); quotations from Kingsley (1894), 12.
10. Beauty and virginity: *PH*, 43; cloak and virginity: Dzielska (1995), 103; quotation from *PH*, 43A–C.
11. In Canfora (1990), 20.
12. Range: Epiphanius, *De Mensuris et Ponderibus*; translation: Byzantine treatise quoted in Canfora (1990), 24.
13. This paragraph is indebted to Ward's wonderful essay in MacLeod, ed. (2005), 170–71.
14. Food and living: MacLeod, ed. (2005), 4; zoo: MacLeod, ed. (2005), 42; Timon, quoted in MacLeod, ed. (2005), 62.
15. Vitruvius, *The Architecture of Marcus Vitruvius Pollio*, Book IX.9–11.
16. The precise number is thanks to a fourth-century register of the city's five districts — see Hahn (2008), 336–37.
17. Rufin (Rufinus of Aquileia), HE 11.29; Hahn (2008), 356, for this as an act of Christianization.
18. Dzielska (1995), 82–83.
19. Socrates, *Ecclesiastical History*, VII.15.
20. Visits: *PH*, 43; friendship of Orestes: Socrates, *Ecclesiastical History*, VII.15.
21. Luminous: Synesius, *Dion*, 9, in Dzielska (1995), 48.
22. *PH*, 43.
23. *Letter of Aristeas*, 9–33.
24. John Chrysostom, *Discourses Against Judaizing Christians*, 1.3.1.
25. Nazis: Laqueur (2006), 48; speech: John Chrysostom, *Discourses Against Judaizing Christians*, 1.3.1; presence of *parabalani*: Dzielska (1995), 96; the conclusion of the riot: John of Nikiu, *Chronicle*, LXXXIV.87.

26. Socrates, *Ecclesiastical History*, VII.13.
27. Socrates, *Ecclesiastical History*, VII.14.
28. Socrates, *Ecclesiastical History*, VII.14.
29. Dzielska (1995), 87; Socrates, *Ecclesiastical History*, VII.14–15.
30. John of Nikiu, *Chronicle*, LXXXIV.87.
31. Standing between Orestes and Cyril: Socrates, *Ecclesiastical History*, VII.15—who to his credit disowns this rumor; on the involvement of the *parabalani* in spreading these rumors: Dzielska (1995), 96; "bestial men": *PH*, 43E; John of Nikiu, *Chronicle*, LXXXIV.87.
32. John of Nikiu, *Chronicle*, LXXXIV.100.
33. John of Nikiu, *Chronicle*, LXXXIV.100.
34. Accounts of the attacks vary: Socrates, the most reliable, has her murdered with "tiles"—presumably flayed by the sharp edges of pottery shards. John of Nikiu (*Chronicle*, LXXXIV.87) has her dragged through the streets till she died; Damascius (fr. 43) has her eyes gouged out. Hesychius, quoted in Dzielska (1995), 93, has her body scattered across the city.

10. TO DRINK FROM THE CUP OF DEVILS

1. Eco (1980), 36.
2. Elderly: Basil, *Address to Young Men on Reading Greek Literature*, tr. Deferrari and McGuire (1934), 365.
3. Basil, *Address to Young Men on Reading Greek Literature*.
4. Aphrodite: *Odyssey*, Book 8.256ff.; Sophocles, *Oedipus the King*, 906–10; Dido: *Aeneid*, IV.129ff.
5. Basil, *Address*, IV.
6. Jerome, Letter 22.29.
7. Catullus, 16, tr. Richlin.
8. Martial, *Epigrams*, 1.90.
9. Ovid, *Amores*, 1.5.
10. Basil, *Address*, IV.
11. Basil, *Address*, IV.
12. Marcus Aurelius, *Meditations*, 6.13.
13. Basil, *Address*, IV.
14. Basil, *Address*, IV.
15. Tertullian, *Apology*, 14.2.
16. Tertullian, *Apology*, 14.3.
17. Basil, *Address*, IV.
18. God-fearing people: Tertullian, *Apology*, 14.6; defiled: Tertullian, *Apology*, 15.3.
19. Diogenes Laertius, 6.2.59.

20. Diogenes Laertius, 6.2.45.

21. Diogenes Laertius, 6.1.4. For a very interesting introduction to ancient atheism, see Tim Whitmarsh's *Battling the Gods* (2015).

22. Basil, *Address*, IV.

23. These observations are indebted to Rohmann (2016), 127 and 60–61.

24. Wilson (1975), 7–9 and 13–14.

25. Basil, *Address*, tr. Deferrari and McGuire (1934), 371–72.

26. Basil, *Address*, tr. Deferrari and McGuire (1934), 370.

27. Basil, *Address*, tr. Padelford (1902), 33.

28. See, for example, Bohn's Classical Library 1875 edition of Martial's *Epigrams*. Epigram IX, xxvii, "To Chrestus," is a good example; it begins (for the benefit of Italian speakers): *"O Chresto, quantunque porti i testicoli spelati, ed una mentola simile al collo d'un Avotojo . . ."* and continues in a similar vein.

29. Catullus, *Poems*, tr. Cornish (1904), 19.

30. Catullus, 16, tr. Whigham (1966).

31. This observation is indebted to Kendrick (1996), 43. Richlin, finally, translates it correctly in 1983: "I will bugger you and I will fuck your mouths."

32. Chrysostom, Homily XV.10, *Concerning the Statues*.

33. Chrysostom, Homily XV.10–12, *Concerning the Statues*.

34. Index in Chrysostom, ed. Parker (1842), 373.

35. Shaw (2001), 4.

36. Chrysostom, *Discourses Against Judaizing Christians*, I.4.1.

37. Protagoras quoted and translated in Plato, *Protagoras*, ed. Denyer (2008), 101.

38. Anathema: quoted in Wilson (1970), 71.

39. 1 Corinthians 3:19.

40. *The Little Labyrinth*, quoted in Eusebius, *HC*, 5.28.13–15.

41. Athanasius, *Life of Antony*, 1.1.

42. Augustine, *Confessions*, 8.7–8.

43. Tertullian, *On the Prescription of Heretics*, VII.

44. Augustine, *City of God*, 2.13.

45. Augustine, *Confessions*, 1.18.28–29.

46. Catullus, 84.

47. Augustine, *On Christian Doctrine*, 2.13.

48. Concierge: Augustine quoted in Brown (1967), 458; ramparts: Augustine, *Expositions on the Psalms*, 54.13, quoted in Shaw (2011), 204.

49. Jerome, Letter 22.30.

50. Jerome, Letter 22.30.

51. Though it was clearly there, in a simple form, earlier in the Gospel of John. But later, it starts to be developed further.

52. Justin Martyr, *Apology*, 1.46.

53. *CC*, IV.38.

54. *The Little Labyrinth*, quoted in *HC*, 5.28.15.

55. Knox and McKeown (2013), 7.

56. Ammianus Marcellinus, *The Later Roman Empire*, 14.6.18.

57. C. Th., 16.4.2.

58. Cartledge (2009), 125.

59. According to the judgment of modern scholars, he succeeded. In the estimation of A.H.M. Jones, he exceeds even Tacitus in his "breadth of view and impartiality of judgement" (quoted by Wallace-Hadrill [1986]). Ammianus Marcellinus, *The Later Roman Empire*, 30.8.

60. *HC*, 8.2ff.

61. Dzielska (1995), 100.

62. Cover-up campaign: Dzielska (1995), 100; for criticism, see Socrates, *Ecclesiastical History*, VII.15: "surely nothing can be farther from the spirit of Christianity than the allowance of massacres, fights, and transactions of that sort"; destroyed the last remains: John of Nikiu, *Chronicle*, LXXXIV.103.

63. Chadwick (1958), passim. This paragraph is indebted to the ever-excellent MacMullen, especially MacMullen (1984), 6, and MacMullen (1997), 3–4.

II. TO CLEANSE THE ERROR OF DEMONS

1. Zachariah of Mytilene, *The Life of Severus*, 37–38.

2. *Rules of Rabbula*, can. 50, quoted in Rohmann (2016), 115.

3. Shenoute, *Vita* tr. Leipoldt, 13.32.1–3, quoted in Rohmann (2016), 135.

4. Pietro Bernardo quoted in Plaisance (2008), 65–67.

5. Augustine, *City of God*, 18.37.

6. Augustine, *City of God*, 18.41, quoted in Rohmann (2016), 114.

7. Chrysostom, Homily on First Corinthians (Argument); see Rohmann (2016), Chapter 4, for an excellent in-depth discussion of Christian attitudes to materialist philosophy to which this paragraph and the following are much indebted.

8. *The Apostolic Constitutions*, 1.6.1–2, quoted in Rohmann (2016), 114.

9. *PH*, 80, 85, 86.

10. *PH*, 63.

11. Gibbon, *Decline and Fall*, Vol. IV, Chapter 40, 265.

12. Zachariah of Mytilene, *The Life of Severus*, 64–69.

13. *The Life of Simeon Stylites the Younger*, 161, quoted in Rohmann (2016), 104.

14. Zachariah of Mytilene, *The Life of Severus*, 59–62.

15. Ammianus Marcellinus, *The Later Roman Empire*, 29.1.23.

16. Ammianus Marcellinus, *The Later Roman Empire*, 29.1.35.

17. Ammianus Marcellinus, *The Later Roman Empire*, 29.2.4.

18. Ammianus Marcellinus, *The Later Roman Empire*, 29.1.41.

19. Ammianus Marcellinus, *The Later Roman Empire*, 29.1.4–29.2.1.

20. Observation and translation indebted to Rohmann (2016), 247.

21. John Chrysostom, Homily 89 in the Acts of the Apostles (PG, 60, 274–75), quoted in Chuvin (1990), 52.
22. Jerome, Letter 70.2.
23. Reynolds and Wilson (1968), 70.
24. Wilson (1970), 72.
25. See Wilson (1975), 10.
26. Quoted in Wilson (1970), 72.
27. Rohmann (2016), 19, and main discussion 290–94.
28. Reynolds and Wilson (1968), 76, to whom this paragraph and the next are much indebted.
29. Reynolds and Wilson (1968), 75–76.
30. Chrysostom, Homily 2 on the Gospel of John, quoted in Rohmann (2016), 201, to whom these paragraphs are much indebted.
31. Chrysostom, *Eiusdem in illud, si qua in Christo*, quoted in Rohmann (2016), 203.
32. Theodoret, *Treatment of Greek Diseases*, 5.64–66, quoted in Rohmann (2016), 120.
33. Augustine, Letter 118.3.21, quoted in Rohmann (2016), 171.
34. H. Gerstinger (1948) and H. Bardon (1952–1956), quoted in Rohmann (2016), 8.
35. Estimate is that of Manfred Fuhrmann, *Geschichte der römischen Literatur*, again quoted in Rohmann (2016), 8.

12. CARPE DIEM

1. Virgil, *Aeneid*, 1.279.
2. Palladas, 10.82. By "Greeks" Palladas here means that he worships the old gods.
3. From the lines that open the "infamous" Chapter 15 of *The Decline and Fall of the Roman Empire* (1896–1900). Not all were so impressed. As the Duke of Gloucester said: "Another damned, thick, square book! Always scribble, scribble, scribble! Eh! Mr. Gibbon?"
4. John Chrysostom, *Testimonies against the Jews*, 56.
5. Justin Martyr, *Apology*, 1.xii.
6. Minucius Felix, *The "Octavius,"* X.
7. Pliny, *Natural History*, 2.4.
8. "The Martyrdom of Montanus and Lucius," in *ACM*, 15.11.
9. See Hopkins (1998), passim, for a discussion of numbers and their implications.
10. Quoted in Judge (2008), 6.
11. Quoted in Judge (2008), 6.
12. Richlin (1983), 146.
13. Kendrick (1996), 7, to whom these paragraphs are indebted.

14. Sanager's *History of Prostitution*, quoted in Kendrick (1996), 25–26.
15. Quoted in Fisher and Langlands (2011).
16. Fanin (1871), vii and title page.
17. Winckelmann quoted in Fisher and Langlands (2011), 309.
18. See Fisher and Langlands (2011), 306ff.
19. Fanin (1871), xvii.
20. Winckelmann (1771) quoted in Fisher and Langlands (2011), 309.
21. Date from Fisher and Langlands (2011), 310.
22. Fanin (1871), xviii.
23. Veyne (1992), 202.
24. Suetonius, *The Twelve Caesars, Julius Caesar* 1.49.
25. Ovid, *Amores*, 1.5.
26. Ovid, *Tristia*, 2.207.
27. Epictetus, *Enchiridion*, 33.8, quoted in Brown, *The Body and Society* (2008).
28. Galen, *On Affected Parts*, 6.5.
29. Ovid, *Amores*, 1.13, 1–3.
30. Macrobius, *Saturnalia*, 2.5.9.
31. Pells (2016).
32. Horace, *Odes*, I.9. The usual translation "Seize the day" doesn't quite catch the flavor of the Latin. *"Carpo"* is a much more delicate action—it's what you do to a flower, or to fruit: to pick it, savor it.
33. Ovid, *The Art of Love*, 1.1ff.
34. Ovid, *Metamorphoses*, 15.871–79.
35. Ovid, *The Art of Love*, 3.779ff.
36. Romans 1:24. As ever, Brown, *The Body and Society* (2008), 44ff., is brilliant and this section is much indebted to his observations.
37. Romans 1:26–27.
38. 1 Corinthians 6:9.
39. Romans 7:24.
40. Clement, *The Instructor*, 2.1.
41. Clement, *The Instructor*, 1.8.
42. Clement, *The Instructor*, 3.9.
43. Clement, *The Instructor*, 2.1.
44. Clement, *The Instructor*, 2.1.
45. Clement, *The Instructor*, 2.2.
46. Chrysostom, *The Homilies, On the Statues*, XV.4.
47. Chrysostom, *The Homilies, On the Statues*, XV.4.
48. Ovid, *The Art of Love*, 1.229ff.
49. Ovid, *The Art of Love*, 3.764ff.
50. Ovid, *The Art of Love*, 1.518ff.
51. Ovid, *The Art of Love*, 1.523–24.
52. Ovid, *The Art of Love*, 3.133ff.
53. Ovid, *The Art of Love*, 3.193.

54. Ovid, *The Art of Love*, 3.199ff.
55. Clement, *The Instructor*: hair curling etc., 2.11; sandals, 2.12; makeup, 3.2.
56. Clement, *The Instructor*: cups, 2.3; bedsheets, 2.3.
57. Clement, *The Instructor*: jewelry, 2.13; fabrics, 2.11.
58. Clement, *The Instructor*, 3.3.
59. Jerome, Letter 14.10.

13. THEY THAT FORSAKE THE WAY OF GOD

1. MacMullen (1990), 150: "The only sadistic literature I am aware of in the ancient world, is the developing Christian vision of Purgatory."
2. Anon., *Apocalypse of Peter*, 22, 28.
3. Anon., *Apocalypse of Peter*, 24.
4. Anon., *Apocalypse of Peter*, 30.
5. Anon., *Apocalypse of Peter*, 26.
6. Libanius, *Oration*, 11.218, quoted in Hall and Wyles, eds. (2008), 18.
7. Libanius, *Oration*, 64.116, quoted in Hall and Wyles, eds. (2008), 397.
8. Pliny the Younger, Letter 9.17.
9. Augustine, *City of God*, 1.32–33.
10. Tertullian, *Apology*, ed. Sider (2001), 99 n. 67.
11. Tertullian, *Spectacles*, 10.12, 10.5.
12. Chrysostom, *AGT*.
13. Severus of Antioch quoted in Sizgorich (2009), 116.
14. Chrysostom, *AGT*.
15. Chrysostom, *Homilies on Matthew*, 7.7.
16. Jacob of Serugh quoted in Sizgorich (2009), 116–17, to whom these paragraphs are indebted.
17. Arnobius, *Adversus gentes*, 42.
18. Ovid, *The Art of Love*, 1.135ff.
19. Chrysostom, *AGT*.
20. Martial, *Epigrams*, 2.42.
21. Quoted in Veyne (1992), 183.
22. Seneca, Epistle 56.
23. Martial, *Epigrams*, 6.93.
24. Chrysostom, *The Homilies, On the Statues*, XVII.9.
25. Tertullian, *Spectacles*, 8.9.
26. Tertullian, *Spectacles*, 18.3.
27. Clement, *The Instructor*, III.V.
28. Jerome, Letter 14.10.
29. Malalas, 18.18.
30. See MacMullen (1990), 142ff., for a very interesting discussion on this general question to which this paragraph and others here are much indebted.
31. Tertullian, *Spectacles*, 30.3ff.

14. TO OBLITERATE THE TYRANNY OF JOY

1. Chrysostom, *Homily* 14 on I Timothy v. 8.
2. Athanasius, *Life of Antony*, 14.
3. Bedjan, *The Life of Simeon Stylites*, 154.
4. Maillet, *Description de l'Égypte* (1735), quoted in Lacarrière (1963), tr. Monkcom (1963).
5. *AP*, Zacharias, 1.
6. *AP*, Euprepius, 4.
7. Smith, *A Smaller Latin-English Dictionary* (1955).
8. Rhetorical manual of Theon, the sophist, quoted in Wilken (1983), 99, to whom this paragraph is indebted.
9. Libanius, *Oration*, 2.32, 30.48.
10. Libanius, *Oration*, 2.32.
11. Libanius, *Oration*, 30.11.
12. Quoted in Lacarrière (1963), 92, to whom this paragraph is much indebted.
13. *AP*, Antony, 10.
14. *AP*, Dioscorus, 1.
15. Jerome on Hilarion, quoted in Lacarrière (1961), tr. Monkcom (1963), 142.
16. Evagrius quoted in Brakke (2006), 58.
17. This observation is indebted to Brown, *The Body and Society* (2008), 220.
18. *AP*, Isaac Priest of the Cells, 7.
19. *AP*, Apollo, 2.
20. *AP*, Evagrius, 1.
21. Palladius, *Lausiac History*, 26.2–4, quoted in Brakke (2006), 140.
22. *AP*, Evagrius, 4.
23. *AP*, John the Dwarf, 9.
24. *AP*, Theophilus the Archbishop, 1.
25. *AP*, Gelasius, 6.
26. Chrysostom, *AGT*.
27. Chrysostom, *Homilies on Genesis*, 6.6, quoted in Chadwick (2001), 486.
28. Constantine, *Oration to the Saints*, 11; for the genuineness or otherwise, see Drake (1985), 335ff.
29. Lactantius, *On the Deaths of the Persecutors*, 48.3; C. Th., 16.10.6; see also C. Th., 16.10.7.
30. C. Th., 16.10.19.3, and C. Th. 16.10.20.4.
31. Chrysostom, *Demonstration Against the Pagans That Christ Is God* 11, quoted in Rohmann (2016), 192.
32. Chrysostom quoted in Sizgorich (2009), 40; Chrysostom's policing of the boundaries of Christian life is discussed brilliantly in Sizgorich (2009), Chapter I, to which these paragraphs are indebted.
33. Chrysostom, *Discourses Against Judaizing Christians*, 8.5.2–4, quoted in Sizgorich (2009), 40.

34. Chrysostom, *AGT*.
35. Chrysostom, *Discourses Against Judaizing Christians*, 7.6.8.

15. "MERCIFUL SAVAGERY"

1. Augustine, *City of God*, 19.17.
2. John Chrysostom described in *EH*, VIII.4, quoted along with the above in Gaddis (2005), 192, to whom these paragraphs are much indebted.
3. Layton (2007), 62.
4. Eunapius, *Lives of the Sophists*, 423.
5. Theodosius quoted in Ambrose, Epistle 41.27.
6. Shenoute, *Let Our Eyes*, 1.5.
7. Shenoute, *Let Our Eyes*, 1.6.
8. Shenoute, *Let Our Eyes*, 1.2.
9. Shenoute, *Let Our Eyes*, 1.4.
10. Bagnall (2008), 31. Bagnall points out that this could have been a statement of Arian tendencies or similar.
11. Shenoute, *Let Our Eyes*, 1–2.4.
12. Shenoute, *Let Our Eyes*, 2.1–4.
13. Shenoute, *Let Our Eyes*, 1.3–2.12.
14. In Shenoute, *Open Letter to a Pagan Notable* (1961); translation from Gaddis (2005), 1.
15. Layton (2007), passim, to whom this section is much indebted.
16. Layton (2007), 60.
17. This observation and these paragraphs are indebted to the excellent Layton (2007), passim.
18. Wealth: Layton (2007), 60; shaving: 60, 62; desire: 47; cucumber: 51; sexual laws: 63; washing: 50; desirous feeling: 69; sitting: 62.
19. Jeremiah 23:24.
20. Layton (2007), 47 n. 4.
21. This paragraph is much indebted to the excellent observations in Lacarrière (1963), 131ff.
22. Account in Shenoute's *In the Night*, described in the excellent Brakke (2006), 3–4, 115–16; retold in Besa, *Life of Shenoute*, 73.
23. Augustine, Letter 93.II.4.
24. Augustine, Letter 93.II.5.
25. Augustine, Letter 185.2.
26. John Chrysostom, *The Homilies, On the Statues*, 1.32; Aphrarat writing of Numbers 25, quoted in Gaddis (2005), 182.
27. This paragraph is much indebted to Thurman (1968), 19–20.
28. *On Buildings*, 1.1, quoted in Thurman (1968), 17.
29. For punishments, see *Apocalypse of Peter*, 22–24; on appositeness: Gaddis (2005), 127–28, to whom this paragraph is indebted.

30. Augustine, *A Summary of the Conference with the Donatists*, 3.II.22, quoted in Shaw (2011), 684, to whom this and the following paragraphs are much indebted.

31. Augustine, *Tract in Ioh*, 5.12 (CCL 36:47), quoted in Shaw (2011), 698.

32. I am indebted to the as ever brilliant observation of Shaw (2011), 674; see Augustine, *Against the Letter of Parmenianus*, 1.10.16.

33. *HC*, 5.1.20.

34. Gaddis (2005), 216.

35. Libanius, *Oration*, 45.26, *For the Prisoners*, quoted in Gaddis (2005), to whom these paragraphs are much indebted.

36. Gregory Nazianzen, *Oration* 43.57.

37. Libanius, *Oration* 30.25–26.

38. Luke 14:23 KJV.

39. Augustine, Letter 104.2.7.

40. Jerome, Letter 109.2.

41. Chrysostom, *AGT*.

42. Augustine, Sermon 279.4, quoted in Shaw (2011), 682: *"Ubi terror, ibi salus. Qui faciebat contra nomen, patiatur pro nomine. O saevitia misericors!"*

43. This observation is much indebted to the brilliant essay by H. A. Drake (1996), 3–6.

16. "A TIME OF TYRANNY AND CRISIS"

1. The manuscript of the Justinian Code is corrupted at this point, making precise dating difficult: AD 529 is the generally accepted date of this. There are two laws that are relevant here; I focus on the second.

2. For Damascius's enthusiasm for her, see *PH*, 106A.

3. Zachariah of Mytilene, *The Life of Severus*, 26–33; *PH*, 53.

4. Zachariah of Mytilene, *The Life of Severus*, 30.

5. *PH*, 119.

6. *PH*, 106.

7. *PH*, 124.

8. Athanassiadi (1993), 4; Marinus, *Life of Proclus*, 10; 26.

9. Simplicius, epilogue on commentary on *Enchiridion*, quoted in Cameron (1969), 14.

10. Isidore, quoted in *PH*, 150.

11. *PH*, 145.

12. Agathias, *Histories*, 2.30.2.

13. According to Cameron (1969), 22.

14. Strömberg (1946), 176–77.

15. C. Th., 16.10.22 of April 423.

16. Geffcken (1978), 228.

17. Cf. C. Just. 1.1.8.35; 1.1.8; 1.1.8.25.

18. C. Just. 1.11.10.

19. C. Just. 1.11.10 and 1.11.10.4.

20. C. Just. 1.11.10.1–7.

21. C. Just. 1.11.10.2.

22. Gibbon, *Decline and Fall*, Vol. IV, Chapter 40, 265.

23. Athanassiadi (1993), 342–47.

24. Shear (1973), 162.

25. *PH*, 43A–C.

26. *PH*, 85A.

27. Cameron (1969), 17.

28. Athanassiadi (1993), 21.

29. *PH*, 36; Olympiodorus in *Commentary on the First Alcibiades*, quoted in Cameron (1969), 15.

30. Marinus, *Life of Proclus*, 30.

31. Vultures: Marinus, *Life of Proclus*, 15; *PH*, 117C; "the tyrant" is in Olympiodorus, *Commentary on the First Alcibiades*, quoted in Cameron (1969), 15.

32. *PH*, 45.

33. Plato more dangerous: Chadwick (1966), 11ff.; Cameron (1969), 9; see also Wilson (1970), 71.

34. *PH*, 63B.

35. Photius, *The Bibliotheca*, 130.7–12, quoted in Watts (2006).

36. C. Just. 1.11.10.2.

37. Cameron (1969), 18, to whose observations these paragraphs are much indebted; Cameron (2016), 222.

38. Simplicius in Cameron (1969), 21.

39. *PH*, 158.

40. *PH*, 146.

41. *PH*, 119C and 121.

42. Homer, *The Iliad*, 1.2–5.

43. Agathias, *Histories*, 2.28–2.31.2.

44. Agathias, *Histories*, 30–31.2.

45. Agathias, *Histories*, 2.31.2–4.

46. Cameron (1969/1970), 176.

47. Al Mas'udi, *Les prairies d'or* (ed. and tr. B. de Meynard, P. de Courtelle, C. Pellat), ii 741, 278, quoted in Athanassiadi (1993), 28.

48. Damascius, ed. Athanassiadi (1999), caption to Plate III.

Bibliography

PRIMARY SOURCES

Agathias, *The Histories*, tr. with intr. and short explanatory notes by J. D. Frendo (Berlin; New York: de Gruyter, 1975).

Ambrose, *Epistles*, in *Some of the Principal Works of St. Ambrose*, tr. H. De Romestin, E. De Romestin, and H.T.F. Duckworth (Oxford: J. Parker & Co., 1896).

Ammianus Marcellinus, *The Later Roman Empire (A.D. 354–378)*, tr. W. Hamilton, intr. A. Wallace-Hadrill (London: Penguin, 1986).

Anon., *The Acts of the Christian Martyrs*, tr. H. Musurillo (Oxford: Clarendon Press, 1972).

———, *The Apocalypse of Peter*, in *The Apocryphal New Testament: Being the Apocryphal Gospels, Acts, Epistles, and Apocalypses, with Other Narratives and Fragments*, ed. M. R. James (Oxford: Clarendon Press, 1924).

———, *Apophthegmata Patrum, The Sayings of the Desert Fathers: The Alphabetical Collection*, tr. B. Ward (Kalamazoo, Mich.: Cistercian Publications, 1975).

———, *Expositio totius mundi et gentium*, tr. J. Rougé (Paris: Éditions du Cerf, 1966).

Antony, *The Letters of St. Antony: Monasticism and the Making of a Saint*, ed. S. Rubenson (Minneapolis, Minn.: Fortress Press, 1995).

[*Aristeas*], *The Letter of Aristeas*, tr. H. St. J. Thackeray (London: Macmillan, 1904).

Arnobius, *The Seven Books of Arnobius adversus gentes*, tr. A. H. Bryce and Hugh Campbell (Edinburgh: T. & T. Clark, 1871).

Athanasius, *Life of Antony*, in *Early Christian Lives*, tr. C. White (London: Penguin, 1998).

Augustine, *City of God*, tr. M. Dods (Edinburgh: T. & T. Clark, 1913).

———, *City of God*, abridged from the translation by Gerald Walsh et al., ed. V. J. Bourke (New York: Image Books, 1958).

———, *City of God and Christian Doctrine*, tr. M. Dods and J. F. Shaw (Buffalo, N.Y.: Christian Literature Co., 1887).

————, *Confessions*, tr. R. S. Pine-Coffin (Harmondsworth: Penguin, 1961).

————, *Exposition on the Psalms, vol. 4, Psalms 73–98*, tr. M. Boulding (New York: Augustinian Heritage Institute, 2002).

————, *Letters*, tr. J. G. Cunningham, in *Letters of Augustine*, tr. Cunningham, vol. 1 (Edinburgh: T. & T. Clark, 1872).

————, *Letters*, tr. J. G. Cunningham, in *Letters of Augustine*, tr. Cunningham, vol. 2 (Edinburgh: T. & T. Clark, 1875).

————, *Vingt-six sermons au peuple d'Afrique; retrouvés à Mayence*, ed. F. Dolbeau (Paris: Institut d'études augustiniennes, 1996).

————, *The Writings Against the Manichaeans*, tr. R. Stothert and A. H. Newman, and *Against the Donatists*, tr. J. R. King; rev. C. D. Hartranft (Buffalo, N.Y.: Christian Literature Co., 1887).

————, *Meditations*, tr. R. Hard (Oxford: Oxford University Press, 2011).

Basil, *Address to Young Men on Reading Greek Literature*, in *The Letters*, vol. 4 of *Letters*, tr. R. J. Deferrari and M.R.P. McGuire, Loeb Classical Library 270 (Cambridge, Mass.: Harvard University Press, 1934).

————, *Address to Young Men on the Right Use of Greek Literature* in *Essays on the Study and Use of Poetry by Plutarch and Basil the Great*, tr. F. M. Padelford, in Yale Studies in English 15 (New York: Henry Holt & Company, 1902).

————, *Epistles*, in *Nicene and Post-Nicene Fathers*, second series, vol. 8, tr. Blomfield Jackson, ed. Philip Schaff and Henry Wace (Buffalo, N.Y.: Christian Literature Publishing Co., 1895; online: newadvent.org/fathers).

[Bedjan, Paul], *The Life of Saint Simeon Stylites: A Translation of the Syriac Text in Bedjan's Acta Martyrum et Sanctorum* by F. Lent (Merchantville, N.J.: Evolution Publishing, 2009).

Besa, *The Life of Shenoute*, tr. D. N. Bell (Kalamazoo, Mich.: Cistercian Publications, 1983).

Catullus, *The Poems of Gaius Valerius Catullus*, tr. F. W. Cornish (Cambridge: Cambridge University Press, 1904).

————, *The Poems of Catullus*, tr. P. Whigham (Harmondsworth: Penguin, 1966).

Celsus, *On the True Doctrine: A Discourse Against the Christians*, tr. R. J. Hoffmann (New York; Oxford: Oxford University Press, 1987).

————, *Discourses Against Judaizing Christians*, tr. P. W. Harkins (Washington, D.C.: Catholic University of America, 1979).

————, *The Homilies of John Chrysostom: Archbishop of Constantinople, on the Statues, or To the People of Antioch* (Oxford: J. H. Parker, 1842).

Cicero, *On the Nature of the Gods*, tr. H. Rackham, Loeb Classical Library 268 (Cambridge, Mass.: Harvard University Press, 1933).

Clement, *The Writings of Clement of Alexandria*, tr. W. Wilson, Ante-Nicene Christian Library, vols. 1, 4, 12 (Edinburgh: T. & T. Clark, 1867–69).

Constantine, *Oration to the Saints*, in *Eusebius Pamphilius: The Life of the Blessed Emperor Constantine, in Four Books* (London: Samuel Bagster & Sons, 1845).

Cyprian, *On the Lapsed, On the Mortality*, and *On the Unity of the Church*, in *The Writings of Cyprian, Bishop of Carthage*, tr. R. E. Wallis (Edinburgh: T. & T. Clark, 1868–69).

Damascius, *The Philosophical History*, ed. P. Athanassiadi (Athens: Apamea Cultural Association, 1999).

Diogenes Laertius, *Diogenes*, in *Lives of Eminent Philosophers*, vol. 2, books 6–10, tr. R. D. Hicks, Loeb Classical Library 185 (Cambridge, Mass.: Harvard University Press, 1925).

Epictetus, *Discourses*, books 3–4, *Fragments, The Enchiridion*, tr. A. Oldfather, Loeb Classical Library 218 (Cambridge, Mass.: Harvard University Press, 1928).

Eunapius, *Lives of the Philosophers and Sophists*, tr. W. C. Wright, Loeb Classical Library 134 (Cambridge, Mass.: Harvard University Press, 1921).

———, *Lives of the Sophists*, in *Eunapius: Lives of the Philosophers and Sophists*, tr. W. C. Wright, Loeb Classical Library 134 (Cambridge, Mass.: Harvard University Press, 1921).

Eusebius, *The History of the Church from Christ to Constantine*, tr. G. A. Williamson (London: Penguin, 1989).

———, *The Life of the Blessed Emperor Constantine, in four books, from AD 306 to 337* (London: S. Bagster & Sons, 1845).

———, *Life of Constantine*, tr. A. Cameron and S. G. Hall (Oxford: Clarendon Press, 1999).

———, *Oration in Praise of Constantine*, in *Eusebius Pamphilius: Church History, Life of Constantine, Oration in Praise of Constantine*, ed. P. Schaff, tr. Richardson et al. (New York: Christian Literature Publishing, 1890).

———, *The Preparation for the Gospel*, tr. E. H. Gifford (Oxford: 1903; repr. Grand Rapids, Mich.: 1981).

Evagrius Ponticus, *The Praktikos: Chapters on Prayer*, tr. J. E. Bamberger (Spencer, Mass.: Cistercian Publications, 1972).

———, *Talking Back: A Monastic Handbook for Combating Demons*, tr. D. Brakke (Trappist, Ky.; Collegeville, Minn.: Cistercian Publications, 2009).

Firmicus Maternus, *The Error of the Pagan Religions*, tr. C. A. Forbes (New York: Newman Press, 1970).

Galen, *De Pulsuum Differentiis* and *On Hippocrates' Anatomy*, quoted in R. Walzer, *Galen on Jews and Christians* (London: Oxford University Press, 1949).

———, *On Anatomical Procedures*, tr. C. Singer (London: Oxford University Press, 1956).

Gregory Nazianzen, *First Invective Against Julian*, in *Julian the Emperor, Contain-*

ing Gregory Nazianzen's *Two Invectives and Libanius' Monody with Julian's Extant Theosophical Works*, tr. W. King (London: G. Bell, 1888).

Herodotus, *The Histories*, tr. A. de Sélincourt, revised J. Marincola (London: Penguin, 1996).

Hesiod, *Theogony*, in *Hesiod: Theogony and Works and Days and Theognis: Elegies*, tr. D. Wender (Harmondsworth: Penguin, 1976).

Homer, *The Iliad*, tr. M. Hammond (Harmondsworth: Penguin, 1987).

———, *The Odyssey*, tr. E. V. Rieu, revised D. Rieu (London: Penguin, 2003).

Horace, *Odes*, in *Odes and Epodes*, tr. N. Rudd, Loeb Classical Library 33 (Cambridge, Mass.: Harvard University Press, 2004).

———, *Satires*, in *Satires, Epistles, The Art of Poetry*, tr. H. Rushton Fairclough, Loeb Classical Library 194 (Cambridge, Mass.: Harvard University Press, 1926).

Jacobus de Voragine, *The Golden Legend: Readings on the Saints*, tr. W. Granger Ryan, intr. E. Duffy (Princeton, N.J.: Princeton University Press, 2012).

James, M. R., ed., *The Apocryphal New Testament: Being the Apocryphal Gospels, Acts, Epistles, and Apocalypses, with Other Narratives and Fragments* (Oxford: Clarendon Press, 1924).

Jerome, *Letters*, in *The Principal Works of St. Jerome*, tr. W. H. Freemantle, G. Lewis, and W. G. Martley, in *A Select Library of Nicene and Post-Nicene Fathers of the Christian Church*, second series, vol. 6 (Oxford: Parker, 1893).

John, Bishop of Nikiu, *The Chronicle of John, Bishop of Nikiu*, tr. R. H. Charles (London: Williams & Norgate for the Text and Translation Society, 1916).

John Chrysostom, *Against the Games and Theatres*, in *John Chrysostom*, ed. W. Mayer and P. Allen (London; New York: Routledge, 2000).

John of Ephesus, *The Third Part of the Ecclesiastical History of John, Bishop of Ephesus*, tr. R. P. Smith (Oxford: Oxford University Press, 1860).

Julian, *Against the Galilaeans*, in *Julian*, vol. 3, tr. W. C. Wright, Loeb Classical Library 157 (Cambridge, Mass.: Harvard University Press, 1923).

Justin Martyr, *The Apology*, in *The Writings of Justin Martyr and Athenagoras*, tr. M. Dods, G. Reith, and B. Pratten, Ante-Nicene Christian Library, vol. 2 (Edinburgh: T. & T. Clark, 1867).

Justinian, *Annotated Justinian Code*, tr. F. H. Blume, ed. T. Kearley, second edition, George W. Hopper Library of the University of Wyoming; online: uwyo.edu/lawlib/blume-justinian.

———, *The Codex of Justinian: A New Annotated Translation, with Parallel Latin and Greek Text Based on a Translation by Justice Fred H. Blume*, ed. B. W. Frier et al. (Cambridge; New York: Cambridge University Press, 2016).

———, *Digest*, book 1, in *The Civil Law*, ed. S. P. Scott, 17 vols. (Cincinnati, 1932), constitution.org.

Juvenal, *Sixteen Satires*, in *Juvenal and Persius*, tr. S. Morton Braund, Loeb Classical Library 91 (Cambridge, Mass.: Harvard University Press, 2004).

Lactantius, *On the Deaths of the Persecutors*, ed. and tr. J. L. Creed (Oxford: Clarendon Press, 1984).

Leo XIII, Encyclical, *On the Nature of Human Liberty* (1888; published now online by Libreria Editrice Vaticana).

Libanius, *Oration 18*, in *Selected Orations*, vol. 1, *Julianic Orations*, tr. A. F. Norman, Loeb Classical Library 451 (Cambridge, Mass.: Harvard University Press, 1969).

———, *Oration 30*, in *Selected Orations*, vol. 2, tr. A. F. Norman, Loeb Classical Library 452 (Cambridge, Mass.: Harvard University Press, 1977).

Livy, *The Early History of Rome*, tr. A. de Sélincourt (London: Penguin, 2002).

Lucian, *Demonax*, in *Lucian*, vol. 1, tr. A. M. Harmon, Loeb Classical Library 14 (Cambridge, Mass.: Harvard University Press, 1913).

———, *The Passing of Peregrinus*, in *Lucian*, vol. 5, tr. A. M. Harmon, Loeb Classical Library 302 (Cambridge, Mass.: Harvard University Press, 1936).

Lucretius, *On the Nature of Things*, tr. W.H.D. Rouse, revised M. F. Smith, Loeb Classical Library 181 (Cambridge, Mass.: Harvard University Press, 1924).

Macrobius, *Saturnalia*, vol. 1, books 1–2, ed. and tr. Robert A. Kaster, Loeb Classical Library 510 (Cambridge, Mass.: Harvard University Press, 2011).

Malalas, *The Chronicle of John Malalas*, tr. E. Jeffreys, M. Jeffreys, and R. Scott (Melbourne: Australian Association for Byzantine Studies; Sydney: Department of Modern Greek, University of Sydney, 1986).

Marcus Aurelius, *Meditations*, in *Marcus Aurelius*, tr. C. R. Haines, Loeb Classical Library 58 (Cambridge, Mass.: Harvard University Press, 1916).

Marinus, *Life of Proclus*, in *Life, Hymns & Works*, tr. K. S. Guthrie (North Yonkers, N.Y.: Platonist Press, 1925).

Mark the Deacon, *The Life of Porphyry, Bishop of Gaza*, tr. G. F. Hill (Oxford: Clarendon Press, 1913).

Martial, *Epigrams*, vol. 2, books 6–10, tr. D. R. Shackleton Bailey, Loeb Classical Library 95 (Cambridge, Mass.: Harvard University Press, 1993).

Minucius Felix, *The "Octavius,"* tr. J. H. Freese (London: SPCK; New York: Macmillan, 1919).

Moschos, John, *The Spiritual Meadow*, tr. J. Wortley (Kalamazoo, Mich.: Cistercian Publications, 1992).

Origen, *Contra Celsum*, tr. H. Chadwick (Cambridge: Cambridge University Press, 1953).

———, *Homilies on Joshua*, tr. B. J. Bruce (Washington, D.C.: Catholic University of America Press, 2002).

Ovid, *The Art of Love*, tr. R. Humphries (Bloomington: Indiana University Press, 1957).

———, *The Art of Love*, in *The Erotic Poems*, tr. P. Green (Harmondsworth: Penguin, 1982).

———, *Fasti*, tr. J. G. Frazer, revised G. P. Goold, Loeb Classical Library 253 (Cambridge, Mass.: Harvard University Press, 1931).

———, *Metamorphoses*, tr. F. J. Miller, revised G. P. Goold, Loeb Classical Library 42 (Cambridge, Mass.: Harvard University Press, 1916).

Palladas, *The Greek Anthology*, vol. 3, book 9, tr. W. R. Paton, Loeb Classical Library 84 (Cambridge, Mass.: Harvard University Press, 1917).

———, *The Greek Anthology*, vol. 3, book 10, *The Hortatory and Admonitory Epigrams*, tr. W. R. Paton (Cambridge, Mass.: Harvard University Press, 1918).

Petronius, *The Satyricon*, in *Petronius, Seneca: Satyricon, Apocolocyntosis*, tr. M. Heseltine, W.H.D. Rouse, revised E. H. Warmington, Loeb Classical Library 15 (Cambridge, Mass.: Harvard University Press, 1913).

Plato, *Protagoras*, ed. N. Denyer (Cambridge: Cambridge University Press, 2008).

Pliny, *Natural History*, vol. 1, books 1–2, tr. H. Rackham, Loeb Classical Library 330 (Cambridge, Mass.: Harvard University Press, 1938).

———, *Natural History*, vol. 10, books 36–37, tr. D. E. Eichholz, Loeb Classical Library 419 (Cambridge, Mass.: Harvard University Press, 1962).

Pliny the Younger, *The Letters of the Younger Pliny*, tr. B. Radice (Harmondsworth: Penguin, 1963).

Plutarch, *On Superstition*, in *Moralia*, vol. 2, tr. F. C. Babbitt, Loeb Classical Library 222 (Cambridge, Mass.: Harvard University Press, 1928).

Procopius, *History of the Wars*, tr. H. B. Dewing (London: Heinemann; New York: Macmillan, 1914).

Prudentius, *Crowns of Martyrdom*, in *Prudentius*, vol. 2, tr. H. J. Thomson, Loeb Classical Library 398 (Cambridge, Mass.: Harvard University Press, 1953).

Quodvultdeus, *Livre des Promesses et des Prédictions de Dieu*, tr. R. Braun (Paris: Cerf, 1964).

Reymond, E.A.E., and J.W.B. Barns, eds., "The Martyrdom of S. Coluthus," in *Four Martyrdoms from the Pierpont Morgan Coptic Codices* (Oxford: Clarendon Press, 1973).

Rufinus of Aquileia, *The Church History of Rufinus of Aquileia: Books 10 and 11*, tr. P. R. Amidon (New York; Oxford: Oxford University Press, 1997).

Seneca, *Epistles*, vol. 1, *Epistles 1–65*, tr. R. M. Gummere, Loeb Classical Library 75 (Cambridge, Mass.: Harvard University Press, 1917).

Shenoute, *Let Our Eyes*, tr. S. Emmel, in "Shenoute of Atripe and the Christian Destruction of Temples in Egypt: Rhetoric and Reality," in *From Temple to*

Church: Destruction and Renewal of Local Cultic Topography in Late Antiquity, ed. J. Hahn, S. Emmel, and U. Gotter (Leiden; Boston, Mass.: Brill, 2008).

———, *Open Letter to a Pagan Notable*, in "Shenute as a Historical Source," tr. J. Barnes, in *Actes du Xe Congrès International de Papyrologues*, ed. J. Wolski (Warsaw/Cracow, 1961), pp. 156–58 with suggested alterations by Gaddis (2005), pp. 151–52.

———, *Selected Discourses of Shenoute the Great: Community, Theology, and Social Conflict in Late Antique Egypt*, ed. and tr. D. Brakke and A. Crislip (Cambridge: Cambridge University Press, 2015).

———, *Vita et omnia opera*, vol. 3, CSCO 42, ed. Johannes Leipoldt (Paris: E Typographeo Republicae, 1908); in Latin, tr. Hermann Wiesmann, CSCO 96 (1953).

Socrates Scholasticus, *The Ecclesiastical History of Socrates Scholasticus: Comprising a History of the Church from A.D. 323 to A.D. 425*, tr. A. C. Zenos (Oxford: Parker, 1891).

Sozomen, *The Ecclesiastical History*, tr. C. D. Hartranft, in *A Select Library of the Nicene and Post-Nicene Fathers of the Christian Church*, ed. P. Schaff and H. Wace, vol. 2 (Oxford: Parker, 1890).

Suetonius, *The Twelve Caesars*, tr. R. Graves, revised J. B. Rives (London: Penguin Classics, 2007).

———, *Vespasian*, in *Suetonius, Lives of the Caesars*, vol. 2, tr. J. C. Rolfe, Loeb Classical Library 38 (Cambridge, Mass.: Harvard University Press, 1914).

Sulpicius Severus, *Life of St. Martin of Tours*, in *Early Christian Lives*, tr. C. White (London; New York: Penguin, 1998).

Symmachus, *Memorandum 3*, in *Pagans and Christians in Late Antiquity: A Sourcebook*, ed. A. D. Lee (London: Routledge, 2000).

Tacitus, *Annals*, tr. C. Damon (London: Penguin, 2012).

———, *The Annals of Imperial Rome*, tr. M. Grant (London: Penguin, 2003).

———, *A History of the Monks of Syria*, tr. R. M. Price (Kalamazoo, Mich.: Cistercian Publications, 1985).

Tertullian, *The Address of Q. Sept. Tertullian to Scapula Tertullus, Proconsul of Africa*, tr. D. Dalrymple (Edinburgh: Murray & Cochrane, 1790).

———, *The Apology, The Crown,* and *Spectacles*, in *Christian and Pagan in the Roman Empire: The Witness of Tertullian*, ed. R. Sider (Washington, D.C.: Catholic University of America Press, 2001).

———, *The Writings of Q.S.F. Tertullianus*, tr. S. Thelwall and P. Holmes (Edinburgh: T. & T. Clark, 1869, 1870).

Themistius, *Speech 5*, in *Pagans and Christians in Late Antiquity: A Sourcebook*, ed. A. D. Lee (London: Routledge, 2000).

Theodoret, *Ecclesiastical History*, in *Theodoret, Jerome, Gennadius and Rufinus:*

Historical Writings, in *Nicene and Post-Nicene Fathers*, second series, vol. 3, ed. P. Schaff and H. Wace (Oxford: Parker, 1892).

Theodosius, *The Theodosian Code and Novels: And the Sirmondian Constitutions*, tr. C. Pharr, in collaboration with T. S. Davidson and M. B. Pharr (Princeton, N.J.: Princeton University Press, 1952).

Virgil, *The Aeneid*, in *Eclogues, Georgics, Aeneid: Books 1–6*, tr. H. Rushton Fairclough, revised G. P. Goold, Loeb Classical Library 63 (Cambridge, Mass.: Harvard University Press, 1916).

Vitruvius, *The Architecture of Marcus Vitruvius Pollio*, tr. J. Gwilt (London: Lockwood, 1874).

Zachariah of Mytilene, *The Life of Severus*, tr. L. Ambjörn (Piscataway, N.J.: Gorgias Press, 2008).

Zosimus, *The History of Count Zosimus, Sometime Advocate and Chancellor of the Roman Empire* (London: J. Davis, 1814).

SECONDARY SOURCES

Aldrete, G. S., *Floods of the Tiber in Ancient Rome* (Baltimore: Johns Hopkins University Press, 2007).

Athanassiadi, P., "Persecution and Response in Late Paganism: The Evidence of Damascius," *Journal of Hellenic Studies* 113 (1993), pp. 1–29.

Attwater, D., *The Penguin Dictionary of Saints* (Harmondsworth: Penguin, 1965).

Bagnall, R. S., "Models and Evidence in the Study of Religion in Late Roman Egypt," in *From Temple to Church: Destruction and Renewal of Local Cultic Topography in Late Antiquity*, ed. J. Hahn, S. Emmel, and U. Gotter (Leiden; Boston, Mass.: Brill, 2008).

Barnes, T. D., "Pre-Decian Acta Martyrum," *Journal of Theological Studies*, n.s., 19 (1968), pp. 509–31.

———, *Tertullian: A Historical and Literary Study* (Oxford: Clarendon Press, 1971).

Beard, M., *The Roman Triumph* (Cambridge, Mass.: Belknap Press of Harvard University Press, 2007).

Beard, M., J. North, and S. Price, *Religions of Rome*, vol. 1, *A History* (Cambridge: Cambridge University Press, 1998).

———, *Religions of Rome*, vol. 2, *A Sourcebook* (Cambridge: Cambridge University Press, 1998).

Benko, S., *Pagan Rome and the Early Christians* (London: B. T. Batsford, 1984).

Blumenthal, H. J., "529 and Its Sequel: What Happened to the Academy," *Byzantion* 48 (1978), pp. 369–85.

Bodel, J., "Dealing with the Dead: Undertakers, Executioners and Potter's

Fields in Ancient Rome," in *Death and Disease in the Ancient City*, ed. V. M. Hope and E. Marshall (London; New York: Routledge, 2000).

Bowersock, G. W., *Julian the Apostate* (Cambridge, Mass.: Harvard University Press, 1978).

————, *Martyrdom and Rome* (Cambridge: Cambridge University Press, 1995).

————, "Parabalani: A Terrorist Charity in Late Antiquity," *Anabases* 12 (2010), pp. 45–54.

Brakke, D., *Demons and the Making of the Monk: Spiritual Combat in Early Christianity* (Cambridge, Mass.: Harvard University Press, 2006).

————, "From Temple to Cell, from Gods to Demons: Pagan Temples in the Monastic Topography of Fourth-Century Egypt," in *From Temple to Church: Destruction and Renewal of Local Cultic Topography in Late Antiquity*, ed. J. Hahn, S. Emmel, and U. Gotter (Leiden; Boston, Mass.: Brill, 2008).

Brown, P., *Augustine of Hippo: A Biography* (1967; Berkeley: University of California Press, 2008).

————, *Authority and the Sacred: Aspects of the Christianisation of the Roman World* (Cambridge: Cambridge University Press, 1997).

————, *The Body and Society—Men, Women, and Sexual Renunciation in Early Christianity*, Twentieth Anniversary Edition with a new introduction (New York; Chichester: Columbia University Press, 2008).

————, "The Challenge of the Desert," in *A History of Private Life*, ed. P. Veyne, vol. 1, *From Pagan Rome to Byzantium*, tr. A. Goldhammer (Cambridge, Mass.; London: Belknap Press of Harvard University Press, 1992).

————, "Christianization and Religious Conflict," in *The Cambridge Ancient History*, ed. A. Cameron and P. Garnsey, vol. 13, *The Late Empire, AD 337–425* (Cambridge: Cambridge University Press, 1997), pp. 632–64.

————, *The Making of Late Antiquity* (Cambridge, Mass.; London: Harvard University Press, 1978).

————, *Power and Persuasion in Late Antiquity: Towards a Christian Empire* (Madison: University of Wisconsin Press, 1992).

————, *The Rise of Western Christendom: Triumph and Diversity AD 200–1000* (Oxford: Blackwell, 1997).

Buckland, William, *Vindiciae Geologicae, or, The Connexion of Geology with Religion Explained* (Oxford: Oxford University Press, 1820).

Bury, J. B., *History of the Later Roman Empire: From the Death of Theodosius I to the Death of Justinian*, reprint of first edition (New York: Dover Publications, 1958).

Cameron, Alan, "The Last Days of the Academy of Athens," *Proceedings of the Cambridge Philological Society* 195 (1969), pp. 7–29.

————, *The Last Pagans of Rome* (Oxford; New York: Oxford University Press, 2011).

————, *Wandering Poets and Other Essays on Late Greek Literature and Philosophy* (Oxford: Oxford University Press, 2016).

Cameron, Averil, "Agathias on the Sassanians," Dumbarton Oaks Papers, vol. 23/24 (1969/1970), pp. 67–183.

————, "Form and Meaning: The Vita Constantini and the Vita Antonii," in *Greek Biography and Panegyric in Late Antiquity*, ed. T. Hägg and P. Rousseau (Berkeley: University of California Press, 2000), pp. 72–88.

Cameron, A., and P. Garnsey, eds., *The Cambridge Ancient History*, vol. 13, *The Late Empire AD 337–425* (Cambridge: Cambridge University Press, 1997).

Cameron, A., B. Ward-Perkins, and M. Whitby, *The Cambridge Ancient History*, vol. 14, *Late Antiquity: Empire and Successors, AD 425–600* (Cambridge: Cambridge University Press, 2000).

Canfora, L., *The Vanished Library: A Wonder of the Ancient World*, tr. M. Ryle from *La biblioteca scomparsa* (Palermo: Sellerio editore, 1987; Berkeley and Los Angeles: University of California Press, 1990).

Cartledge, P., *Ancient Greek Political Thought in Practice* (Cambridge: Cambridge University Press, 2009).

Chadwick, H., *The Church in Ancient Society: From Galilee to Gregory the Great* (Oxford: Oxford University Press, 2001).

————, *Early Christian Thought and the Classical Tradition: Studies in Justin, Clement, and Origen* (Oxford: Clarendon Press, 1966).

————, *The Early Church* (London: Hodder & Stoughton, 1968).

————, "Ossius of Cordova and the Presidency of the Council of Antioch, 325," *Journal of Theological Studies*, n.s., 9 (1958), pp. 292–304.

Chitty, D., *The Desert a City: Introduction to the Study of Egyptian and Palestinian Monasticism Under the Christian Empire* (Oxford: Basil Blackwell, 1966).

Chuvin, P., *A Chronicle of the Last Pagans*, tr. B. A. Archer from *Chronique des derniers païens* (Cambridge, Mass.; London: Harvard University Press, 1990).

Clarke, J. R., *Looking at Lovemaking: Constructions of Sexuality in Roman Art, 100 B.C.–A.D. 250* (Berkeley: University of California Press, 1998).

Cohn-Haft, L., *The Public Physicians of Ancient Greece* (Northampton, Mass.: Smith College, 1956).

Constantelos, D. J., "Paganism and the State in the Age of Justinian," in *Catholic Historical Review* 50 (1968), pp. 372–80.

Copeland, K. B., "Sinners and Post-Mortem 'Baptism' in the Acherusian Lake," in *The Apocalypse of Peter*, ed. J. Bremmer and I. Czachesz (Leuven: Peeters, 2003).

Corke-Webster, J., "Author and Authority: Literary Representations of Moral Authority in Eusebius of Caesarea's the Martyrs of Palestine," in *Christian Martyrdom in Late Antiquity (300–450 AD): History and Discourse, Tradition and Religious Identity*, ed. P. Gemeinhardt and J. Leemans (Berlin; Boston, Mass.: De Gruyter, 2012), pp. 51–78.

———, "Mothers and Martyrdom: Familial Piety and the Model of the Maccabees in Eusebius' Ecclesiastical History," in *Eusebius of Caesarea: Traditions and Innovations*, ed. Aaron Johnson and Jeremy Schott (Washington, D.C.: Center for Hellenic Studies, 2013), pp. 51–82.

Dalrymple, W., *From the Holy Mountain: A Journey in the Shadow of Byzantium* (1997; London: HarperCollins, 2005).

Davis, J. B., "Teaching Violence in the Schools of Rhetoric," in *Violence in Late Antiquity: Perceptions and Practices*, ed. H. A. Drake (Aldershot: Ashgate, 2014), pp. 197–204.

de Hamel, C., *Meetings with Remarkable Manuscripts* (London: Allen Lane, 2016).

de Ste. Croix, G.E.M., *Christian Persecution, Martyrdom, and Orthodoxy* (Oxford: Oxford University Press, 2006).

———, "Why Were the Early Christians Persecuted?" *Past & Present*, no. 26 (November 1963), pp. 6–38.

———, "Why Were the Early Christians Persecuted? A Rejoinder," *Past & Present*, no. 27 (1964), pp. 28–33.

Dodds, E. R., *Pagan and Christian in an Age of Anxiety* (Cambridge: Cambridge University Press, 1965).

Dodwell, H., "De paucitate martyrum," in *Dissertationes Cyprianae* (Oxford, 1684).

Drake, H. A., "The Edict of Milan: Why We Still Need It," in *Serdica Edict (311 AD): Concepts and Realizations of the Idea of Religious Toleration* (Sofia: Tangra, TanNakRa, 2014), pp. 63–78.

———, "Intolerance, Religious Violence, and Political Legitimacy in Late Antiquity," in *Journal of the American Academy of Religion* 79, no. 1 (March 2011), pp. 193–235.

———, "Lambs into Lions: Explaining Early Christian Intolerance," *Past & Present*, no. 153 (November 1996), pp. 3–36.

———, "Suggestions of Date in Constantine's Oration to the Saints," *American Journal of Philology* 106, no. 3 (Autumn 1985), pp. 335–49.

———, ed., *Violence in Late Antiquity: Perceptions and Practices* (Aldershot: Ashgate, 2006).

Dunbabin, K., *The Roman Banquet: Images of Conviviality* (Cambridge: Cambridge University Press, 2003).

Dzielska, M., *Hypatia of Alexandria*, tr. F. Lyra (Cambridge, Mass.: Harvard University Press, 1995).

Eco, U., *The Name of the Rose*, tr. W. Weaver from *Il nome della rosa* (1980) (London: Minerva, 1983).

Edwards, C., *Politics of Immorality in Ancient Rome* (Cambridge: Cambridge University Press, 1993).

———, "Unspeakable Professions: Public Performance and Prostitution in Ancient Rome," in *Roman Sexualities*, ed. J. P. Hallett and M. B. Skinner (Princeton, N.J.: Princeton University Press, 1997).

Emmel, S., "Shenoute of Atripe and the Christian Destruction of Temples in Egypt: Rhetoric and Reality," in *From Temple to Church: Destruction and Renewal of Local Cultic Topography in Late Antiquity*, ed. J. Hahn, S. Emmel, and U. Gotter (Leiden; Boston, Mass.: Brill, 2008).

———, U. Gotter, and J. Hahn, "From Temple to Church: Analysing a Late Antique Phenomenon of Transformation," in *From Temple to Church: Destruction and Renewal of Local Cultic Topography in Late Antiquity*, ed. J. Hahn, S. Emmel, and U. Gotter (Leiden; Boston, Mass.: Brill, 2008).

Engberg, J., "Truth Begs No Favours—Martyr-Literature and Apologetics," in *Critique and Apologetics: Jews, Christians and Pagans in Antiquity*, ed. D. Brakke, A.-C. Jacobsen, and J. Ulrich (Frankfurt; Oxford: Peter Lang, 2009).

Evans, G. R., *The University of Oxford: A New History* (London: I. B. Tauris, 2010).

Fagan, G. G., *Bathing in Public in the Roman World* (Ann Arbor: University of Michigan Press, 1999).

Fanin, *The Royal Museum at Naples, Being Some Account of the Erotic Paintings, Bronzes and Statues Contained in That Famous "Cabinet Secret"* (London: Privately printed, 1871).

Fisher, K., and R. Langlands, "The Censorship Myth and the Secret Museum," in *Pompeii in the Public Imagination from Its Rediscovery to Today*, ed. S. Hales and J. Paul (Oxford: Oxford University Press, 2011), pp. 301–15.

Fleming, R., "Galen's Imperial Order of Knowledge," in *Ordering Knowledge in the Roman Empire*, ed. J. König and T. Whitmarsh (Cambridge: Cambridge University Press, 2007), pp. 241–77.

Fowden, G., "Between Pagans and Christians," *Journal of Roman Studies* 78 (1988), pp. 173–82.

———, "Bishops and Temples in the Eastern Roman Empire, AD 320–435," *Journal of Theological Studies*, ser. 2, 29 (1978), pp. 53–78.

———, "Polytheist Religion and Philosophy," in *The Cambridge Ancient History*, vol. 13, *The Late Empire, AD 337–425*, ed. A. Cameron and P. Garnsey (Cambridge: Cambridge University Press, 1998).

Francis, J. A., *Subversive Virtue: Asceticism and Authority in the Second-Century Pagan World* (University Park: Pennsylvania State University Press, 1995).

Frankfurter, D., "Iconoclasm and Christianization in Late Antique Egypt: Christian Treatments of Space and Image," in *From Temple to Church:*

Destruction and Renewal of Local Cultic Topography in Late Antiquity, ed. J. Hahn, S. Emmel, and U. Gotter (Leiden; Boston, Mass.: Brill, 2008).

Frantz, A., *From Paganism to Christianity in the Temples of Athens*, Dumbarton Oaks Papers, vol. 19 (1965).

Frend, W.H.C., *The Donatist Church: A Movement of Protest in Roman North Africa* (Oxford: Clarendon Press, 1952).

———, "The Donatist Church—Forty Years On," in *Windows on Origins: Essays on the Early Church*, ed. C. Landman and D. P. Whitelaw (Pretoria: University of South Africa, 1985), pp. 70–84.

———, *Martyrdom and Persecution in the Early Church: A Study of Conflict from the Maccabees to Donatus* (Oxford: Blackwell, 1965).

Friedland, E. A., "Visualizing Deities in the Roman Near East: Aspects of Athena and Athena-Allat," in *The Sculptural Environment of the Roman Near East: Reflections on Culture, Ideology, and Power*, ed. Y. Z. Eliav, E. A. Friedland, and S. Herbert (Leuven: Peeters, 2008).

Gaddis, M., *There Is No Crime for Those Who Have Christ: Religious Violence in the Christian Roman Empire*, Transformation of the Classical Heritage 39 (Berkeley: University of California Press, 2005).

Garnsey, P., *Food and Society in Classical Antiquity* (Cambridge: Cambridge University Press, 1999).

———, "Religious Toleration in Classical Antiquity," in *Persecution and Toleration*, ed. W. J. Sheils, Studies in Church History 21 (Oxford: Oxford University Press, 1984), pp. 1–27.

Gassowska, B., "Maternus Cynegius, Praefectus Praetorio Orientis and the Destruction of the Allat Temple in Palmyra," *Archeologia* 33 (1982), pp. 107–23.

Gawlikowski, M., "The Statues of the Sanctuary of Allat in Palmyra," in *The Sculptural Environment of the Roman Near East: Reflections on Culture, Ideology, and Power*, ed. Y. Z. Eliav, E. A. Friedland, and S. Herbert (Leuven: Peeters, 2008).

Geffcken, J., *The Last Days of Greco-Roman Paganism*, tr. Sabine MacCormack from *Der Ausgang des griechisch-römischen Heidentums*, revised edition (Amsterdam; Oxford: North-Holland Publishing, 1978; originally published Heidelberg, 1929).

Gibbon, E., *The History of the Decline and Fall of the Roman Empire, with the Notes by H. H. Milman* (London: Methuen, 1896–1900).

———, "Memoirs of My Life and Writings," in *The Miscellaneous Works of Edward Gibbon, Esq., with Memoirs of his Life and Writings, Illustrated from His Letters, with Occasional Notes and Narrative, by John, Lord Sheffield* (London: B. Blake, 1837).

———, *A Vindication of Some Passages in the Fifteenth and Sixteenth Chapters of the History of the Decline and Fall of the Roman Empire* (Dublin: W. & H. Whitestone, 1779).

Gill, C., T. Whitmarsh, and J. Wilkins, "Introduction," in *Galen and the World of Knowledge*, ed. C. Gill, T. Whitmarsh, and J. Wilkins (Cambridge: Cambridge University Press, 2009).

Gleason, M., "Shock and Awe: The Performance Dimension of Galen's Anatomy Demonstrations," in *Galen and the World of Knowledge*, ed. C. Gill, T. Whitmarsh, and J. Wilkins (Cambridge: Cambridge University Press, 2009), pp. 85–114.

Gordon, R., "Religion in the Roman Empire: The Civic Compromise and Its Limits," in *Pagan Priests: Religion and Power in the Ancient World*, ed. M. Beard and J. North (London: Duckworth, 1990), pp. 235–55.

Grant, R. M., "Porphyry Among the Early Christians," in *Romanitas et Christianitas*, ed. W. den Boer et al. (Amsterdam: North-Holland, 1973), pp. 181–87.

Greenblatt, S., *The Swerve: How the Renaissance Began* (London: Vintage, 2012).

Grindle, G., *The Destruction of Paganism in the Roman Empire from Constantine to Justinian* (Oxford: Blackwell, 1892).

Gross, C. C., "Galen and the Squealing Pig," *Neuroscientist* 4, no. 3 (1998), pp. 216–21.

Grubb, J. E., "Constantine and Imperial Legislation on the Family," in *The Theodosian Code: Studies in the Imperial Law of Late Antiquity*, ed. J. Harries and I. Wood (London: Duckworth, 1993), pp. 120–42.

Hadot, I., and M. Chase, "Studies on the Neoplatonist Hierocles," *Transactions of the American Philosophical Society* 94, part 1 (2004), pp. 99–124.

Hahn, J., "The Conversion of the Cult Statues: The Destruction of the Serapeum 392 AD and the Transformation of Alexandria into the 'Christ-Loving' City," in *From Temple to Church: Destruction and Renewal of Local Cultic Topography in Late Antiquity*, ed. J. Hahn, S. Emmel, and U. Gotter (Leiden; Boston, Mass.: Brill, 2008).

Hall, E., and R. Wyles, eds., *New Directions in Ancient Pantomime* (Oxford: Oxford University Press, 2008).

Harries, J., "Introduction: The Background to the Code," in *The Theodosian Code: Studies in the Imperial Law of Late Antiquity*, ed. J. Harries and I. Wood (London: Duckworth, 1993).

Hopkins, K., "The Age of Roman Girls at Marriage," *Population Studies* 18, no. 3 (March 1965), pp. 309–27.

———, "Christian Number and Its Implications," *Journal of Early Christian Studies* 6, no. 2 (Summer 1998), pp. 185–226.

Hunt, D., "Christianising the Roman Empire: The Evidence of the Code," in

The Theodosian Code: Studies in the Imperial Law of Late Antiquity, ed. J. Harries and I. Wood (London: Duckworth, 1993), pp. 143–58.

Jakab, A., "The Reception of the *Apocalypse of Peter* in Ancient Christianity," in *The Apocalypse of Peter*, ed. J. Bremmer and I. Czachesz (Leuven: Peeters, 2003), pp. 174–86.

Jenkins, R.J.H., "The Bronze Athena at Byzantium," *Journal of Hellenic Studies* 67 (1947), pp. 31–33.

Judge, E. A., *The First Christians in the Roman World: Augustan and New Testament Essays*, ed. J. R. Harrison (Tübingen: Mohr Siebeck, 2008).

Kaegi, W. E., "The Fifth-Century Twilight of Byzantine Paganism," *Classica et Mediaevalia* 27 (1968), pp. 243–75.

Kaltsas, N. E., *Ancient Greek and Roman Sculpture in the National Archaeological Museum, Athens*, tr. D. Hardy (Los Angeles: J. Paul Getty Museum, 2002).

Karageorghis, V., *Sculptures from Salamis I* (Nicosia: Department of Antiquities, Cyprus, 1964).

Kendrick, W., *The Secret Museum: Pornography in Modern Culture* (Berkeley: University of California Press, 1996).

Kingsley, C., *Hypatia: or New Foes with an Old Face* (London: Macmillan, 1894).

Kitzinger, E., *The Cult of Images in the Age Before Iconoclasm*, Dumbarton Oaks Papers, vol. 8 (1954).

Knox, P. E., and J. C. McKeown, *The Oxford Anthology of Roman Literature* (New York: Oxford University Press, 2013).

Kristensen, T. M., *Making and Breaking the Gods: Christian Responses to Pagan Sculpture in Late Antiquity*, Aarhus Studies in Mediterranean Antiquity (Aarhus: Aarhus University Press, 2013).

Lacarrière, J., *The God-Possessed*, tr. Roy Monkcom from *Les hommes ivres de dieu* (Paris: Arthaud, 1961; London: George Allen & Unwin, 1963).

Lane Fox, R., *Augustine: Conversions and Confessions* (London: Allen Lane, 2015).

———, *Pagans and Christians* (San Francisco: Harper & Row, 1988).

Laqueur, W., *The Changing Face of Antisemitism: From Ancient Times to the Present Day* (Oxford: Oxford University Press, 2006).

Layton, B., "Rules, Patterns, and the Exercise of Power in Shenoute's Monastery: The Problem of World Replacement and Identity Maintenance," *Journal of Early Christian Studies* 15, no. 1 (Spring 2007), pp. 45–73.

Lo Cascio, E., "Did the Population of Imperial Rome Reproduce Itself?" in *Urbanism in the Preindustrial World: Cross-Cultural Approaches*, ed. G. R. Storey (Tuscaloosa: University of Alabama Press, 2006).

Löfsted, E., *Late Latin* (Oslo: Aschehoug, 1959).

MacLeod, R., "Introduction: Alexandria in History and Myth," in *The Library of Alexandria: Centre of Learning in the Ancient World*, ed. R. MacLeod (London; New York: I. B. Tauris, 2004), pp. 1–15.

MacMullen, R., *Changes in the Roman Empire: Essays in the Ordinary* (Princeton, N.J.; London: Princeton University Press, 1990).

———, *Christianity and Paganism in the Fourth to Eighth Centuries* (New Haven, Conn.; London: Yale University Press, 1997).

———, *Christianizing the Roman Empire (AD 100–400)* (New Haven, Conn.; London: Yale University Press, 1984).

Mango, C., *Antique Statuary and the Byzantine Beholder*, Dumbarton Oaks Papers, vol. 17 (1963).

Mattern, S. P., *The Prince of Medicine: Galen in the Roman Empire* (Oxford: Oxford University Press, 2013).

Molloy, M. E., *Libanius and the Dancers* (Hildesheim; New York: Olms-Weidmann, 1996).

Moss, C., *The Myth of Persecution: How Early Christians Invented a Story of Martyrdom* (New York: HarperOne, 2013).

Nutton, V., "The Chronology of Galen's Early Career," *Classical Quarterly* 23, no. 1 (May 1973), pp. 158–71.

Paine, R. R., and G. R. Storey, "Epidemics, Age at Death, and Mortality in Ancient Rome," in *Urbanism in the Preindustrial World: Cross-Cultural Approaches*, ed. G. R. Storey (Tuscaloosa: University of Alabama Press, 2006).

Palmer, A.-M., *Prudentius on the Martyrs* (Oxford: Clarendon Press, 1989).

Pells, R., "Archaeologists Discover Ancient Mosaic with Message: 'Be Cheerful, Enjoy Your Life,'" *Independent*, 24 April 2016.

Perry, E., "Divine Statues in the Works of Libanius of Antioch: The Actual and Rhetorical Desacralization of Pagan Cult Furniture in the Late Fourth Century CE," in *The Sculptural Environment of the Roman Near East: Reflections on Culture, Ideology, and Power*, ed. Y. Z. Eliav, E. A. Friedland, and S. Herbert (Leuven: Peeters, 2008).

Plaisance, M., *Florence in the Time of the Medici: Public Celebrations, Politics, and Literature in the Fifteenth and Sixteenth Centuries*, tr. and ed. N. Carew-Reid (Toronto: Centre for Reformation and Renaissance Studies, 2008).

Pollini, J., "Christian Destruction and Mutilation of the Parthenon," in *Mitteilungen des deutschen archäologischen Instituts*, Athenische Abteilung 122 (2007), pp. 207–28.

———, "Gods and Emperors in the East: Images of Power and the Power of Intolerance," in *The Sculptural Environment of the Roman Near East: Reflections on Culture, Ideology, and Power*, ed. Y. Z. Eliav, E. A. Friedland, and S. Herbert (Leuven: Peeters, 2008), pp. 165–95.

Ratcliffe, S., ed., *Little Oxford Dictionary of Quotations*, fifth edition (Oxford: Oxford University Press, 2012).

Rebillard, É., *Christians and Their Many Identities in Late Antiquity, North Africa, 200–450 CE* (Ithaca, N.Y.: Cornell University Press, 2012).

Reynolds, L. D., and N. G. Wilson, *Scribes and Scholars: A Guide to the Transmission of Greek and Latin Literature* (Oxford: Oxford University Press, 1968, 1974; reprinted 1978).

Richlin, A., *The Garden of Priapus: Sexuality and Aggression in Roman Humour* (Oxford: Oxford University Press, 1983).

Rohmann, D., *Christianity, Book-Burning and Censorship in Late Antiquity: Studies in Text Transmission* (Boston, Mass.: De Gruyter, 2016).

Rousselle, A., *Porneia: On Desire and the Body in Antiquity* (Oxford: Oxford University Press, 1988).

Rovelli, C., *Reality Is Not What It Seems: The Journey to Quantum Gravity* (London: Allen Lane, 2016).

Russell, N., *Theophilus of Alexandria* (London: Routledge, 2007).

Salzman, M. R., "Rethinking Pagan-Christian Violence," in *Violence in Late Antiquity: Perceptions and Practices*, ed. H. A. Drake (Aldershot: Ashgate, 2014), pp. 265–85.

Saradi, H., "The Christianization of Pagan Temples in the Greek Hagiographical Texts," in *From Temple to Church: Destruction and Renewal of Local Cultic Topography in Late Antiquity*, ed. J. Hahn, S. Emmel, and U. Gotter (Leiden; Boston, Mass.: Brill, 2008).

Sauer, E., *The Archaeology of Religious Hatred in the Roman and Early Medieval World* (Stroud: Tempus, 2003).

Scobie, A., "Slums, Sanitation and Mortality in the Roman World," *Klio* 68 (1986), pp. 399–433.

Shaw, B. D., "Bad Boys: Circumcellions and Fictive Violence," in *Violence in Late Antiquity: Perceptions and Practices*, ed. H. A. Drake (Aldershot: Ashgate, 2014), pp. 179–96.

———, "Bandits in the Roman Empire," *Past & Present*, no. 105 (November 1984), pp. 3–52.

———, *Sacred Violence: African Christians and Sectarian Hatred in the Age of Augustine* (Cambridge: Cambridge University Press, 2011).

Shear, T. L., "The Athenian Agora: Excavations of 1971," *Hesperia: The Journal of the American School of Classical Studies at Athens* 42, no. 2 (April–June 1973), pp. 121–79.

Sherwin-White, A. N., "Why Were the Early Christians Persecuted?—An Amendment," *Past & Present* 27 (1964), pp. 23–27.

Sienkiewicz, H., *Quo Vadis: A Narrative of the Time of Nero* (1895), tr. S. F. Conrad (New York: Hippocrene, 1992).

Sizgorich, T., *Violence and Belief in Late Antiquity: Militant Devotion in Christianity and Islam* (Philadelphia: University of Pennsylvania Press, 2009).

Smith, W., *A Smaller Latin-English Dictionary*, revised J. F. Lockwood (London: John Murray, 1855; third edition, seventh impression, 1955).

Stark, R., *The Rise of Christianity: A Sociologist Reconsiders History* (Princeton, N.J.: Princeton University Press, 1996).

Stevenson, J., ed., *A New Eusebius: Documents Illustrating the History of the Church to AD 337* (London: SPCK Publishing, 1957; revised edition 1987).

Stewart, P., "The Destruction of Statues in Late Antiquity," in *Constructing Identities in Late Antiquity*, ed. R. Miles (New York; London: Routledge, 1999), pp. 159–89.

Stoneman, R., *Palmyra and Its Empire: Zenobia's Revolt against Rome* (Ann Arbor: University of Michigan Press, 1992).

Strömberg, R., "Damascius: His Personality and Significance," *Eranos* 44 (1946), pp. 175–92.

Thurman, W. S., "How Justinian I Sought to Handle the Problem of Religious Dissent," *Greek Orthodox Theological Review* 13 (1968), pp. 15–40.

Traversari, G., "Tetimimo e Colimbetra: Ultime manifestazioni del teatro antico," *Dioniso* 13 (1950), pp. 18–35.

Trombley, F. R., "The Destruction of Pagan Statuary and Christianization (Fourth–Sixth Century CE)," in *The Sculptural Environment of the Roman Near East: Reflections on Culture, Ideology, and Power*, ed. Y. Z. Eliav, E. A. Friedland, and S. Herbert (Leuven: Peeters, 2008), pp. 143–64.

Tsafrir, Y., "The Classical Heritage in Late Antique Palestine: The Fate of Free-standing Sculptures," in *The Sculptural Environment of the Roman Near East: Reflections on Culture, Ideology, and Power*, ed. Y. Z. Eliav, E. A. Friedland, and S. Herbert (Leuven: Peeters, 2008), pp. 117–41.

Veyne, P., "Pleasures and Excesses," in *A History of Private Life*, vol. 1, *From Pagan Rome to Byzantium*, ed. P. Veyne, tr. A. Goldhammer (Cambridge, Mass.; London: Belknap Press of Harvard University Press, 1992).

Walker, J. T., "The Limits of Late Antiquity: Philosophy between Rome and Iran," *Ancient World* 33 (2002), pp. 45–69.

Walters, J., "Invading the Roman Body: Manliness and Impenetrability in Roman Thought," in *Roman Sexualities*, ed. J. P. Hallett and M. B. Skinner (Princeton, N.J.: Princeton University Press, 1997), pp. 29–43.

Walzer, R., *Galen on Jews and Christians* (Oxford: Oxford University Press, 1949).

Ward, J. O., "Alexandria and Its Medieval Legacy: The Book, the Monk and the Rose," in *The Library of Alexandria: Centre of Learning in the Ancient World*, ed. R. MacLeod (London: I. B. Tauris, 2000; reprinted 2005), pp. 163–79.

Watts, E. J., *City and School in Late Antique Athens and Alexandria*, Transformation of the Classical Heritage 41 (Berkeley: University of California Press, 2006).

———, *The Final Pagan Generation*, Transformation of the Classical Heritage 53 (Oakland: University of California Press, 2015).

Whitmarsh, T., *Battling the Gods: Atheism in the Ancient World* (New York: Knopf, 2015).

Wilken, R. L., *The Christians as the Romans Saw Them* (New Haven, Conn.; London: Yale University Press, 1984, second, revised edition, 2003).

———, *John Chrysostom and the Jews: Rhetoric and Reality in the Late 4th Century* (Berkeley, Calif.; London: University of California Press, 1983).

Wilson, M. R., *Our Father Abraham: Jewish Roots of the Christian Faith* (Grand Rapids, Mich.; Dayton, Ohio: William B. Eerdmans, 1989).

Wilson, N. G., "The Church and Classical Studies in Byzantium," *Antike und Abendland* 16 (1970).

———, *Saint Basil on the Value of Greek Literature* (London: Duckworth, 1975).

Wood, I., and J. Harries, eds., *The Theodosian Code, Studies in the Imperial Law of Late Antiquity* (London: Duckworth, 1993).

Yegül, F. K., *Baths and Bathing in Classical Antiquity* (Cambridge, Mass.: MIT Press, 1992).

Index